EVIDENCE-BASED PRACTICE IN THE EARLY CHILDHOOD FIELD

EVIDENCE-BASED PRACTICE
IN THE
EARLY CHILDHOOD FIELD

Edited by

VIRGINIA BUYSSE

PATRICIA W. WESLEY

ZERO TO THREE
Washington, D.C.

Published by

ZERO TO THREE
2000 M St., NW, Suite 200
Washington, DC 20036-3307
(202) 638-1144
Toll-free orders (800) 899-4301
Fax: (202) 638-0851
Web: http://www.zerotothree.org

The mission of the ZERO TO THREE Press is to publish authoritative research, practical resources, and new ideas for those who work with and care about infants, toddlers, and their families. Books are selected for publication by an independent Editorial Board.

The views contained in this book are those of the authors and do not necessarily reflect those of ZERO TO THREE: National Center for Infants, Toddlers and Families, Inc.

Cover design: Kirk DouPonce, DogEared Design
Text design and composition: Design Consultants.

Library of Congress Cataloging-in-Publication Data

Evidence-based practice in the early childhood field / edited by
Virginia Buysse and Patricia W. Wesley.
    p. cm.
  Includes bibliographical references.
  ISBN-13: 978-0-943657-95-0
  ISBN-10: 0-943657-95-4
  1. Child development. 2. Early childhood education. I. Buysse,
Virginia. II. Wesley, Patricia W.
  HQ772.E95 2006
  372.21--dc22
                            2006010661

10 9 8 7 6 5 4 3 2
ISBN 0-943657-95-4
Printed in the United States of America

Suggested citations:

Book citation: Buysse, V., & Wesley, P. W. (Eds.). (2006). *Evidence-based practice in the early childhood field*. Washington, DC: ZERO TO THREE Press.

Chapter citation: Snyder, P. (2006). Best available research evidence: Impact on research in early childhood. In V. Buysse & P. W. Wesley (Eds.), *Evidence-based practice in the early childhood field* (pp. 35–70). Washington, DC: ZERO TO THREE Press.

In memory of Emily Fenichel,
whose insights, intellect, and eloquence continue to inspire us.

TABLE OF CONTENTS

FOREWORD

Why won't practitioners do what the research says?
Why don't researchers study what really matters in practice?

Researchers and practitioners in many disciplines and professions have been asking these questions for decades. Since the beginning of this century, leaders in the multidisciplinary field of early childhood development have come to understand that the distance between practitioners and researchers stems from the fact that the study of child development and the delivery of services for young children and their families reflect related yet distinct cultures. Moreover, a third domain, the formulation and implementation of social policies, has its own unique perspective, which powerfully shapes the context in which early childhood researchers and practitioners do their work.

Evidence-based practice, as the editors and contributors for this impressive volume describe it, has the potential to become a truly integrated culture that incorporates the "different ways of knowing" that characterize early childhood science, policy, and practice. In order to better appreciate the promise that such integration brings to the early childhood field, it is useful to examine these three cultures and the tensions among them.

Scientists are on a quest for knowledge. They construct theories, test hypotheses, and refine conceptual models over time. Scientists are aware that any study result could be the product of chance or be explained by an alternative and equally plausible interpretation. Thus, those who study child development must be comfortable with complexity, ambiguity, and uncertainty. In fact, many investigators say that unexplained phenomena are the key attraction of research into the mysteries of early childhood development. Stated simply, science is focused on *what we do not know*.

Service delivery is focused on *what we should do*. Practitioners who provide health, education, early intervention, and mental health services for infants, toddlers, and families have a primary obligation to "the child and family in front of them." Unlike researchers, practitioners cannot reserve judgment until they have collected more data. In order to respond to immediate human needs, they must make decisions even though their information base may be inadequate. Practitioners rely heavily on professional experience—their own and that of colleagues. Their knowledge is influenced by what they learn from practice, which may or may not be grounded in systematic data collection and analysis.

Makers of social policy, who determine the resources that are available to scientists and practitioners, demand simplicity. In the policy world, science is just one point of view, and frequently it is not the most influential. Policy makers are driven by political, economic, and social forces. Compelling stories and the selective use of evidence may persuade them to take a course of action that affects thousands, if not millions, of young children and their families. For policymakers, science competes with both values and "common sense" as a guide to decision making.

Because of the tensions that exist among the cultures of science, practice, and policy, there are significant gaps between what we know and what we do to promote the healthy development of young children. To achieve successful cross-cultural interaction to close these gaps, we must first recognize: (1) the various rules of evidence that govern each of these three distinctive worlds; (2) the influence of values on child development research, service delivery, and policy making; and (3) the impact of frequent societal disregard for the professional status of those whose work focuses on young children and families.

The distance between the boundaries of "hard" science and the information needs of conscientious policymakers and practitioners will always exist, but we certainly can work to reduce it. Such an effort requires clear criteria for the responsible translation and application of what we have learned about children's development. As a first step, researchers, practitioners, and policymakers must reach consensus on how to differentiate among three categories of child development information: (1) established knowledge; (2) reasonable hypotheses; and (3) unwarranted or irresponsible assertions. (Shonkoff, 2000).

The scientific community defines *established knowledge*, which is governed by strict rules of evidence and monitored by a rigorous process of peer review. The volume of established knowledge is relatively limited, and its boundaries are strictly enforced.

Reasonable hypotheses may be generated by scientists, policymakers, practitioners, parents, and others concerned with the well-being of young children. Reasonable hypotheses are anchored to established knowledge but move beyond the limits of what we know. The critical defining feature of any single hypothesis is its "falsifiability"—that is, an appropriately designed experiment can prove it true or false. If validated through scientific experimentation, a reasonable hypothesis becomes part of the established knowledge base of a field of inquiry. In the worlds of policy and practice, reasonable hypotheses embody the essence of responsible action based on incomplete information.

Anyone, unfortunately, can propagate *unwarranted assertions*. These statements may stray far beyond the boundaries of established knowledge. Sometimes they blatantly distort or misrepresent state-of-the-art science. Unlike reasonable hypotheses, irresponsible assertions neither advance knowledge nor guide responsible policymaking or service delivery. Their greatest threat is the extent to which they masquerade as science and therefore undermine its credibility in the eyes of the general public.

If we are serious in our wish to enhance the well being of young children and their families, we must combine the best of the three perspectives of science, practice, and policy. This is not a question of the relative value of thinking versus acting. It is not a matter of assigning greater weight to empirical data over professional judgment (or vice versa). The challenge is to develop creative ways of blending all three cultures—to be open to different ways of thinking about the needs of children and families, and to consider alternative strategies for mobilizing knowledge on their behalf.

Evidence-based practice may prove to be the long-sought bridge that closes the gap between research and practice in the early childhood field. Buysse and Wesley and their colleagues define evidence-based practice as "a decision-making process that integrates the best available research evidence with family and professional wisdom and values." As such, evidence-based practice draws on research knowledge, craft knowledge (also known as professional wisdom), and the values and beliefs of practitioners and those of the families and communities they serve.

Buysse and Wesley argue that closing the gap between research and practice in the early childhood field requires consideration of all the ways in which members of a profession acquire knowledge. These ways of knowing include conceptualization, empirical testing, consensus-building within and across disciplines and settings, and employments of a variety of rigorous research methodologies—descriptive, qualitative, and quantitative.

Interestingly, evidence-based practice in the early childhood field builds on the tenets of evidence-based medicine, which itself has come into prominence only in the last decade and a half. Buysse and Wesley underscore this linkage by citing five steps that constitute the practice of evidence-based medicine at the practitioner level, as described by Sackett, Straus, Richardson, Rosenberg, and Haynes (2000): (1) convert the need for information into an answerable question; (2) track down the best evidence to answer the question; (3) appraise the evidence for its validity, impact, and applicability; (4) integrate the appraisal with clinical expertise and the patient's unique circumstances and values; and (5) evaluate the effectiveness of steps 1–4 and seek ways to improve them in the future.

Although the evidence-based practice movement in medicine recommends involving consumers to generate, assemble, and use knowledge, it is not yet clear what shape that involvement will take in all domains. In some areas of the early childhood field, however, notably early intervention for infants and young children with developmental disabilities, parents and professionals have been working on the parameters of that special partnership for more than 20 years. This collaborative relationship, which is actually mandated by federal law, has served to define, establish, expand, and evaluate a rich and highly robust field of practice, policy, and research that continues to evolve.

Buysse, Wesley, and their colleagues have provided a thorough, thoughtful, and thought-provoking guide to evidence-based practice in the early childhood field—its origins, its applications, its challenges, and its potential. Like evidence-based practice itself, Buysse and Wesley's recommendations draw on ideas from within and outside the early childhood field, as well as from their own observations, reflections, and questions as explorers of uncharted terrain. They are acutely aware that the early childhood arena can no longer advance strictly on the basis of ideology and collective wisdom, but must be informed by the thoughtful integration of ongoing scientific investigation. Thus they urge the early childhood field to reach consensus on the meaning of the term evidence-based practice; decide what constitutes evidence and how its various forms will be weighted; guide practitioners in assessing evidence that comes from different sources; pay attention to knowledge dissemination and utilization; develop communities of practice as a way to involve practitioners, families, and local researchers in establishing the knowledge base of the field; and align continuous professional development to evidence-based practice, making sure to embrace the complexity and acknowledge the uncertainty that exists in any work with infants, toddlers, and their families.

The early childhood field embodies a rich diversity of perspectives. At its core, it combines a keen respect for knowledge and a deep passion to make a difference in the lives of young children and their parents. Buysse and Wesley have produced an important volume that paves the way to a higher level of understanding and impact. The immediate needs of children and families, and the long term interests of society as a whole, will be served well by thoughtful reflection on what they and their colleagues have to say.

REFERENCES

Sackett, D. L., Straus, S. E., Richardson, W. S., Rosenberg, W., & Haynes, R. B. (2000). *Evidence-based medicine: How to practice and teach EBM.* Edinburgh, UK: Churchill Livingstone.

Shonkoff, J. (2000). Science, policy, and practice: Three cultures in search of a shared mission. *Child Development, 71:* 181–187.

PREFACE

Writing and editing *Evidence-Based Practice in the Early Childhood Field* was a journey of discovery and learning. We began with a much narrower focus in mind, intending to address a topic that we had spent considerable time thinking and writing about—the community-of-practice approach for bringing together practitioners, parents, researchers, and others in pursuit of shared knowledge. The original goal was to demonstrate how building collaborative relationships among these diverse stakeholder groups could be the key to closing the research–practice gap that had plagued the early childhood professions (and indeed most other professions) since their inception. But at almost every turn, we encountered a growing transnational movement that was having a significant effect across many different disciplines and professions—evidence-based practice. As we delved into the literature and attempted to trace the origins of this movement, we came to understand the potential for evidence-based practice to transform radically the way in which knowledge was generated, disseminated, and used in our field. Once we grasped the notion that evidence-based practice could alter practically everything we do within the early childhood field, from making public policy to conducting research to educating professionals, we were led rapidly to another realization: We were in way over our heads. So, in the spirit of scholarly collaboration, we turned to our colleagues—Mary Ruth Coleman, Jennifer Neitzel, Patricia Snyder, and Pamela Winton—and the book became an edited volume that benefited greatly from the contributions of these authors.

This book's purpose is to take a critical look at the evidence-based practice movement in the early childhood field, a disparate collection of disciplines and professions that includes early childhood education, early childhood special education, early intervention, child care, infant and child mental health, developmental and clinical psychology, social work, the medical and allied health professions, among others. The book is organized around three key questions:

- What is evidence-based practice, and how did it emerge?
- How will evidence-based practice affect the early childhood field?
- What are some promising practices, strategies, and future directions for implementing evidence-based practice?

WHAT IS EVIDENCE-BASED PRACTICE, AND HOW DID IT EMERGE?

In chapter 1, we examine the challenges of integrating research and practice that helped pave the way for the evidence-based practice movement; we trace the origins of the evidence-based practice movement in medicine and the standards movement in education; and we briefly discuss some future directions for building and disseminating the professional knowledge base. Drawing on the work of Sackett, Straus, Richardson, Rosenberg, and Haynes (2000) in medicine, we offer the following definition of evidence-based practice for the early childhood profession: Evidence-based practice is a decision-making process that integrates the best available research evidence with family and professional wisdom and values. What is at the heart of this definition and what represents the most dramatic shift from previous thinking is the notion that evidence-based practice is essentially a process—a way of empowering individuals to deliver the most effective interventions on behalf of children and families. Previous attempts to influence practice knowledge have emphasized products such as written sets of recommended practices sanctioned by expert groups or professional organizations. In contrast to this approach, evidence-based practice represents a democratization of knowledge in which knowledge is transparent and accessible to all, thus requiring that practitioners identify, evaluate, and interpret the evidence and apply it to solve practice problems.

How Will Evidence-Based Practice Affect the Early Childhood Field?

In chapter 2, Patricia Snyder examines how evidence-based practice is changing the conduct of research. She begins with an in-depth explanation of the distinction between evidence-based practice and systematically promulgated lists of recommended or developmentally appropriate practices as well as the processes used to arrive at these products. Next, she conducts a critical analysis of various appraisal systems that have been developed in response to the evidence-based practice movement to accumulate research knowledge and to assess the quality of available empirical evidence. She suggests that the focus on methodological quality that evidence-based practice has spawned should be broadened to include several other characteristics of scientifically based research, namely, relevance, significance, transparency, and social validity. She also discusses the power of random assignment, suggests appropriate ways in which randomized controlled studies could be applied in the early childhood field, and questions whether other forms of evidence should count.

In chapter 3, Pamela Winton considers how the evidence-based practice movement is changing the way in which we think about generating and sharing practice knowledge in the early childhood professions. She defines the concept of knowledge utilization and outlines the issues and promising strategies associated with three of its components: knowledge generation, knowledge organization and translation, and knowledge mediation and application. She discusses existing Web sites that were developed to organize and translate research-based knowledge on specific areas of practice and concludes that a future direction should be to link these resources to professional development programs and standards. She also summarizes innovative models that currently are being evaluated and are designed to support knowledge utilization and professional development.

In chapter 4, we consider the relationship between research and policy. We begin by describing traditional assumptions and processes by which several key policies in the early childhood field were developed and implemented and then consider how policymakers might go about the business of creating policy using an evidence-based framework. We suggest that additional evidence is needed to illuminate the links between intended policy outcomes and policy objectives. We also identify current obstacles to evidence-based policy and offer possible analytic frameworks that can be used to understand how various sources of evidence inform the policymaking process.

What Are Some Promising Practices, Strategies, and Future Directions for Implementing Evidence-Based Practice?

In chapter 5, we explore the community of practice model that prompted our initial inquiry into the evidence-based practice movement, largely because of its potential to alter the linear relationship between researchers as knowledge generators and practitioners as the consumers of knowledge. We first define *community of practice* in terms of its core membership, purpose, and activities and then distinguish it from similar models such as learning organizations or a community of learners. We also describe three approaches to conducting communities of practice in early education and intervention and offer suggestions for how to use communities of practice to build the evidence base for the early childhood field.

In chapter 6, Mary Ruth Coleman, Virginia Buysse, and Jennifer Neitzel apply evidence-based practice concepts to address a real-world practice problem. They describe an initiative designed to build the evidence base around an emerging area of practice—an early intervening system called Recognition and Response that is designed to help struggling learners during pre-kindergarten before they experience school failure and before they are referred to special education services. They describe the key national organizations and state partners that have formed a community of practice to develop the Recognition and Response system and delineate the sources of evidence on which the model is based: empirical, theoretical, as well as family and professional wisdom and values.

In chapter 7, we review key concepts from each chapter, revisit the recommendations to the field presented at the end of chapter 1, and raise critical questions about the potential for the evidence-based practice movement to improve early childhood interventions and programs. We end on a somewhat provocative note, suggesting that the field shift its focus from advocacy and information-gathering activities to more practical implementation issues, the most important of which is addressing the question of how to integrate research-based knowledge with professional and family wisdom and values.

We have entered a new era of evidence that demands that we substantiate our claims about which services and supports should be provided to children and families. In many respects, this new era has leveled the playing field. Practitioners, researchers, and policymakers alike are all equally unsure about what constitutes evidence in this new paradigm and how in the world one combines various levels or types of evidence to make sound decisions. Proponents of evidence-based practice often look to the natural sciences as a guide in this regard because that field's experimentation under carefully controlled conditions is known to produce indisputable evidence. But global warming is an example of an area in which scientists are limited from conducting controlled experiments on planet earth and must rely instead on natural experiments to demonstrate that changes in our atmosphere are directly related to human activities such as harmful emissions from coal-fired power plants (Schlesinger, 2005). In our pursuit of evidence on which to base individual and collective practice, we in the early childhood profession must ensure that we do not ignore the results of natural experiments and other equally viable sources of knowledge that could lead to more effective professional practices and improved outcomes for children and families.

REFERENCES

Sackett, D. L., Straus, S. E., Richardson, W. S., Rosenberg, W., & Haynes, R. B. (2000). *Evidence-based medicine: How to practice and teach EBM.* Edinburgh, NY: Churchill.

Schlesinger, W. H. (2005, February 7). We've experimented with the atmosphere. *The News and Observer*, p. 9.

CHAPTER 1

EVIDENCE-BASED PRACTICE: HOW DID IT EMERGE AND WHAT DOES IT REALLY MEAN FOR THE EARLY CHILDHOOD FIELD?

Virginia Buysse and Patricia W. Wesley

Within the past several years, the words *evidence-based practice* have entered the lexicon with little fanfare and with little attention to the origins of this term and what it means for the early childhood professions. The growing use of the phrase in conference programs, journal articles, grant announcements, and the World Wide Web seems to suggest that there are definitive answers to a host of complex practice-related issues. Most would agree in principle that early childhood professionals should rely on evidence to make important decisions about which services and supports will be provided to young children and families. Practitioners need evidence to help them address the needs and priorities of children and families and to resolve specific practice dilemmas. Researchers rely on evidence to formulate their research questions and to interpret their findings. Policymakers must consider evidence on the effectiveness of specific interventions and programs to make sound policy decisions and to allocate scarce resources. In addition, a sense of urgency and importance surround the term, which suggests something else: evidence-based practice is more than a passing trend; it has become a movement.

But what does the evidence-based practice movement mean? What is evidence and what standards will be used to evaluate it? How will the early childhood field establish evidence for existing and emerging practices? How will the push for evidence change or reinforce notions of what constitutes high-quality early care and intervention for young children, and how will it alter our thinking about the best way to prepare them to succeed in school?

What are the most effective ways of sharing evidence-based knowledge with families, practitioners, and policymakers, and how have traditional methods of knowledge dissemination failed? A report of the National Research Council (National Research Council Committee on Research in Education, 2005) concluded that the push for evidence to support our practices is changing almost everything we do: the way in which we design and implement professional development programs; the standards for reviewing grant proposals and journal articles; the types of research questions we pose and the way in which we design studies to address them.

But how did we arrive at the need for evidence-based practice and what precisely does it mean for the early childhood professions? This chapter examines (a) the longstanding challenge of integrating research and practice that helped pave the way for the evidence-based practice movement, (b) the history and origins of evidence-based practice in medicine, (c) the way in which evidence-based medicine is being redefined in education and other fields, and finally, (d) future directions for the early childhood field as it comes to terms with a new paradigm for building and disseminating the professional knowledge base.

THE AGE-OLD PROBLEM: CONNECTING RESEARCH AND PRACTICE

In recent years, the early childhood field has witnessed heroic efforts to integrate scientific knowledge about early development and the critical role of early experiences that support or inhibit children's development (National Research Council & Institute of Medicine, 2000). There is generally broad consensus about the value of creating a shared knowledge base for any field, but particularly for one that encompasses many different disciplines and professions, as is the case with the early childhood field. There also is wide acceptance of the core concepts that have been proposed to frame early childhood professionals' understanding of how young children develop and learn (e.g., "Children are active participants in their own development, reflecting the intrinsic human drive to explore and master one's environment" from National Research Council & Institute of Medicine, 2000, p. 4).

But reaching consensus about what we know to be effective practice in early childhood does not necessarily imply that teachers, parents, and others will actually use this knowledge and incorporate it into their daily practices with young children and families as a way to improve these practices. From the tension that has long existed between research and practice (e.g., Why won't practitioners do what the research says? Why don't researchers study what really matters in practice?) to the complex process of applying new knowledge to a wide range of practice contexts, little has changed in the past decade. At its core, the evidence-based practice movement appears to represent the newest twist on the now familiar refrain about the need to close the research–practice gap. But there are aspects of the evidence-based practice movement that make it fundamentally different from previous attempts to integrate research and practice and from previous efforts to create practice guidelines, as we will see in chapter 2.

At this time, the early childhood field has not reached consensus on a definition of evidence-based practice; however, most would agree that a clear understanding of the concept is needed. The term *evidence-based practice* has emerged only within the past several years, but as noted in an early childhood newsletter, "that movement toward evidence-based education is expected to have a significant impact on early childhood education" and related fields in the future ("Evidence-Based Education in Early Childhood," 2002, p. 1). Although the term originated in the field of medicine, the emphasis on applying evidence to make informed practice decisions also has its foundation in the No Child Left Behind Act of 2001 and in the larger accountability movement in education. As we begin to understand the contributions of the evidence-based practice movement to our field, it may be helpful to take a critical look at attitudes toward and assumptions about how we generate and use knowledge.

What We Know About Knowledge

When we think about the way that knowledge informs practice in the early childhood field, the word *dissemination* often comes to mind. Indeed, we frequently use dissemination as the "gap-filler" to explain the process by which research findings get translated into practice (Hood, 2002). But there is more to informing practice than simply providing access to research findings, although even that process is fraught with problems related to the different ways in which people seek information and the availability of technology and other resources. Rather than focus on knowledge dissemination, however, let us consider the nature of knowledge itself.

First, it is important to recognize that knowledge about one's profession can be represented in multiple forms. Our current assumption appears to be that research knowledge is the best foundation on which to build the professional knowledge base (Hiebert, Gallimore, & Stigler, 2002), but in recent years, evidence-based practice has challenged this assumption. A number of scholars have suggested, for example, that more emphasis be given to craft knowledge (the particular type of professional knowledge used by practitioners), which is characterized by its concreteness and contextual richness and, therefore, is a very different form of knowledge than that which is produced through scientific research (Estabrooks, 1998; Gallagher, 1998; Hiebert et al., 2002). Furthermore, it is generally accepted that craft knowledge (also referred to as professional wisdom) is influenced heavily by the values and beliefs of practitioners and those of the families and communities that they serve.

If we hold firm to the idea that the problem of integrating research and practice is essentially one of knowledge dissemination or of finding the most effective ways of translating research into practice, then we not only have been waiting for a train that will not arrive but also we have been waiting at the wrong station (Giddens, 1976, cited in Gallagher, 1998).[1]

Second, if we allow ourselves for a moment to entertain the notion that there are different ways of knowing, it is easy to see that solving the research–practice gap will require that we consider all of the ways in which members of a profession acquire knowledge. These ways of knowing include, for example, various forms of scholarship (e.g., philosophical and theoretical approaches, conceptual models or frameworks), consensus building activities (e.g., written lists of recommended or developmentally appropriate practices, professional standards and competencies, national panels, position papers published by professional organizations), and various research methods (e.g., qualitative methods and traditions that emphasize rich description and interpretation).

Third and even more important, perhaps, is the need to identify the sources of early childhood practice knowledge. In the nursing profession, sources of practice knowledge have been classified into the following categories: empirics (the science of nursing), aesthetics (the art of nursing), ethics (the moral aspects of nursing), and personal knowledge (Estabrooks, 1998). In the early childhood field, there is little discussion in the literature concerning the manner in which practice knowledge is generated. Weikart (2004) wisely observed that the early childhood education field is influenced heavily by its own beliefs. He stated, "Early childhood education, like education in general, has always been a field based on beliefs, not evidence-based educational approaches" (p. 155). To support his assertion, he noted that the field has adopted various approaches to early education such as Montessori, Reggio Emilia, and the Creative Curriculum—all of which are well conceptualized and generally appealing to teachers, but none of which have scientific evidence to support their effectiveness. This situation is beginning to change, however, with efforts under way and resources now available to evaluate many of these programs and models.

Achieving a clearer understanding about the sources of practice knowledge in the early childhood profession could lead to changes that would produce more useful forms of knowledge for practitioners. Hiebert et al. (2002) have suggested that these changes would require that we organize knowledge in such a way that it (a) responds to practitioners' immediate needs and the specific problems of practice, (b) focuses directly on improving child and family outcomes, (c) integrates all of the different types of knowledge that practitioners are required to use (e.g., content and process knowledge, knowledge about social and cultural contexts, knowledge of individual differences), and (d) is available for public scrutiny and use in ways that can be understood by both researchers and practitioners.

The early childhood field faces enormous challenges if it embraces the goal of producing more useful forms of practice knowledge as part of an evidence-based practice approach. Let us assume, for example, that a child-care director who recently attended a conference session on emergent literacy wants to work with teachers in her program to improve the language and literacy outcomes in classrooms serving 3-year-olds. These professionals need access to practical information that will lead to necessary improvements in creating a literacy-rich environment and that will help them to select curricular strategies that are developmentally and individually appropriate for a group of children who likely are diverse with respect to their cultures, languages, and abilities.

Synthesizing this form of practice knowledge, making it available to all who need it, and delineating a process by which this knowledge can be implemented in practice in a way that addresses the local context is a rather tall order for the field. Yet it is just such a challenge that the early childhood field has addressed, even though only partially, through previous attempts to develop practice guidelines. It is important to differentiate evidence-based practice from previous efforts to define and guide early childhood practices, a point that is discussed more fully in chapter 2. In contrast to previous attempts to guide practices through products consisting of sets of written recommendations, evidence-based practice represents a process by which parents and professionals can make practice decisions that are tailored to the needs and priorities of individual children, families, and programs. In an evidence-based practice approach, written practice guidelines represent one tangible source of evidence that might be used in making informed practice decisions. Although it will take time to determine precisely how the field must change in response to the evidence-based movement, we can easily reach agreement on one thing: maintaining our current research agenda to address questions that researchers deem relevant using their preferred methods (with randomized controlled studies considered the gold standard) likely will lead only to more knowledge in a form that is difficult for practitioners to understand and use (Hiebert et al., 2002).

The Debate Over Research Methods

So far, we have considered the possibility that one viable solution to the age-old problem of connecting research and practice lies in producing a distinctly different, more immediately useful form of practice knowledge. A second, but related, school of thought is that the problem stems primarily from using the wrong research methods. On the extreme end of this argument are researchers who reject the scientific method altogether. Gallagher (1998) noted that human affairs are inherently unpredictable, yet researchers in the social sciences have held to the belief that through repeated experimentation they will arrive at the point when the results of their interventions can be predicted and controlled systematically. Arguing that this type of a scientific knowledge base is unobtainable, Gallagher suggested that a more tenable approach would be to draw on the interpretative, hermeneutical tradition found in qualitative research methods and to make teachers' craft knowledge the centerpiece of our efforts to improve practices.

Other scholars have embraced the so-called scientific revolution in education and have attributed the lack of incremental increases in knowledge in education that is characteristic of improvements in the hard sciences to the field's tendency to move from fad to fad rather than in response to empirical data (Slavin, 2002). As evidence of this perspective, many have pointed to the paucity of intervention research and the overreliance on descriptive and correlational studies in education and other social science fields. This view is a criticism that also can be leveled at the early childhood field.

Seeking a middle-ground perspective are those who have suggested that experimental designs are not always appropriate and that research methods should be selected to fit the particular research questions that they were designed to answer (Odom et al., 2005). Proponents of this viewpoint would argue that it is important to distinguish, for example, whether the intention of the research is to produce a desired outcome or external product or whether it is oriented toward internal processes that may help to understand a phenomenon (Brew, 2003). Weiss (2002) suggested that there are circumstances such as community-based interventions in which random assignment is difficult or impossible to implement. In these situations, researchers commonly face challenges such as the inability to assign entire communities to groups, small numbers of participants, and variability across sites. As an alternative to using experimental designs, Weiss recommended several promising methods that stem from the qualitative research tradition: theory-based evaluation in which researchers examine what is expected to happen at each stage during intervention and an approach called "ruling out alternative explanations" that often complements theory-based evaluation. Finally, advancing a view called *scientific realism*, Chatterji (2005) argued that carefully documenting contextual and site-specific variables is a prerequisite to designing sound field experiments in which the goal is to evaluate the effectiveness of an intervention.

To provide further guidance about what constitutes rigorous scientific research in education, the National Research Council produced a landmark publication that proposed a set of six fundamental principles that underlie scientific inquiry in every field (National Research Council Committee on Scientific Principles for Education Research, 2002). Table 1.1 presents these six core scientific principles. Although it is easy to acknowledge the importance of each of these guidelines in theory, applying these principles to research in the early childhood field is more complex. As is the case in education and the broader social sciences, the early childhood field is value laden, it consists of an amalgam of different disciplines and professional organizations, and its practices occur within a variety of geographic and sociopolitical contexts. Attention to each of these factors is critical to understanding how various theories and research findings generalize to diverse groups of children and families in many situations (National Research Council Committee on Scientific Principles for Education Research, 2002). Still, the National Research Council report reminds us of the importance of scientific rigor as a critical component in establishing the evidence base for specific interventions and practices, a component to which the early childhood field must pay closer attention in the future.

Table 1.1. Scientific Principles Presented by the National Research Council.

1. Pose significant questions that can be investigated empirically.
2. Link research to relevant theory.
3. Use methods that permit direct investigation of the question.
4. Provide a coherent and explicit chain of reasoning.
5. Replicate and generalize across studies.
6. Disclose research to encourage professional scrutiny and critique.

Note: From *Scientific Research in Education*, by National Research Council Committee on Scientific Principles for Education Research, 2002, Washington, DC: National Academy Press.

The Separation Between the Research and Practice Communities

The separation that exists between the research and practice communities is yet another explanation that has been offered to understand the almost insurmountable difficulties of integrating research and practice (Buysse, Sparkman, & Wesley, 2003; Hiebert et al., 2002; Palincsar, Magnusson, Marano, Ford, & Brown, 1998). Drawing on our earlier example of the program in need of improved literacy practices, let us consider whether that director would be more inclined to contact the unfamiliar researcher who conducted the conference presentation on early literacy or to seek advice from another colleague whom she trusts. Experience tells us (and there is at least some empirical evidence to support this observation) that practitioners generally do not turn to research findings in developing or refining practices and that researchers do not turn to practice for inspiration in framing new research questions or interpreting the implications of their results. In developing an explanation for this phenomenon, Hood (2002) noted that researchers and practitioners live in very different communities of practice, each of which is rooted in different cultures with dissimilar assumptions, beliefs, and frames of reference. It is not surprising then that the ways in which each of these groups engage in efforts to make sense of information, appraise claims, and construct knowledge are markedly different. Yet, the concept of evidence-based practice requires that we find new ways to bridge these cultural worlds so both science and professional wisdom can contribute to the evidence base.

Although the vast majority of early childhood practitioners work to improve their practices almost daily on an individual level (e.g., testing their own hypotheses about the best way to intervene in the lives of young children and families and developing explanations based on the observed results), the field lacks a mechanism for collecting, scrutinizing, and sharing this evolving craft knowledge with the broader early childhood community (Buysse et al., 2003; Hiebert et al., 2002; Wesley & Buysse, 2001). The field needs a new model and an infrastructure that would allow practitioners, researchers, parents, and others to work together to build the knowledge base, both as a way to improve individual practices and as a way to advance the profession as a whole. In contrast to the old model that concentrates on knowledge transmission, a new model termed "communities of practice" would shift the focus to a process in which individuals and groups negotiate meanings, engage in shared inquiry and learning, and co-construct knowledge (Brew, 2003; Lave & Wenger, 1991).

The Role of Public Policy

It is also important to recognize the role of public policy in influencing the way in which early childhood practices are defined and delivered. Policymakers consistently have demonstrated an interest in connecting research to practice in two primary ways: (a) by using research evidence to promote quality services and accountability systems that measure inter-vention effectiveness and (b) by relying on research to inform their decisions about which programs and services are most effective and for whom. At the federal level, no specific, comprehensive public policy or set of policies govern all types of early childhood programs and services, but it is important to examine how various federal policies are promoting evidence-based practices and the type of evidence on which policymakers rely to shape these policies. Later in this chapter, we trace the history of key public poli-cies that have influenced the evidence-base practice movement in the early childhood field.

The issues surrounding the problem of integrating research and practice are complex, but it is clear that changing the way we think about knowledge generation and utilization is one of the keys to reaching consensus on what constitutes evidence-based practice knowledge for the early childhood field. Of course, this problem of integrating research and practice is not unique to the early childhood field. The next section explores the origins of the evidence-based practice movement in medicine as a response to some of the very issues we have discussed.

THE ORIGINS OF THE MOVEMENT IN MEDICINE

The origins of the evidence-based practices in education and the early child-hood field can be traced back to its roots in medicine. Gordon Guyatt and his colleagues at McMaster University in Canada coined the term *evidence-based medicine* in 1992, but ideas about incorporating critical appraisals of evidence in clinical decision making existed before this term was introduced (Sackett, Straus, Richardson, Rosenberg, & Haynes, 2000). Archie Cochrane (the namesake of the Cochrane Collaborative that is described later) is credited for launching evidence-based medicine in the 1970s in the United Kingdom primarily by promoting the use of randomized controlled trials in the evaluation of treatment approaches and by pioneering the use of systematic reviews and meta-analyses of clinically relevant research (Reynolds, 2000).

Each year, thousands of articles on evidence-based medicine are published, and the interest on this topic has led to the creation of a number of evidence-based journals and countless Internet Web sites. Until the advent of evidence-based medicine, a major criticism of the medical field had been the lack of a mechanism for conducting systematic reviews of studies of effectiveness of various treatments. The international Cochrane Collaborative in health care (http://www.cochrane.org) was created in 1993 to fill this gap. It now consists of an electronic library that contains information on hundreds of thousands of randomized trials on health interventions and more than 1,000 systematic reviews to synthesize the accumulation of knowledge across studies.[2]

Evidence-based medicine emphasizes the need for practitioners to understand certain rules of evidence to correctly interpret and apply research findings on causation, diagnosis, and treatment. In contrast to traditional practices, evidence-based medicine has been referred to as a paradigm shift for the field (Evidence-Based Medicine Working Group, 1992). Health-care professionals who follow evidence-based medicine guidelines are expected to make an independent assessment of the evidence by conducting a search of the literature, selecting the most relevant studies, and applying rules of evidence to determine their validity. In addition to research evidence, health-care professionals are expected to rely on informed clinical judgment and patient values in making decisions about applying specific interventions to individual patients.

The newest edition of a book on evidence-based medicine written by David Sackett and his colleagues (Sackett et al., 2000) is considered one of the most reliable sources on this topic. Written for the "busy practitioner," the book provides an introduction to evidence-based medicine and offers guidelines for finding the current best evidence related to diagnosis, prognosis, and treatment. We use this book as our primary source for getting across to our readers the way in which the medical field defines and operationalizes the term evidence-based medicine. We also discuss the connection between evidence-based medicine and evidence-based practice in the early childhood field.

Defining Evidence-Based Medicine and Evidence-Based Practice

What precisely is evidence-based medicine? Sackett and his colleagues offer the following definition: "Evidence-based medicine (EBM) is the integration of *best research evidence* with *clinical expertise* and *patient values*" (2000, p. 1, emphasis added). Table 1.2 draws from the work of Sackett et al. (2000) to define each of the three major components of this definition for medicine (i.e., best research evidence, clinical expertise, and patient values) and then applies these concepts to the early childhood field. The early childhood field has not yet reached consensus on a definition of evidence-based practice, as Dunst, Trivette, and Cutspec (2002) noted. If we were going to adopt a definition of evidence-based practice for the early childhood field that is based on the one for evidence-based medicine, we might substitute the words *family and professional wisdom* for clinical expertise. Similarly, we might expand patient values to include the *values of families and the profession* (while also being mindful of the characteristics of individual children and their families as well as the social, cultural, geographic, and political contexts in which interventions are planned and implemented). With these considerations in mind, we offer the following definition of evidence-based practice for the early childhood field: Evidence-based practice is a decision-making process that integrates the best available research evidence with family and professional wisdom and values.

Table 1.2. Components of the Definition of Evidence-Based Medicine Applied to the Early Childhood Field

Component	Medicine	Early Childhood
Best research evidence (Medicine and Early Childhood)	"…clinically relevant research…into the accuracy and precision of diagnostic tests…, the power of prognostic markers, and the efficacy and safety of therapeutic, rehabilitative, and preventive regimens" (p. 1).	Scientifically based research on the efficacy and effectiveness of specific early childhood practices and interventions
Clinical expertise (Medicine) Family and professional wisdom (Early Childhood)	"…the ability to use our clinical skills and past experience to rapidly identify each patient's unique health status and diagnosis, their individual risks and benefits of potential interventions, and their personal values and expectations" (p. 1).	Individual and collective wisdom of families and professionals gained through observation, experience, reflection, and consensus
Patient values (Medicine) Family and professional values (Early Childhood)	"…unique preferences, concerns and expectations each patient brings to a medical encounter and which must be integrated into clinical decisions" (p. 1).	Characteristics of individual children and families as well as local circumstances, values, and contexts that must be integrated into all practice decisions

Note: From *Evidence-Based Medicine: How to Practice and Teach EBM*, (2nd ed.), by D. L. Sackett, S. E. Straus, W. S. Richardson, W. Rosenberg, & R. B. Haynes, 2000. Edinburgh, UK: Churchill Livingstone.

Problems That Paved the Way for Evidence-Based Practice

Table 1.3 summarizes the major shortcomings of the medical field that led to the creation of evidence-based medicine. It is not difficult for those of us in the early childhood professions to relate to each of those criticisms. Early childhood practitioners, administrators, and faculty in professional development programs all require information on a daily basis, but they face obstacles in finding relevant, up-to-date content material to develop training

Table 1.3. Factors That Created the Need for Evidence-Based Medicine

1. "Our need for valid information about diagnosis, prognosis, therapy, and prevention..." (p. 2).
2. "The inadequacy of traditional sources for this information because they are out of date (textbooks), frequently wrong (experts), ineffective (didactic continuing medical education), or too overwhelming in their volume and too variable in their validity for practical clinical use" (p. 2).
3. "The disparity between our diagnostic skills and clinical judgment, which increase with experience, and our up-to-date knowledge and clinical performance, which decline" (p. 2).
4. "Our inability to afford more than a few seconds per patient..., or to set aside more than half an hour per week for general reading and study" (p. 2).

Note: From *Evidence-Based Medicine: How to Practice and Teach EBM*, (2nd ed.), by D. L. Sackett, S. E. Straus, W. S. Richardson, W. Rosenberg, & R. B. Haynes, 2000. Edinburgh, UK: Churchill Livingstone.

programs and to make informed practice decisions. Because there is no single repository for information on a particular topic, those professionals need to conduct separate searches in journals, textbooks, online publications, and so forth as well as to integrate information that is written for various audiences at different levels of technical difficulty. In addition, established guidelines for evaluating research on effectiveness do not exist; however, they are essential for determining the validity and relevance of these findings for other situations. Although we often assume that wisdom and expertise accompany professional experience in the early childhood field, we also should consider the very real possibility that, without systematic methods of sharing practice knowledge and ensuring its utilization, professional competence may actually decline over time. Moreover, health-care professionals also face another easily recognized challenge: the limited time allotted to focus on professional development activities.

Creating Information Systems That Provide Systematic Reviews of Effective Practices

Table 1.4 summarizes some of the major developments associated with the wide-based acceptance of evidence-based medicine, including systematic reviews of effective treatments and information systems that provide professionals with easy access to this information. Aside from the What Works

Table 1.4. Developments Associated With Acceptance of Evidence-Based Medicine

1. "The development of strategies for effectively tracking down and appraising evidence" (p. 2).
2. "The creation of systematic reviews and concise summaries of the effects of health care" (p. 2).
3. "The creation of evidence-based journals of secondary publications (that publish the 2% of articles that are both valid and of immediate clinical use)" (p. 3).
4. "The creation of information systems for bringing [the above] to us in seconds" (p. 3).
5. "The identification and application of effective strategies for lifelong learning and for improving our clinical performance" (p. 3).

Note: From *Evidence-Based Medicine: How to Practice and Teach EBM,* (2nd ed.), by D. L. Sackett, S. E. Straus, W. S. Richardson, W. Rosenberg, & R. B. Haynes, 2000. Edinburgh, UK: Churchill Livingstone.

Clearinghouse (www.whatworks.ed.gov), which was created in conjunction with the No Child Left Behind Act of 2001 (discussed in the next section) and modeled on similar evidence-based medicine systems to produce systematic reviews on the quantity, quality, and relevance of available research evidence, the efforts to address issues similar to those in Table 1.4 are only just being conceived in education and the early childhood field (see chapter 3). The What Works Clearinghouse has developed standards for determining study effectiveness and has established criteria for deciding what evidence will be included in a synthesis of research on effectiveness. Currently, the mission to create research syntheses in particular areas has a K–12 focus, but there are plans to include early childhood topics in the future. These efforts, however, seem geared primarily toward knowledge dissemination, and much more work is needed to enhance the understanding of knowledge and to support its application in practice.

An Evidence-Based Decision-Making Process

Table 1.5 summarizes the key steps in practicing evidence-based medicine. A helpful approach in more clearly understanding the evidence-based medicine process is to contrast the way in which traditional medicine was practiced before adoption of evidence-based medicine with the way it was designed to be practiced in accordance with evidence-based medicine. To make this

Table 1.5. Steps in Practicing Evidence-Based Medicine

1. Converting the need for information into an answerable question
2. Tracking down the best evidence to answer the question
3. Appraising the evidence for its validity, impact, and applicability
4. Integrating the appraisal with clinical expertise and the patient's unique circumstances and values
5. Evaluating the effectiveness of steps 1–4 and seeking ways to improve them in the future

Note: From *Evidence-Based Medicine: How to Practice and Teach EBM*, (2nd ed.), by D. L. Sackett, S. E. Straus, W. S. Richardson, W. Rosenberg, & R. B. Haynes, 2000. Edinburgh, UK: Churchill Livingstone.

comparison, we draw from an example presented in an article about evidence-based medicine published in *JAMA* at the time when this concept was first being introduced to physicians (Evidence-Based Medicine Working Group, 1992). Consider a situation that characterizes traditional medicine: a resident in a teaching hospital admits a man who experienced a grand mal seizure but who has no history of previous seizures. Faced with the question of how to calculate the man's future risk of seizure, the resident turns to a senior resident (who seeks verification from the attending physician) and is informed that the risk of future seizures is quite high. The patient is informed of this risk and told that he should continue his medication and discontinue driving. Now consider this same scenario under the evidence-based medicine paradigm. The resident conducts a computerized literature search on epilepsy and comes up with 25 citations, one of which appears to be directly relevant to this situation. She uses established criteria to evaluate the study and determines that it meets the criteria as a valid investigation. She further determines that the study is relevant for this particular patient. The results of the study show that the risk of seizure recurrence changes over time, 43% to 51% within 1 year, 51% to 60% after 3 years, and less than 20% after an 18-month seizure-free period. The resident devises a treatment approach to fit the risk (i.e., she advises the patient to continue his medication and to reassess the need for medication if he remains seizure-free for 18 months) and the patient leaves with very specific information about his prognosis.[3]

It is difficult to imagine a scenario within the early childhood field that even remotely resembles the ability of this physician to assess the problem and develop an intervention that could be applied with such confidence and precision. This scenario also raises many questions about the applicability of the evidence-based medicine process to education and the early childhood professions. Let us return once again to the example of the child-care program in search of improved literacy practices. Similar to the doctor who asked questions about one patient's risk for future seizures, the child-care director likely will pose a set of complex questions directed at understanding how specific literacy practices will need to be adapted for particular children and how these interventions will be integrated with many other practices that constitute the total curriculum.

Some scholars have pointed to medicine as a model of how to integrate research and practice (e.g., Feuer, Towne, & Shavelson, 2002a, 2002b). But is it realistic to expect that adoption of evidence-based practice in the social sciences will lead to the equivalence of the Salk vaccine in those fields? Some scholars have noted that even the most sophisticated medical research has resulted in conflicting or transitory results that are not easily translated into consistent treatment approaches. Others have questioned the extent to which science (as opposed to clinical judgment) actually informs medical practice. Citing the results of a survey of physicians in the United Kingdom, Sackett et al. (2000) noted that 72% reported using evidence-based summaries generated by others and 84% followed evidence-based practice guidelines or protocols; however, only a minority reported that they understood the appraisal tools (35%) and confidence intervals (20%). If the early childhood field models its evidence-based practices on evidence-based medicine, we likely will face similar questions about practitioners' abilities to understand rules of evidence and use resources designed to identify and evaluate the research evidence.

This section presented an admittedly brief summary of the history, origins, and meaning of evidence-based practice in medicine. Although evidence-based medicine is widely recognized in the health-care professions as the preferred method of diagnosis and treatment, full implementation presents the medical field with a number of challenges. Ironically, there is little empirical evidence that evidence-based medicine leads to better care and improved outcomes for patients, even though that poorly substantiated conclusion is the widely accepted rationale for using evidence-based medicine. Other issues that must be addressed before full implementation of evidence-based medicine include the challenges of (a) teaching medical professionals to be expert in searching and appraising the research literature and (b) finding the resources and time required for professionals to access the evidence in all types of clinical settings (Sackett et al., 2000). Finally, as is the case in all professions, there are some medical practices that simply do not have a sufficient evidence base, which perhaps is the challenge to which we can relate most readily in the early childhood profession as we begin to think about a system that could parallel the one that exists in evidence-based medicine.

In the next section, we examine how evidence-based practice is being defined in the field of education by tracking the history of major policies and legislation. We also begin a discussion (continued in chapter 4) about the implications of these policies for the early childhood field. Although a number of fields outside of health care (e.g., mental health, nursing, social work) have begun to use the term evidence-based practice, we now turn to education to examine how this field has applied concepts from evidence-based medicine to achieve significant school reforms.

EVIDENCE-BASED PRACTICE IN EDUCATION

When we think about policies that spawned the evidence-based practice movement in education, the first thing that comes to mind for most people is the No Child Left Behind Act of 2001 (NCLB) with its emphasis on scientifically based research. But the standards movement and legislation that underpin it actually paved the way for NCLB. Table 1.6 displays key provisions across the major policies that have influenced the evidence-based practice movement in education and the early childhood field. The following sections provide an overview of these policies.

The standards movement. In 1983, a landmark federal study titled *A Nation at Risk* (National Commission on Excellence in Education, 1983) began a movement in which public schools were encouraged to adopt more rigorous and measurable standards and higher expectations for student performance (Ripley & Steptoe, 2005). Since the late 1980s and throughout the 1990s, reforms in education have been driven largely by one thing: the need to set standards that determine what every student should know and be able to do and to use these standards to guide all other education decisions. The primary goal of the standards movement (also referred to as standards-based reform) was to align the curriculum, assessments, and professional development to clear measurable standards that set high expectations for all students. The standards movement linked efforts to reform education with student outcomes, relying on standardized tests to reveal patterns of student achievement among groups, and made public schools accountable for student outcomes. The standards movement has been criticized for its failure to find ways to align standards to student assessments, curricular and instructional strategies, accountability systems, and professional development programs (American Federation of Teachers, 2003); however, the emphasis on the need to monitor student outcomes for all students can be seen across all of the other major policies that followed.

Government Performance and Results Act (GPRA) of 1993. In an effort to collect more systematic information about the effects of all government-sponsored programs on children and families, Congress enacted the Government Performance and Results Act (GPRA) in 1993. This legislation required that each federal agency identify the goals and indicators for all of its programs and report annual progress toward accomplishing these goals. Under Part C (the Infant Toddler Program) of the Individuals With Disabilities Education Act (IDEA), the indicators are increases in the following areas: the proportion of children from the general population who receive services, the percentage of children who receive services in natural environments, the percentage of children who demonstrate developmental improvements, and the percentage of families that report increased capacity to enhance their child's development (Harbin, Rous, & McLean, 2004). Other programs such as Head Start, Children With Special Health Care Needs,

Table 1.6. Federal Policies Underpinning the Evidence-Based Practice Movement in Education

Federal Legislation and Policies	Education Reforms
The accountability movement and standards-based reform (1980s and 1990s)	• Created expectations for student performance standards • Emphasized large-scale standardized tests to reveal patterns of achievement across groups
Government Performance and Results Act (GPRA) of 1993	• Mandated each federal agency to identify goals and indicators for all of its programs and services
Improving America's School Act of 1994	• Promoted high standards for all children • Emphasized professional development opportunities • Required statewide assessments to measure student progress in reading and math
Head Start Act of 1998	• Required all Head Start agencies to collect data on child outcomes • Resulted in the *Head Start Child Outcomes Framework* (Head Start, 1998), which provides 100 indicators of what children in Head Start should know and be able to do
No Child Left Behind Act of 2001 (NCLB)	• Requires annual yearly progress for all students in Grades 3–8, with reading and math scores broken out by poverty, race, ethnicity, disability, and limited English proficiency • Requires highly qualified teachers • Makes major investments in early reading and literacy • Promotes "scientifically based" research
Good Start, Grow Smart Initiative (2002)	• Proposed that Head Start develop standards of learning in early literacy, language, and numeracy • Proposed that states develop voluntary guidelines for early childhood programs on prereading and language skills that align with K–12 standards • Provided resources to identify effective prereading and language curricula and teaching strategies
Education Sciences Reform Act of 2002	• Reorganized the Department of Education to establish the role of the Institute of Education Sciences

Temporary Aid to Needy Families (TANF), and the Developmental Disabilities Programs are engaged in similar, but separate, efforts to comply with federal GPRA accountability requirements.

Improving America's School Act of 1994. In 1994, the Improving America's School Act (P.L. 103-382) reauthorized the Elementary and Secondary Education Act of 1965 (ESEA). The key provisions of this legislation built on the foundations of the standards movement (see Table 1.6). Once again, the focus was on helping all children to achieve high standards, with progress in statewide assessments in reading and math representing a key component of a state's accountability system. The legislation also offered provisions that emphasized high-quality professional development programs that were integrated with the schoolwide improvement efforts. The NCLB Act (2001) that followed contained these same key elements, but added a progression of consequences for states that did not achieve adequate yearly progress in reaching its goals for student achievement.

Head Start Act of 1998. The influence of the standards movement also can be seen in the *Head Start Child Outcomes Framework* (Head Start, 1998). The *Framework* was intended to guide Head Start programs in their efforts to find appropriate tools to assess progress in individual children, align child assessment with the curriculum, and evaluate the program as a whole. The *Framework* contains eight domains and 100 indicators of children's skills, abilities, knowledge, and behaviors. Specific skills in the areas of language, literacy, and numeracy were legislatively mandated and indicated with a star. The *Framework* was based on the Head Start Program Performance Standards, the Head Start Program Performance Measures, and provisions of the Head Start Act of 1998.

No Child Left Behind Act (NCLB) of 2001. The landmark NCLB Act was enacted in 2001 and represents a cornerstone of the Bush administration. As with prior reauthorizations of the ESEA, the major provisions of this act were written primarily with the K–12 school community in mind, but there are aspects of NCLB that have implications for the early childhood field, as we will see. Under NCLB, schools that receive Title I funds are required to show annual yearly progress, with the ultimate goal being that all students will reach academic proficiency by the end of the 2013–14 school year.

Progress in reading and math must be shown annually for all children in Grades 3–8 across the following subgroups: economically disadvantaged students, limited-English-proficiency students, students with disabilities, and students in various racial and ethnic groups. There are no provisions that require schools to report annual yearly progress for children in prekindergarten through Grade 2.

Another provision under NCLB is that all teachers in core academic subjects must be highly qualified. Highly qualified elementary teachers are defined as teachers with bachelor's degrees, full state certification, and subject-matter competence as demonstrated through test scores (for newly hired teachers) or through state-defined standards (for teachers already in the classroom). There are no provisions in the legislation that define the standards for highly qualified prekindergarten teachers. Another NCLB provision related to highly qualified teachers is the provision for professional development programs. One such program is the Early Childhood Educator Professional Development (ECEPD) Program (http://www.ed.gov/programs/eceducator/index.html), which provides competitive grants to support professional development for teachers who serve young children (birth to 5) and their families in low-income communities.

NCLB also includes provisions for two early reading and literacy initiatives to ensure that every child learns to read by the end of third grade. The Reading First State Grant program (http://www.ecs.org/clearinghouse/43/61/4361.doc) provides funding to states and schools to implement scientifically based[4] reading interventions to students in Grades K–3 who are from low-income communities and who are most at risk of reading failure. The Early Reading First Program (http//:www.ed.gov/programs/readingfirst/index.html) targets low-income students in prekindergarten programs and requires research-based curricula to address the language, cognitive, and early reading skills that young children need to succeed when they enter kindergarten.

Good Start, Grow Smart Initiative. In 2002, the Bush Administration proposed an early childhood initiative—Good Start, Grow Smart—to strengthen early learning programs throughout the country. Key provisions of this initiative were (a) to ensure that every Head Start center assess learning standards in early literacy, language, and numeracy for children ranging in

age from 3 to 5, (b) to provide Head Start teachers with intensive early literacy training activities, (c) to encourage states to develop for children ages
3–5 voluntary state guidelines on literacy, language, and prereading skills
that align with state K–12 standards, (d) to encourage states to develop a
plan for offering education and training activities to child-care and prekindergarten teachers and administrators, (e) to offer regional Early Childhood Educator Academies to deliver "scientifically based" research on
cognitive development, and (f) to provide guidance to states on the coordination of early childhood services to avoid duplication of services and to
facilitate smooth transitions to elementary school.

Education Sciences Reform Act of 2002. In 2002, the U.S. Department of
Education was reorganized under the Education Sciences Reform Act to
establish the Institute of Education Sciences (IES), which replaced the former Office of Educational Research and Improvement. The overarching goal
of this legislation was to reform federally funded education research to make
it more scientific. This legislation also established the following entities
within IES: the National Board for Education Sciences, the Commission of
the National Education Centers, the National Center for Special Education
Research, the National Center for Education Research, the National Center
for Education Statistics, and the National Center for Education Evaluation
and Regional Assistance.

Implications of the Standards Movement for the Early Childhood Field

What are the implications of the standards movement for the early childhood field, and how is that movement influencing the evidence-based practice movement? Our review of the key federal policies and legislation that
have defined the standards movement over the past two decades along with
other state and local initiatives leads us to several conclusions.

First, throughout the early childhood field, multiple accountability initiatives are seeking evidence of the effectiveness of programs and services for
young children and families; unfortunately, these efforts are not coordinated,
nor are they necessarily tapping into the most important dimensions of the
interventions they are attempting to assess (Harbin et al., 2004). One of the

challenges of having multiple accountability systems stems from the fact that young children and their families commonly encounter early childhood services from more than one program. For example, a child enrolled in a Head Start program may also receive speech and language therapy through Part B, Section 619 (the Preschool Program) of IDEA. Yet the ways in which programs measure progress in meeting their specific goals are not consistent and do not take into account the duplication of services or the fact that children may receive different services from multiple agencies. In developing their individual accountability systems, each program should recognize and attempt to rectify these inconsistencies.

Second, it should be noted that many early childhood accountability systems that have been created or are currently being considered are based on accountability systems that were developed for older children (primarily children in Grades K–12 in public schools), and it is important to recognize that components of these systems may not be developmentally appropriate for children from birth through 8 years (Harbin et al., 2004). Despite the fact that NCLB does not have accountability provisions for early childhood programs, many other federal early childhood programs such as Head Start and IDEA reflect the national emphasis on testing by requiring annual outcome data. The Good Start, Grow Smart initiative has prompted the creation of new state standards to assess children's school achievement in prekindergarten. Rather than focus on the expectations for the learning environment or program, these early learning standards specify clear results and expectations for prekindergarten children as a way to align child outcomes with the curriculum and to guide instruction and learning across all developmental domains and approaches to learning (Scott-Little, Kagan, & Frelow, 2003a, 2003b). It is not yet clear how these standards will be applied to diverse learners such as children with disabilities or English-language learners, but we should expect that these standards will have a significant effect on the curriculum and on children's learning goals.[5] As we move forward in implementing these new initiatives, it is critical that the early childhood profession institute safeguards to ensure that all early learning standards and accountability measures are developmentally appropriate and used to make decisions that improve programs rather than to label or harm children in any way (Kauerz & McMaken, 2004).

Third, recent national policies have created concerns among many in the early childhood community that the emphasis on academic accountability will trickle down to young children and lead to inappropriate instructional and assessment practices in early childhood classrooms (Kauerz & McMaken, 2004; Wesley & Buysse, 2003). The emphasis on literacy and children's preparation to read as key goals, for example, appears to be changing the definition of school readiness (see entire issue of *Zero To Three*; Fenichel, 2004). Some have questioned whether a sufficient research base exists to support developmentally appropriate interventions that focus on early literacy learning for prekindergarten children. The new emphasis on literacy has led to a number of publications in which early childhood scholars have reiterated basic early childhood tenets about the interrelatedness of development across all domains and the importance of social–emotional development (see for example, Ewing Marion Kauffman Foundation, 2002; Love, 2001; National Research Council & Institute of Medicine, 2000; Raver, 2002; Sherrod, 2002). The essence of many of these publications reflects uneasiness with policies and programs that place too much importance on learning to read at an early age and signals a concern that academic and cognitive skills will be emphasized to the exclusion of children's social and emotional adjustment.

Fourth, provisions within NCLB and other accountability efforts remind us of the critical importance of having highly qualified professionals throughout the early childhood system. Although the provisions for highly qualified teachers in NCLB apply primarily to K–12 teachers, this situation does not prohibit states from setting high standards for teachers in early childhood programs, particularly when these programs are administered as part of elementary school systems (Kauerz & McMaken, 2004). The early childhood field should consider ways to improve and align the uneven qualifications of early childhood professionals from various programs (Head Start, child-care centers, mental health programs, early intervention, public school prekindergarten classrooms, family child care) through comprehensive, intensive, integrated, and continuous professional development efforts. In addition, issues related to compensation of early childhood professionals must receive additional attention because it is widely acknowledged that low compensation makes it difficult to recruit and retain highly qualified early childhood professionals.

Finally, it is also important to consider the ways in which current early childhood policies and initiatives may benefit young children and families. Although some have expressed concerns about the increased emphasis on academic learning during the prekindergarten period, others view this emphasis as an opportunity to expand and improve children's learning in these areas (Kaurez & McMaken, 2004). Many states are making an investment in developing prekindergarten programs as a way to promote early school success and academic achievement among children from low-income families and those with diverse linguistic and cultural backgrounds. Now more than ever, policymakers appear to recognize the importance of early learning and the connections between positive early childhood experiences and later school success. Finally, the standards movement underscores the need to assess the effectiveness of our programs and services for all young children, including those who traditionally have been excluded from accountability systems.

COMING TO TERMS WITH EVIDENCE-BASED PRACTICE: WHERE DO WE GO FROM HERE?

Given the recent emphasis on standards, guidelines, and other accountability measures, it is essential that early childhood professionals find ways to engage in discussions about the best way to implement new federal and state policies that emphasize children's academic outcomes. This effort will require collective questioning and problem solving to address a host of issues resulting from the push for evidence to demonstrate the effectiveness of our practices. We end this chapter with five specific recommendations that we examine more thoroughly in chapter 7. These recommendations reflect our response to some of the most pressing issues and challenges that emanate from the evidence-based practice movement. It may be helpful to keep these recommendations in mind throughout the remaining chapters in which the authors explore specific aspects of the evidence-based practice movement as it relates to research, knowledge utilization, public policy, and constituent participation.

Recommendation 1: Reach consensus on the meaning of evidence-based practice. The early childhood field must reach consensus on the meaning of evidence-based practice in much the same way that medicine has developed a definition for its practitioners. In this chapter, we proposed a definition of evidence-based practice for the early childhood field that was adapted from the one used in evidence-based medicine. As part of the definition of evidence-based practice, we must describe the process by which early childhood professionals are expected to make practice decisions. We must decide whether evidence-based medicine should be a model for developing such a process or whether another approach would be better suited to the needs of early childhood professionals. Furthermore, we must align separate personnel, program, and practice guidelines endorsed by various early childhood professional organizations (e.g., Division of Early Childhood Recommended Practices, the National Association for the Education of Young Children Developmentally Appropriate Practices, Head Start Performance Standards) and determine how these standards and guidelines (based on empirical knowledge, professional wisdom, or both and endorsed through consensus) figure into an evidence-based practice decision-making framework.

Recommendation 2: Make the standards of evidence explicit. We must determine how we will establish the evidence base for the early childhood field and make these standards or rules explicit. Will there be levels of evidence, as some have suggested, that enable us to evaluate research on a continuum from most to least rigorous (with randomized controlled studies being the most rigorous)? If we use various research methods (including qualitative methods), how will these findings be incorporated into the evidence base? We must decide whether and how we will integrate the best available research evidence with professional and family wisdom and values. In doing so, we must be mindful that early childhood practices rarely exist in isolation but, often, are used in combination to achieve broad-based goals, for example, to lower the incidence of child abuse and neglect. What standards of evidence will be used to recommend particular sets of practices to achieve broad-based goals? In addition, we must decide how we will address areas of practice for which a sufficient evidence base does not exist.

Recommendation 3: Develop information systems to promote knowledge dissemination and utilization. The early childhood field must develop mechanisms for collecting, scrutinizing, and synthesizing research and then disseminating it to a wide early childhood audience. The information systems should be widely available and accessible in a variety of formats and should respond to immediate problems of practice. In addition, information systems should include mechanisms for appraising, verifying, and improving practice knowledge information. Beyond the creation of these information systems, there is a need to develop methods that support knowledge utilization within practice settings in conjunction with professional development programs.

Recommendation 4: Identify ways of involving consumers as participants in establishing the evidence base. The field should consider viable strategies for strengthening partnerships between research and practice communities. These partnerships are essential for ensuring that local traditions and individual differences are considered in the application of evidence-based interventions and for promoting the engagement of professionals, families, and communities in improving the care and education of all young children.

Recommendation 5: Align professional development with evidence-based practices. The early childhood field must align its professional development efforts with the evidence-based practice movement. This effort will involve ensuring that professional development activities have clear linkages to professional competencies and standards. It also will entail teaching early childhood professionals how to search and appraise the best available research evidence (or to use critical appraisals already performed by others) and to apply this information in a way that improves practice in a variety of programs and contexts. In addition to promoting a deep understanding of practices in which there is an adequate level and amount of evidence supporting them, another important component of professional development will be helping early childhood professionals understand how they can participate in advancing the knowledge base of their profession.

CONCLUSION

This chapter explored the history of the evidence-based practice movement. We first considered how problems associated with integrating research and practice helped pave the way for reform and then reviewed the origins of evidence-based practice in medicine and in the accountability movement in education. Although recent policies emphasizing standards, guidelines, and other accountability measures are having a clear effect on the early childhood profession, the specific implications of each of these initiatives with respect to early learning and development have not always been considered or explicitly discussed. Consequently, it is incumbent on the field to engage in scholarship and discussions to determine the conditions under which effective learning goals and standards can be accomplished and evidence can be established. To this end, we will want to be mindful of the following distinctive characteristics of the early childhood period that should influence and guide all of these efforts (National Association for the Education of Young Children & National Association of Early Childhood Specialists in State Departments of Education, 2002):

- The younger children are, the harder it is to create generalized expectations for their development and learning, because children's development varies greatly and is so heavily dependent on experiences. This variability also creates greater challenges in assessing young children's progress in meeting standards or achieving desired results.

- To a greater extent than when children are older, young children's development is connected across developmental domains, with progress in one area being strongly influenced by others.

- Young children's development and learning are highly dependent on their family relationships and environments.

- Our youngest children are our most culturally diverse. Early learning standards must take this diversity into account.

- Early childhood programs include an increasing number of children with disabilities and developmental delays. These children must be given especially thoughtful consideration when states or others develop, implement, and assess progress in relation to early learning standards.

- Finally, settings for early education before kindergarten vary greatly in their sponsorship, resources, and organization—far more than the K–12 system—and the vast majority of those programs are not regulated by public schools. (p. 3)

Subsequent chapters extend our discussion of evidence-based practice by exploring its effect on research, knowledge utilization, and policy in the early childhood field.

END NOTES

1. Giddens used this analogy to describe a slightly different problem, namely, how the methods of empiricism are inappropriately applied to generate practice knowledge.

2. The Campbell Collaboration (http://www.campbellcollaboration.org/) was created in 2000 and was modeled on the Cochrane Collaborative to produce similar syntheses of knowledge in the social sciences.

3. Because of the existence of Cochrane Reviews and the like, health-care professionals can conserve time by seeking out critical appraisals already performed by others and, therefore, eliminate step 3, appraisal (Sackett et al., 2000).

4. A number of scholars have noted that the phrase *scientifically based research* occurs more than 100 times in the NCLB Act (e.g., Feuer et al., 2002a; Slavin, 2002). Under NCLB, the term is defined as "research that involves the application of rigorous, systematic, and objective procedures to obtain reliable and valid knowledge relevant to education activities and programs." For a comprehensive discussion on this topic, see a report by the Education Commission of the States at http://www.ecs.org/html/issue.asp?issueid=195&subIssueID=11.

5. For additional information on the developmental appropriateness of early learning standards, see the joint statement by the National Association for the Education of Young Children and the National Association of Early Childhood Specialists in State Departments of Education at http://www.naeyc.org/resources/position_statements/position_statement.pdf.

REFERENCES

American Federation of Teachers. (2003). *Where we stand: Standards-based assessment and accountability*. Retrieved September 15, 2004, from http://www.aft.org/pubs-reports/downloads/teachers/StandAssessRes.pdf

Brew, A. (2003). Teaching and research: New relationships and their implications for inquiry-based teaching and learning in higher education. *Higher Education Research & Development, 22*(1), 3–18.

Buysse, V., Sparkman, K. L., & Wesley, P. W. (2003). Communities of practice: Connecting what we know with what we do. *Exceptional Children*, 69(3), 263–277.

Chatterji, M. (2005). Evidence on "what works": An argument for extended-term mixed method (ETMM) evaluation designs. *Educational Researcher*, 34(5), 14–24.

Dunst, C. J., Trivette, C. M., & Cutspec, P. A. (2002). Toward an operational definition of evidence-based practices. *Centerscope*, 1(1), 1–10. Retrieved September 13, 2004, from http://www.evidencebasedpractices.org/centerscope/centerscopevol1no1.pdf

Education Sciences Reform Act of 2002, Pub. L. 107-229, Title I-B, 20 U.S.C. §§ 9533, 9562.

Elementary and Secondary Education Act of 1965, Pub. L. 89-313.

Estabrooks, C. A. (1998). Will evidence-based nursing practice make practice perfect? *Canadian Journal of Nursing Research*, 30(1), 15–36.

Evidence-based education in early childhood. (2002, Fall). *ERIC/EECE Newsletter*, 14(2), 1–6.

Evidence-Based Medicine Working Group. (1992). Evidence-based medicine. *JAMA*, 268(17), 2420–2425.

Ewing Marion Kauffman Foundation. (2002). *The Kauffman Early Education Exchange: Vol. 1. Set for success: Building a strong foundation for school readiness based on social-emotional development of young children*. Kansas City, MO: Author.

Fenichel, E. (2004). *Zero to Three*, 25(1).

Feuer, M. J., Towne, L., & Shavelson, R. J. (2002a). Reply [To special section authors]. *Educational Researcher*, 31(8), 28–29.

Feuer, M. J., Towne, L., & Shavelson, R. J. (2002b). Scientific culture and educational research. *Educational Researcher*, 31(8), 4–14.

Gallagher, D. J. (1998). The scientific knowledge base of special education: Do we know what we think we know? *Exceptional Children*, 64(4), 493–502.

Government Performance and Results Act of 1993. Pub. L. 103-62. Retrieved November 1, 2004, from http://govinfo.library.unt.edu/npr/ library/misc/s20.html

Harbin, G., Rous, B., & McLean, M. (2004). *Issues in designing state accountability systems.* Lexington: University of Kentucky, Interdisciplinary Human Development Institute.

Head Start. (1998). Head Start Child Outcomes Framework. Washington, DC: Author. Retrieved October 20, 2004, from http://www.kaplanco.com/ ncludes/content/classroom/UGCOF.pdf

Head Start Act of 1998. Pub. L. 97-35, 42 U.S.C. §§ 9801, et seq. Retrieved October 20, 2004, from http://www.acf.hhs.gov/programs/hsb/ budget/headstartact.htm

Hiebert, J., Gallimore, R., & Stigler, J. W. (2002). A knowledge base for the teaching profession: What would it look like and how can we get one? *Educational Researcher, 31*(5), 3–15.

Hood, P. (2002). *Perspectives on knowledge utilization in education.* Retrieved November 10, 2004, from http://www.wested.org/online_pubs/ perspectives.pdf

Improving America's School Act of 1993. Pub. L. 103-382.

Individuals With Disabilities Education Improvement Act of 2004, Pub. L. 108–446.

Kaurez, K., & McMaken, J. (2004). *No child left behind policy brief: Implications for the early learning field.* Denver, CO: Education Commission of the States.

Lave, M., & Wenger, E. (1991). *Situated learning: Legitimate peripheral partic- ipation.* New York: Cambridge University Press.

Love, J. M. (2001, December). *Instrumentation for state readiness assessment: Issues in measuring children's early development and learning.* Paper presented at the State of State Assessments symposium, Atlanta, GA.

National Association for the Education of Young Children, & National Association of Early Childhood Specialists in State Departments of Education. (2002). *Early learning standards: Creating the conditions for success.* Washington, DC: NAEYC.

National Commission on Excellence in Education. (1983). *A Nation at Risk: The Imperative for Educational Reform.* Washington, DC: U.S. Government Printing Office. Retrieved September 4, 2004, from http://www.ed.gov/pubs/NatAtRisk/index.html

National Research Council Committee on Research in Education. (2005). *Advancing scientific research in education.* Washington, DC: The National Academy Press.

National Research Council Committee on Scientific Principles for Education Research. (2002). *Scientific research in education.* Washington, DC: National Academy Press.

National Research Council, & Institute of Medicine. (2000). *From neurons to neighborhoods: The science of early childhood development* (J. P. Shonkoff & D. A. Phillips, Eds.). Committee on Integrating the Science of Early Childhood Development; Board on Children, Youth, and Families; Commission on Behavioral and Social Sciences and Education. Washington, DC: National Academy Press.

No Child Left Behind Act of 2001, Pub. L. 107-110, 115 Stat. 1425 (2002). Retrieved October 30, 2004, from http://www.nochildleftbehind.gov/next/overview/index.html

Odom, S. L., Brantlinger, E., Gersten, R., Horner, R. H., Thompson, B., & Harris, K. R. (2005). Research in special education: Scientific methods and evidence-based practices. *Exceptional Children, 71*(2), 137–148.

Palincsar, A. S., Magnusson, S. J., Marano, N., Ford, D., & Brown, N. (1998). Designing a community of practice: Principles and practices of the GIsML community. *Teaching and Teacher Education, 14,* 5–19.

Raver, C. C. (2002). Emotions matter: Making the case for the role of young children's emotional development for early school readiness. *Social Policy Report, 16*(3), 3–19.

Reynolds, S. (2000). The anatomy of evidence-based practice: Principles and methods. In L. Trinder & S. Reynolds (Eds.), *Evidence-based practice: A critical appraisal* (pp. 17–34). Oxford, UK: Blackwell.

Ripley, A., & Steptoe, S. (2005, May 9). Inside the revolt over Bush's school rules, *TIME,* 31–33.

Sackett, D. L., Straus, S. E., Richardson, W. S., Rosenberg, W., & Haynes, R. B. (2000). *Evidence-based medicine: How to practice and teach EBM*. Edinburgh, UK: Churchill Livingstone.

Scott-Little, C., Kagan, S. L., & Frelow, V. S. (2003a). Early learning standards for young children: A survey of the states. *Young Children, 58*(5), 58–64.

Scott-Little, C., Kagan, S. L., & Frelow, V. S. (2003b). *Standards for preschool children's learning and development: Who has standards, how were they developed, and how are they used: Executive summary*. Greensboro, NC: Southeastern Regional Vision for Education.

Sherrod, L. R. (2002). From the editor. *Social Policy Report, 16*(3), 2.

Slavin, R. E. (2002). Evidence-based education policies: Transforming educational practice and research. *Educational Researcher, 31*(7), 15–21.

Weikart, D. P. (2004). Head Start and evidence-based educational models. In E. Zigler & S. J. Styfco (Eds.), *The Head Start debates* (pp. 143–159). Baltimore: Brookes.

Weiss, C. H. (2002). What to do until the random assigner comes. In F. Mosteller & R. Boruch (Eds.), *Evidence matters: Randomized trials in education research* (pp. 198–224). Washington, DC: Brookings Institution Press.

Wesley, P. W., & Buysse, V. (2001). Communities of practice: Expanding professional roles to promote reflection and shared inquiry. *Topics in Early Childhood Special Education, 21*(2), 114–123.

Wesley, P. W., & Buysse, V. (2003). Making meaning of school readiness in schools and communities. *Early Childhood Research Quarterly, 18*(3), 351–375.

CHAPTER 2

BEST AVAILABLE RESEARCH EVIDENCE: IMPACT ON RESEARCH IN EARLY CHILDHOOD

Patricia Snyder

The purpose of this chapter is to highlight the "best available research evidence" component of the evidence-based practice definition provided in chapter 1, to describe appraisal systems being used to analyze and compile the best available research evidence, and to discuss how the evidence-based practice movement is influencing research in early education and care. The chapter begins by reviewing the three integrated elements associated with the term *evidence-based practice*: (a) best available research evidence, (b) stakeholder wisdom, and (c) consumer values (cf. Sackett, Straus, Richardson, Rosenberg, & Haynes, 2000). Of particular relevance to this chapter, the term *evidence-based practice* is differentiated from terms often used synonymously with it (e.g., empirically supported treatments, scientifically valid practices). Evidence-based practice is characterized as an active decision-making process and is distinguished from tangible lists of practices, including practice guidelines or recommended practices. This chapter also discusses appraisal systems being used to evaluate the best available research evidence, and it considers strengths and limitations associated with these systems. In addition to the rigor of the research evidence, issues related to relevance, significance, transparency, and social validity of empirical evidence are suggested as important features when evaluating the best available evidence. Pros and cons associated with designating randomized controlled trials as the "gold standard" for empirical evidence in early childhood education and care are also presented. The chapter concludes with consideration of how evidence-based practice is affecting research priorities and initiatives in early childhood education and care.

EVOLUTION OF EVIDENCE-BASED PRACTICE IN RELATION TO THE BEST AVAILABLE RESEARCH EVIDENCE: AVOIDING CATEGORY ERROR

The ERIC/EECE newsletter, "Evidence-Based Education in Early Childhood" (2002), noted that "the movement toward evidence-based education is expected to have a significant impact on early childhood education over the next few years" (p. 1). Few would dispute the accuracy of this prediction. As noted in chapter 1, the term evidence-based practice has entered the early childhood professional lexicon, dominated conference proceedings, emerged in request for funding proposals, become part of organizational mission statements, and appeared on the pages of research- and practice-oriented journals in the field. Given its ubiquitous presence, a clear understanding of the concept is needed. Despite uses of the term that often imply other meanings, evidence-based practice in early childhood education and care might best be viewed as a process that integrates empirical evidence, experience, and values to inform decisions about policies, services, supports, or instruction for young children and their families and the personnel who serve them. As discussed in chapter 1, this definition incorporates elements derived from evidence-based approaches described in medicine and education.

The origins of evidence-based practice often are traced to McMaster Medical School in the early 1980s, where the term evidence-based medicine was used to designate a clinical teaching–learning approach that faculty had been developing for more than a decade (McCabe, 2004). David Sackett, who was affiliated with McMaster University at that time, recognized that several basic elements of biostatistics and epidemiology could help him critically appraise research evidence for its use in clinical decision making. Sackett later brought the major tenets of evidence-based medicine to John Ratliff Hospital where he and his students and patients practiced evidence-based medicine "in real time in a busy (200 + admissions per month) inpatient service" (Sackett et al., 2000, p. x). Evidence-based medicine was initially viewed as the "conscientious, explicit and judicious use of current best [research] evidence in making decisions about the care of individual patients" (Sackett, Rosenberg, Muir Gray, Haynes, & Richardson, 1996). The initial focus of evidence-based medicine emphasized bringing critical appraisal to the bedside and detailed procedures clinicians could use to appraise published studies to inform their clinical decision making. Recognizing that this definition of evidence-based medicine failed to include other factors that influence clinical decision making, Sackett and his colleagues later incorporated clinical expertise and patient values into their definition (Sackett et al., 2000). They defined evidence-based medicine as the "integration of best research evidence with clinical expertise and patient values" (p. 1). Sackett et al. (2000) noted that when these three elements are integrated to inform clinical decision making, "clinicians and patients form a diagnostic and therapeutic alliance which optimizes clinical outcomes and quality of life" (p. 1). As acknowledged in the 2001 Institute of Medicine Report titled "*Crossing the Quality Chasm: A New Health System for the 21st Century,*" contemporary definitions of evidence-based medicine also clarify that evidence is intended to refer not only to randomized controlled trials but also to other types of systematically acquired information. The promises of evidence-based medicine are that it will contribute to improvements in health care delivery systems and that wide variation in performance across health care practitioners and settings in relation to patient outcomes will be reduced.

Grover J. (Russ) Whitehurst, former assistant secretary for the Office of Educational Research and Improvement and current director of the Institute of Education Sciences at the U.S. Department of Education, leads an institute whose expressed goal is "to generate continuous improvement in education in the nation by making the practice of evidence-based education routine" (www.ed.gov/about/offices/list/ies/director.html). In a presentation delivered to the Student Achievement and School Accountability Conference in October 2002, Whitehurst defined evidence-based education as "the integration of professional wisdom with the best available empirical evidence in making decisions about how to deliver instruction." Similar to evidence-based medicine, the promise of evidence-based education is that education will be continually improved and wide variation in performance across schools and classrooms will be eliminated (Whitehurst, 2002).

Table 2.1 shows a side-by-side comparison of how the key elements associated with evidence-based medicine and evidence-based education are defined. Both definitions acknowledge the importance of integrating empirical

Table 2.1. Comparison of Definitions for Key Elements Associated
With Evidence-Based Medicine and Evidence-Based Education
in Relation to Other Terminology

| Key element | Definition | | Related terms |
	Evidence-based medicine	Evidence-based education	
Best available evidence	*Best research evidence* refers to clinically relevant research, often from the basic health and medical sciences, but especially from patient-centered clinical research into the accuracy and precision of diagnostic tests (including the clinical examination); the power of prognostic markers; and the efficacy and safety of therapeutic, rehabilitative, and preventive regimens.	*Best available empirical evidence* refers to scientifically based research from fields such as psychology, sociology, economics, and neuroscience and especially from research in educational settings and objective measures of performance used to compare, evaluate, and monitor progress.	Empirically supported interventions or treatments Scientifically valid practices
Clinical expertise or professional wisdom	*Clinical expertise* means the ability to use clinical skills and past experience to rapidly identify each patient's unique health state and diagnosis, individual risks and benefits of potential interventions, and personal values and expectations.	*Professional wisdom* is the judgment that individuals acquire through experiences and consists of personal experience and consensus views.	Craft knowledge Maxims
Patient or consumer values	*Patient values* refer to the unique preferences, concerns, and expectations that each patient brings to a clinical encounter and that must be integrated into clinical decisions if they are to serve the patient.		Values Norms Preferences

Note. Information in column 2 (evidence-based medicine) is from *Evidence-Based Medicine: How to Practice and Teach EBM* (p. 1), by D. L. Sackett, S. E. Strauss, W. S. Richardson, W. Rosenberg, and R. B. Haynes, 2000, New York: Churchill Livingstone. The information in column 3 (evidence-based education) is from *Evidence-Based Education* (slides 3–5), by G. J. Whitehurst, 2002, Washington, DC: Institute of Education Sciences, U.S. Department of Education. Available at http://www. ed.gov/about/offices/list/ies/director.html evidence and professional wisdom or clinical judgment to make informed decisions about practice. Notably, however, the definition of evidence-based education does not include integration of consumer values into the decision-making process. This omission might be viewed as problematic by stakeholders in early education and care, given the strong emphasis placed on honoring family values in the design and delivery of services and supports for young children and their families. Adopting the proposed definition for evidence-based practice in early education and care acknowledges the critical and integrated roles that empirical evidence, experience, and values play in making informed decisions to benefit young children and their families and to guide the conduct of research.

As use of the term evidence-based practice has become widespread, it often is used interchangeably with terms such as empirically supported treatments or scientifically valid practices. Evidence-based practice is not a synonym for best available research evidence, empirically supported treatments, or scientifically valid practices. Using these terms interchangeably represents category error (cf. Westen, Novotny, & Thompson-Brenner, 2005), confusing parts (best available evidence, empirically supported treatments, scientifically valid practices) with a whole (evidence-based practice). As shown in Table 2.1, empirically supported treatments and scientifically valid practices are associated with the best available evidence component of evidence-based practice. However, evidence-based practice represents more than a collection of empirically supported treatments or scientifically valid practices. Regardless of whether the term evidence-based medicine, evidence-based education, or evidence-based practice is used, all three terms refer to a process for making informed decisions that involves considering not only the best available research evidence about certain treatments or practices but also knowledge gained through experience and values.

DISTINGUISHING EVIDENCE-BASED PRACTICE FROM RECOMMENDED PRACTICES AND PRACTICE GUIDELINES

The process of evidence-based practice should be further distinguished from recommended practices, clinical practice standards, or clinical practice guidelines. These latter terms refer to systematically promulgated lists of practices or treatment protocols that are designed to help practitioners and consumers make informed education or care decisions under specific circumstances. McCabe (2004) defined practice standards as firm recommendations that represent blueprints for care with variation from the standards discouraged. He acknowledged that practice guidelines are more flexible and, although they contain specificity, variation from the guidelines is acceptable when clinical experience suggests that a more appropriate course of action for a particular individual might be warranted.

In the context of early education and care, two terms often are used to represent practice guidelines: (a) recommended practices in early intervention and early childhood special education (Sandall, Hemmeter, Smith, & McLean, 2005), and (b) developmentally appropriate practice in early education and care (Bredekamp & Copple, 1997). Based on both scientific and experiential knowledge, these guidelines offer formal guidance or recommendations about effective practices for attaining improved outcomes for young children, their families, or those working with or on behalf of young children and their families.

The processes used to arrive at the lists of recommended practices or developmentally appropriate practice guidelines are detailed by Smith, McLean, Sandall, Snyder, and Ramsey (2005) and by Bredekamp and Copple (1997). Recommended practices in early intervention and early childhood special education comprise 240 practices organized under seven logical strands that represent direct services and indirect supports relevant to the provision of early intervention and early childhood special education (Sandall et al., 2005). Direct services include (a) assessment, (b) child-focused practices, (c) family-based practices, (d) interdisciplinary models, and (e) technology applications. Indirect supports include (a) policies, procedures, and systems change, and (b) personnel preparation. The recommended practices in early intervention and early childhood special education are those supported by empirical research, the experiences and values of stakeholders, and field validation (Smith et al., 2005). In addition, the process of arriving at the recommended practices was guided by five criteria suggested by Peters and Heron (1993) related to designating a practice as recommended: (a) Does the practice have a sound theoretical base? (b) Is the methodological integrity of the research convincing and compelling? (c) Is there consensus with existing literature? (d) Is there evidence that desired outcomes are consistently produced? and (e) Is there evidence of social validity?

Developmentally appropriate practice guidelines are defined as "those that result from the process of professionals making decisions about the well-being and education of children based on at least three important kinds of information or knowledge" (Bredekamp & Copple, 1997, p. 8). The three types of information are (a) what is known about child development and learning; (b) what is known about the strengths, interests, and needs of each individual child; and (c) knowledge of the social and cultural contexts in which children live.

The procedures used to generate recommended practices or practice guidelines might involve appraising the best available research evidence, gathering consensus views about experiential knowledge, and verifying practices through field validation. Several features, however, distinguish evidence-based practice from practice guidelines or lists of recommended practices. First, evidence-based practice refers to a systematic process that stakeholders use to make informed decisions, whereas practice guidelines or recommended practices are tangible lists. To help inform their evidence-based practice decisions, however, practitioners and families might consult recommended practice lists or practice guidelines. Second, evidence-based practice requires attention to local circumstances, consumer values, and knowledge about individual children and families. Recommended practices or practice guidelines offer general guidance that might not be appropriate in all circumstances.

Several additional caveats about recommended practices or practice guidelines should be considered. Recommended practices or practice guidelines vary in the degree to which they are derived from and consistent with an external evidence base. For example, of the 240 recommended practices in early intervention and early childhood special education, 86 (36%) of the practices were based solely on consensus views and professional wisdom; 64% were supported not only by consensus views and professional wisdom but also by the empirical literature (Sandall, Smith, Snyder, & McLean, 2006). To reflect best available evidence consistently, recommended practices or practice guidelines must be updated as evidence accumulates over time (Odom & McLean, 1993). In addition, recommended practices might evolve or new practices might be validated over time as scientific research supports or refutes existing practices. Thus, the term *recommended* is used in lieu of *best*.

The development of recommended practices or practice guidelines also generally relies on expert panels or focus groups to arrive at specific conclusions. As noted by the Institute of Medicine (2001), judgment often must be used in this process because the evidence base is sometimes weak or conflicting or because it lacks the specificity needed to develop recommendations based solely on empirical evidence. Whether the judgment of the expert panels or focus groups actually represent the range of views about what might constitute effective practice should be considered by those who use recommended practice guidelines, particularly when the practice is based largely or solely on experiential knowledge.

Finally, as discussed in chapter 4, the premise that the research-to-practice gap will be reduced solely by developing and disseminating practice guidelines is a simplistic solution to a complex problem. A number of authors (Cabana, Rand, Powe, Wu, Wilson, Abboud, et al., 1999; Hayward, 1997; Lomas, Anderson, Domnick-Pierre, Vayda, Enkin, & Hannah, 1989; Woolf, 1993) have asserted that without systematic attention to other elements of knowledge utilization, as detailed in chapter 4, the promulgation of guidelines alone have minimal effects on clinical practice.

Despite these and other noted limitations about recommended practices or practice guidelines (Christenson, Carlson, & Valdez, 2002), practices or guidelines are generally acknowledged as superior to clinical judgment alone. In the context of early childhood and care, developmentally appropriate practice guidelines and recommended practices in early intervention and early childhood special education represent commendable initial efforts to organize and synthesize empirical, experiential, and subjective knowledge and to acknowledge which practices are differentially supported by these various sources of knowledge.

USE OF THE TERM *SCIENTIFICALLY* ABOUNDS

Evidence-based practice decision-making frameworks frequently invoke use of the terms *scientific* or *scientifically*. Odom et al. (2005) described efforts occurring across disciplines to identify and disseminate practices that have scientific evidence of effectiveness. The No Child Left Behind Act of 2001 defines scientifically based research as research that involves the application of rigorous, systematic, and objective procedures to obtain reliable and valid knowledge relevant to education activities and programs. No Child Left Behind also mandates that teachers use scientifically proven practices in instruction. In fact, as described in chapter 1, the term scientifically based research appears more than 100 times in the Act. The Education Sciences Reform Act of 2002 also refers to scientifically based research standards and scientifically valid research. According to this Act, scientifically valid research includes "applied research, basic research, and field-initiated research in which the rationale, design, and interpretation are soundly developed in accordance with scientifically based research standards" (p. 5). Scientifically based research standards refer to applying "rigorous, systematic, and objective methodology to obtain reliable and valid knowledge relevant to education activities and programs" and to presenting findings and making claims that are "appropriate to and supported by the methods that have been employed" (p. 4). Table 2.2 shows the other elements of scientifically based research standards as defined in the Education Sciences Reform Act of 2002.

Whitehurst (2002) distinguished scientifically based research as one type of empirical evidence in his evidence-based practice framework, distinguishing scientifically based research from empirical information. He defined scientifically based research as "research that uses conceptual models, research designs, data, statistical analyses, and logical inferences that are appropriate to the questions addressed and that support the conclusions drawn."

From an evidence-based practice perspective, few would disagree with the assertion that science or scientifically valid practices should help guide practice in early childhood education and care. As Odom et al. (2005) noted, however, "the devil is in the details" (p. 3). What qualifies as scientific evidence? How much evidence is sufficient to characterize a practice as scientifically proven?

Table 2.2. Scientifically Based Research Standards Listed in the
Education Sciences Reform Act of 2002

Employing systematic, empirical methods that draw on observation or experiment
Involving data analyses that are adequate to support the general findings
Relying on measurements or observational methods that provide reliable data
Making claims of causal relationships only in random assignment experiments or other designs (to the extent such designs substantially eliminate plausible competing explanations for the obtained results)
Ensuring that studies and methods are presented in sufficient detail and clarity to allow for replication or, at a minimum, to offer the opportunity to build systematically on the findings of the research
Obtaining acceptance by a peer-reviewed journal or approval by a panel of independent experts through a comparably rigorous, objective, and scientific review
Using research designs and methods appropriate to the research question posed

Note: From Education Sciences Reform Act of 2002. Available at
http://www.ed.gov/about/offices/list/ies/index.html

CHARACTERIZING SCIENTIFICALLY BASED RESEARCH IN SUPPORT OF EVIDENCE-BASED PRACTICE

Within the context of evidence-based practice frameworks, a variety of research appraisal approaches have been used to identify and to summarize the rigor of the best available empirical evidence. Strategies have been proposed to evaluate the quality of evidence at the level of the individual study and across groups of studies focused on specific topics (e.g., influences of hippotherapy on motor and social–emotional behavior of young children with disabilities; the relationship of phonological awareness to early reading skill development). The second type of evaluation is concerned with knowledge accumulation, which is essential to inform appraisals of the best available evidence within an evidence-based practice framework.

Levels-of-Evidence Frameworks

Levels-of-evidence frameworks have been proposed as one way to characterize the strength and level of available evidence (e.g., Law, 2000). Using this approach, evidence is ranked based on experimental "rigor," and randomized controlled trials often are viewed as offering the strongest evidence in support of a practice. Table 2.3 shows three examples of levels-of-evidence hierarchies: one disseminated by the Treatment Outcomes Committee Editorial Review Panel of the American Academy for Cerebral Palsy and Developmental Medicine (AACPDM, 2002), one proposed by McCabe (2004) to evaluate behavioral health interventions, and another described by Law (2000) for use in early intervention. As shown in Table 2.3, most levels-of-evidence frameworks identify randomized controlled trials (i.e., group experimental designs where participants are randomly assigned to either treatment or control conditions) as producing the most rigorous and credible type of evidence (i.e., Level I). Randomized controlled trials have been referred to as "research's gold standard for establishing what works" (Institute of Education Sciences, 2003). Level V evidence is the "weakest" form of evidence. Few level-of-evidence frameworks acknowledge single-case experimental designs or rank various single-case experimental designs using a level-of-evidence framework. The AACPDM and Law hierarchies are notable exceptions.

Levels-of-evidence frameworks are useful for displaying the types of evidence available for a particular intervention or practice. For example, Butler and Darrah (2001) conducted a best available evidence appraisal of the effects of neurodevelopmental treatment (NDT) for cerebral palsy using a levels-of-evidence framework approved by the American Academy of Cerebral Palsy and Developmental Medicine Treatment Outcomes Committee. The appraisal contains several tables that display the strength of the evidence for NDT versus other interventions or control conditions in relation to various motor outcomes using the level-of-evidence coding system shown in Table 2.3. In brief, the authors found that the preponderance of the evidence did not show an advantage to NDT over the alternatives with which it was compared. They offer several cautions about the evidence presented, however, noting threats to internal validity that were present in the existing research (e.g., small sample sizes, variance in experimental treatments, heterogeneity of participants). Nevertheless, this appraisal offers important information about the strength of existing evidence for a treatment commonly used with young children with motor disabilities.

Table 2.3. Three Examples of Levels-of-Evidence Hierarchies

Evidence level	Types of evidence at a given level		
	AACPDM (2002)	**McCabe (2004)**	**Law (2000)**
I	Randomized controlled trial All or none case series N-of-1 randomized controlled trial	Evidence from true experimental designs	Randomized controlled trial Randomized single-case design (repeated over several participants)
II	Nonrandomized controlled trial Prospective cohort study with concurrent control group ABABA design Alternating treatments design Multiple baseline across subjects	Evidence from quasi-experimental designs	Cohort study with comparison group Single-case design using alternating treatments or multiple baseline methods
III	Case-control study Cohort study with historical control group ABA design	Evidence from expert consensus	Case-control study
IV	Before and after case series without control group AB design	Evidence from qualitative literature reviews and other publications	Before–after study
V	Descriptive case series or case reports Anecdote Expert opinion Theory based on physiology, bench, or animal research Common sense/first principles	"Someone once told me…"	Case reports Opinions of clinical experts

Note. Information in column 2 from AACPDM *Evidence Report: Effects of Neurodevelopmental Treatment (NDT) for Cerebral Palsy* by AACPDM Treatment Outcomes Committee Editorial Review Panel, 2002, retrieved November 15, 2004 from http://www.aacpdmorg/resources/NDTEvidence.pdf. Information in column 3 from "Crossing the Quality Chasm in Behavioral Health Care: The Role of Evidence-Based Practice" by O. L. McCabe, 2004, *Professional Psychology: Research and Practice, 35,* 571–579. Information from column 4 from "Strategies for Implementing Evidence-Based Practice in Early Intervention" by M. Law, 2000, *Infants and Young Children,* 13(2), 32–40.

Although levels-of-evidence appraisals have utility, they often are difficult for most consumers to understand if those consumers have not had advanced training in various research designs or have not completed a research design and methodology course. Most individuals would need assistance from researchers to help translate what the various designs mean. For example, a cohort study with a historical control group refers to a design where participants are enrolled as a treatment group (i.e., cohort) and outcomes for the treatment group are compared with a group who in the past did not receive the treatment (i.e., historical control group). An example of this design applied in early childhood might involve a study in which a group of preschool children from a prekindergarten program (i.e., cohort) are assigned to participate in a targeted early literacy curriculum. Reading achievement scores of these children at the end of first grade might be compared with a group of preschool children who were enrolled in the same prekindergarten program but at an earlier time (e.g., previous year). The historical group would be the group who did not receive the targeted early literacy program. Once translated, the design is easier to understand, which suggests that levels-of-evidence hierarchies should typically be accompanied by user-friendly descriptions such as a glossary of terms.

In addition to translational challenges, levels-of-evidence hierarchies have been criticized because they imply that certain types of research designs are "better" than others (Dunst, Trivette, & Cutspec, 2002). Within the context of evidence-based practice, these types of rankings might be problematic because different types of research questions require different types of research designs (Odom et al., 2005; Sackett et al., 2000; Whitehurst, 2003). As noted in the report issued by the National Research Council Committee on Scientific Principles for Education Research (2002), "Some [design] methods are better than others for particular purposes and scientific inferences are constrained by the type of design employed" (p. 98). As applied to level-of-evidence hierarchies, the key point is that Level I evidence is not "better" than Level V evidence; rather, Level I evidence permits inferences that are different from Level V evidence.

Functional Approaches

Dunst et al. (2002) have proposed a functional approach for characterizing the best available evidence. This approach emphasizes that different types of empirical evidence, which is produced using various research methods (e.g., group experimental, single-subject, correlational, qualitative), might converge to support particular practices. Rather than use a level-of-evidence appraisal approach, Dunst et al. examined relationships between characteristics and consequences of particular practices with explicit consideration of the processes that mediate these relationships. They described six types of relationships that constitute a hierarchy as shown in Table 2.4. According to these authors, the credibility of the evidence is stronger when the highest conditions in the hierarchy (i.e., relationship 6) are met.

Consistent with their functional approach to analyzing empirical evidence, Dunst and colleagues have produced a series of practice-based research syntheses focused on various intervention approaches or practices. Grouped under the heading *Bridges*, these syntheses are available on the Internet (www.researchtopractice.info). In addition to the research syntheses, Dunst and colleagues have produced other materials that summarize findings from the syntheses in consumer-friendly ways. These materials are designed to support knowledge dissemination and utilization of promising intervention practices based on the best available evidence.

Quality Indicators

Quality indicators have been promulgated by several groups including the What Works Clearinghouse (www.w-w-c.org), the Division for Research of the Council for Exceptional Children (Odom et al., 2005), both Division 12 (Kratochwill & Stoiber, 2002) and Division 16 (Chambless et al., 1998) of the American Psychological Association, and the Agency for Healthcare Research and Quality (2002) for use in evaluating individual studies or groups of studies with respect to whether appropriate and rigorous procedures were used in conducting the study, based on the type of methodology used.

Quality indicators have been developed for different methodologies, including group experimental, single-case experimental, correlational, qualitative,

Table 2.4. Six Types of Relationships Between Characteristics and Consequences of an Intervention

Number	Relationship
1	The consequences of a particular practice or intervention are measured to establish a change in a behavior or outcome.
2	The characteristics of a practice or intervention are measured to establish that the environmental events or experience was applied.
3	Both the characteristics and consequences of an intervention or practice are measured, but are not related to one another in a way that establishes a statistical or functional relationship between the two variables.
4	Both the characteristics and the consequences of an intervention or practice are measured and related to one another in a way that establishes a statistical or functional relationship between variables.
5	Both the characteristics and consequences of an intervention or practice are measured and related to one another empirically, and alternative explanations for the relationship are ruled out.
6	The relationship between the characteristics and consequences of an intervention or practice is replicated across cases or studies, empirical dependencies are established, and alternative explanations for the relationship are ruled out.

Note: From "Toward an Operational Definition of Evidence-Based Practices" by C. J. Dunst, C. M. Trivette, and P. A. Cutspec, 2002, *Centerscope,* 1(1), p. 3. Copyright 2002 by the Orlena Hawks Puckett Institute. Reprinted with permission.

and evaluation research. Some groups have developed quality indicators focused only on evaluating experimental designs (e.g., What Works Clearinghouse); others have developed quality indicators to evaluate a variety of designs (e.g., Kratochwill & Stoiber, 2002; Odom et al., 2005).

Typically, quality indicators outline key design features or key evidence components that relate to research design of interest. Some quality indicators systems apply numerical ratings to specify the degree to which each key feature is met in the study. For example, when evaluating single-subject experimental designs, one quality indicator system (Shernoff, Kratochwill, & Stoiber, 2002) identifies nine key features: (a) measurement, (b) evaluating quality of baseline, (c) measures support key outcomes, (d) educational and clinical significance, (e) durability of effects, (f) identifiable components, (g) implementation fidelity, (h) replication, and (i) site of implementation. Each key feature is defined operationally, and examples of how these features "come alive" in applied research are provided to help translate terminology. In this system, coders rate the extent to which criteria associated with each key feature is met. For example, for the measurement feature, a rating of 3 (strong) would be applied if the dependent (outcome) measure scores produced a reliability coefficient of .85 or higher. A rating of 0 would be given if dependent measure reliability scores were less than .70.

The What Works Clearinghouse, established in 2002 by the Institute of Education Sciences in the U.S. Department of Education, has developed quality review standards designed to appraise the strength of evidence for various educational interventions (e.g., middle school math curricula). For each identified intervention topic, a review team is established, a work plan is created, and a protocol is developed that tailors the quality indicator standards to the identified topic. A comprehensive literature review is conducted to gather published and unpublished research on the topic. Studies are screened for relevance on three dimensions: (a) relevance of the intervention of interest, (b) relevance of the sample to the population of interest and recency of the study, and (c) relevance and validity of the outcome measure. If a study does not meet one or more of these criteria, it is identified as "does not meet evidence screens."

After the screening is completed, the study is reviewed to determine whether the findings offer strong evidence of causal validity (meets evidence standards), weak evidence of causal validity (meets evidence standards with reservations), or insufficient evidence of causal validity (does not meet evidence screens). According to the What Works Clearinghouse, studies that receive the designation of "meets evidence standards" include (a) randomized controlled trials that do not have problems with randomization, attrition, or disruption and (b) regression–discontinuity designs without attrition or disruption problems. Studies that "meet evidence standards with reservations" include (a) quasi-experimental designs with equivalent groups and no attrition or disruption problems; (b) randomized controlled trials with randomization, attrition, or disruption problems; and (c) regression discontinuity designs with attrition or disruption problems. All studies that either meet evidence standards or meet evidence standards with reservations are further reviewed along established quality indicator dimensions, including (a) intervention fidelity; (b) reliability and validity of scores on outcome measures; (c) extent to which relevant people, settings, and measure timings are included in the study; (d) extent to which the study allowed for testing of intervention effect within subgroups; (e) statistical analysis; and (f) statistical reporting.

Three types of reports that summarize the reviewed studies are produced and made available on the What Works Clearinghouse Web site (www.w-w-c.org). Study reports are the reviews of individual studies that passed the screen for relevance and design and were reviewed using the quality indicator dimensions previously described. Intervention reports are topic-focused reports produced for interventions that had one or more studies that met the evidence standards. These reports summarize the findings from each of the studies included, describe the intervention, and include tables that show findings across the reviewed studies. Topic reports are produced for interventions that had studies meeting relevance and design requirements of the What Works Clearinghouse. These reports describe the literature review procedures that were used, the key features of the intervention, the findings from the quality indicator assessment, and the overall strength of the evidence for a particular intervention.

Although the What Works Clearinghouse acknowledges that study designs providing the strongest evidence of causal effects are randomized controlled trials, regression discontinuity designs, quasi-experimental designs, and single-subject designs, the quality indicators focused on study design permit coding of only the first three design types; single-subject designs are not included. In addition, the What Works Clearinghouse has not yet reviewed any topics or interventions relevant to early childhood although they have announced early childhood as a pressing education issue. On the Web site, the early childhood topic area is defined as "interventions for children age 3–5 that are intended to improve children's readiness for school (e.g., cognitive development and early literacy skills). All reviewed programs have preschool curriculums and training materials. The review will include research that assesses intervention effectiveness for children with disabilities and English language learners."

Several groups that have developed quality indicator systems also have suggested the levels of evidence necessary to support a practice as being scientifically valid. The Division for Research (Gersten et al., 2005), for example, characterizes a practice as "evidence-based" when experimental or quasi-experimental group designs are used and when (a) either two or more high-quality studies or four or more acceptable-quality studies support the practice and (b) the weighted effect size is greater than zero. High-quality and acceptable-quality are defined using the quality indicators.

Significant time, effort, and resources have been devoted to developing a variety of quality indicator systems. Benefits of these systems include that they (a) offer guidance for those planning research about important study design features, (b) offer a structure by which reviewers of research (e.g., members of research journal editorial boards, graduate students) can evaluate a research study or a group of research studies related to a specific intervention or practice, and (c) might help improve the quality of reporting research findings (Christenson et al., 2002; Des Jarlais, Lyles, Crepaz, and the TREND group, 2004).

Unfortunately, despite these benefits, a number of challenges exist related to the usefulness of these systems to compile information about the best available research evidence and to inform evidence-based practice decision making. First, the sheer number of systems suggests that individuals from related and diverse fields of study have yet to agree on common design features and how these design features should be evaluated. How many different ways, for example, can critical features of group experimental designs be expressed? Although efforts are under way to unify criteria by which features of educational research will be evaluated in the United States through the What Works Clearinghouse, this initiative is limited by its current emphasis on developing a quality indicator system focused on education that applies to group experimental designs.

In the context of early childhood, wherein knowledge from different disciplines informs practices and different research methodologies are used to answer important questions and generate knowledge, stakeholders are likely to be faced with the need to understand and use several different quality indicator systems if they are interested in evaluating the quality of available research evidence. Second, the extent to which coders reliably and competently appraise evidence using quality indicator systems deserves empirical attention so consumers can have confidence in conclusions reached about the quality of evidence (Christenson et al., 2002; Institute of Medicine, 2001; National Research Council Committee on Research in Education, 2005). Third, issues related to "who gets to wear an evidence-based badge" and how evidence-based pronouncements are accomplished once quality indicator analyses are completed must be addressed if quality indicator systems are to be useful (Levin, 2002, p. 487).

Beyond Evidence Quality

Beyond strategies for evaluating the rigor of research evidence, proponents of evidence-based practice suggest several other important characteristics of scientifically based research. As noted by the National Research Council Committee on Research in Education (2005) in *Advancing Scientific Research in Education*, "the national conversation about methodological quality is but a part of a needed broader focus on how to define and uphold quality in scientific education research" (p. 2). Other quality characteristics described in the literature are relevance, significance, transparency, and social validity.

Relevance. Relevance is the extent to which research participants, interventions, and outcomes are deemed similar to those encountered in applied contexts. When evaluating the relevance of research, early childhood practitioners might ask, Do these research findings relate to the children and families with whom we work and can the intervention or practice be applied in the context of our program? As Reyna (2002) noted, quality and appropriately applied methods alone do not constitute the best scientific research: "It [research] has to be relevant to your practice" (p. 12). Producing scientifically valid research that is relevant for use in applied contexts is an age-old challenge. As noted in chapter 1, practitioners often believe that most scientific research is not relevant to their day-to-day work, and therefore, it does little to inform their practice (cf. Philibert, Snyder, Judd, & Windsor, 2003). In his invited address to the American Educational Research Association in 2003, Whitehurst addressed the issue of relevance in educational research when he noted that "education won't be transformed by applications of research until someone engineers systems and approaches, and packages that work in the settings in which they will be deployed" (p. 4). The essence of relevance is a judgment that a practice might work in a typical practice setting because characteristics of the participants, practice, and outcomes in an empirical study and those encountered in applied contexts are similar. Relevance has direct application to evidence-based practice in early childhood. Stakeholders must view evidence as relevant to their unique circumstances if they are to consider it seriously in the context of an evidence-based practice framework.

Significance. In the early childhood education field, research is considered significant when it addresses important questions related to the core issues in teaching, learning, and schooling (Feuer & Towne, 2002). Significant research advances theory or practice in the field, challenges traditionally held views, and contributes to the cumulative nature of knowledge. Although significance might be in the eye of the beholder, the National Research Council Committee on Scientific Principles for Education Research (2002) adapted a framework proposed by Stokes (1997) that they asserted might be useful for thinking about how to pose significant questions to advance scientific knowledge in education. This framework, the quadrant model of scientific research, is shown in Figure 2.1. Whitehurst (2003) suggested that although all four quadrants can generate significant questions that inform practice in education, research activities focused in Quadrant 4 (pure applied research) are most significant for addressing the research-to-practice gap because they give high consideration to use, are practical, and are relevant to practitioners and policymakers.

Transparency. Transparency is the extent to which research findings are reported with sufficient clarity and detail to provide readers a clear understanding of what did and did not occur during the conduct of the study (Des Jarlais et al., 2004). Transparency is particularly important for analyzing the rigor, relevance, and significance of individual studies or groups of related studies. In the context of evidence-based practice, transparency is crucial for characterizing the best available evidence. For example, if a researcher conducting an experimental design study does not operationally define the

Figure 2.1. Quadrant Model of Scientific Research.

		Consideration of Use in Applied Contexts?	
		No	Yes
Quest for Fundamental Understanding?	Yes	Quadrant 1: Pure basic research	Quadrant 2: Use-inspired research
	No	Quadrant 3: Research with no use determined	Quadrant 4: Pure applied research

From *Pasteur's Quadrant: Basic Science and Technological Innovation* (p. 73) by D. E. Stokes, 1997, Washington, DC: Brookings Institution Press. Copyright 1997 by Brookings Institution Press. Reprinted with permission.

categories of treatment or describe the method of measuring treatment fidelity (i.e., the extent to which the intervention or practice was implemented as planned), then the results are not transparent. That is, consumers are unable to evaluate what happened during the course of the study and they cannot evaluate whether results were due to the treatment or to some other factor unrelated to the treatment.

Social validity. Research might be deemed to be high quality, relevant, significant, and transparent. However, if stakeholders do not view an intervention or practice to be acceptable, or if they believe it will require too much time or effort in relation to the outcomes achieved, then it is unlikely they will consider using the intervention or practice. Almost 30 years ago, Kazdin

(1977) and Wolf (1978) articulated the importance of attending to social validity in scientific research. As Wolf noted,

> If the participants don't like our treatment then they may avoid it, or run away, or complain loudly. And thus, society will be less likely to use our technology [applied behavior analysis], no matter how effective and efficient it might be. (1978, p. 206)

RANDOMIZED CONTROLLED TRIALS IN EVIDENCE-BASED PRACTICE: FRIEND OR FOE?

Discussions related to evaluating the rigor, relevance, significance, and social validity of research evidence invariably turn to debates about the pros and cons of randomized controlled trials. At one end of the spectrum, there are those who believe that randomized controlled trials are the sine qua non of scientific research and refer to these designs as the "gold standard" to which all other research designs should be compared. At the other extreme are those who reject experimental methods and positivistic approaches to the philosophy of science. These individuals question the tenets of the scientific method and the existence of objective reality. They assert all knowledge is subjective and context dependent.

Frequently, these extreme positions pit quantitative methods against qualitative methods in ways that diminish the value of both approaches, even though the arguments actually emanate from differing philosophies of science and not from research methods per se. As Thompson (1989) noted, nothing would prevent use of qualitative methods by those who ascribe to a positivistic philosophy of science, nor would a postmodernist have to avoid quantitative methods.

Fortunately, a more reasoned and moderate position, and one endorsed by almost all proponents of evidence-based practice (e.g., National Research Council Committee on Research in Education, 2005; Odom et al., 2005; Sackett et al., 2000; Whitehurst, 2003), is that randomized controlled trials are special types of experimental design that are useful in some, but not all, circumstances. Qualities inherent in the design of randomized controlled trials, including (but not exclusively) randomization to experimental conditions, permit causal inferences to be made with more certainty when compared with inferences that can be made when other types of group experimental designs are used (National Research Council Committee on Research in Education, 2004). Randomized controlled trials are frequently characterized as having strong internal validity, which means that threats (i.e., extraneous factors) that compromise the ability to relate functionally the experimental effect to changes in the dependent variable have been significantly reduced or eliminated by procedures such as random assignment and use of control groups. Randomized controlled trials produce efficacy evidence, which is defined as a measure of the benefit of an intervention that is implemented with fidelity under highly structured (controlled) conditions (McCabe, 2004). Evidence of effectiveness occurs when interventions are implemented with integrity in natural settings and achieve meaningful outcomes with or without concurrent controls. Effectiveness studies are focused on generalizability and consider issues related to the feasibility, use, and acceptability of the intervention or practice in different contexts or with different participants (Kratochwill & Stoiber, 2002).

The "Power" of Random Assignment

The professed "power" of random assignment in the context of randomized controlled trials is that it creates probabilistic equivalence between treatment and control groups before treatment is applied. Random assignment helps ensure that assignment to treatment or control conditions is independent of researchers' personal judgment or participants' preferences. Random assignment "provides the greatest confidence that no systematic biases exist with respect to a group's collective attributes that might differentially affect the dependent (outcome) variable" (Portney & Watkins, 2000, p. 155). Random assignment also is expected to control for random events that occur during the course of study, assuming that these events are equally likely to be experienced by participants in treatment and control groups. The promise of random assignment in relation to probabilistic equivalence of groups is typically more powerful as sample sizes increase. When fewer participants are randomly assigned to groups (e.g., 20 participants randomly assigned to either a treatment or control condition), it is more likely individuals in the two groups might differ, on average, on an attribute that has relevance to the dependent variable. Mosteller and Boruch (2002) have edited a text that presents in-depth discussion about the power and potential pitfalls of random assignment in randomized controlled trials. In addition, the National Research Council Committee on Research in Education has issued a report titled *Implementing Randomized Field Trials in Education: Report of a Workshop* (2004) that characterizes the opportunities and challenges associated with conducting randomized trials in applied settings. Interested readers are referred to these sources for additional discussion about randomized controlled trials.

When Might Randomized Controlled Trials Be Useful in Early Education and Care?

If the question of interest is causal, then a randomized controlled trial might be a useful design to use because it will provide a relatively unbiased estimate of the efficacy or effectiveness of an intervention for study participants. A well-designed randomized controlled trial or, better yet, several well-designed randomized controlled trials focused on the same intervention, can offer important evidence to inform evidence-based practice decisions. An important and often overlooked caveat related to randomized controlled trials, however, is that these designs provide information about how well a practice or intervention works "on average" for participants enrolled in the study. Average effects imply that, in most cases, the intervention works better for some participants than others. When stakeholders in early childhood attempt to apply an intervention or practice that worked well for the average participant in a randomized controlled trial to young children with whom they work, particularly those who might not fall within an "average" range (i.e., children with disabilities or learning challenges) and who might not have been represented in the initial study samples, then different results might be achieved. This issue partially explains the key role that single-subject experimental designs play in applied research in early childhood, particularly early childhood special education. Single-subject designs permit experimental analysis of whether an intervention or practice is efficacious or effective for a particular child or family. This analysis is accomplished through time series manipulation of an independent variable and the demonstration, over time, of a functional relationship between manipulation of the independent variable and changes in level, trend or variability of treatment outcomes of interest. As stated previously, decisions about whether to use a group experimental or single-subject experimental design should be guided by the research question of interest. If the research question is focused on examining average treatment effects, then a randomized controlled trial might be an appropriate choice. To address causal research questions related to a particular child or small group of children (e.g., $n = 3$), single-subject experimental designs would be suitable choices.

Randomized controlled trials would not be useful when the research question is not causal (National Research Council Committee on Scientific Principles for Education Research, 2002). Randomized controlled trials also are not appropriate when randomization to an intervention or practice condition is not possible. For example, if the question of interest is Do children with severe disabilities impose greater caregiving stress on families than children with mild disabilities, then it is unlikely that researchers would consider randomly assigning family members to children with and without severe disabilities. Because of ethical concerns, randomized controlled trials might not be appropriate in circumstances where interventions previously demonstrated to be efficacious or effective are proposed to be withheld. Boruch, de Moya, and Snyder (2002) suggested that randomized controlled trials might not be warranted if other research designs produce satisfactory evidence about intervention or practice effectiveness.

Do Other Forms of Evidence Count?

Beyond demonstrating cause–effect relationships between independent (x) and dependent (y) variables of interest, researchers often are interested in explicating processes or mechanisms by which x and y are functionally related. Researchers also might be interested in describing phenomena or relationships among variables of interest. In *Scientific Research in Education* (National Research Council Committee on Scientific Principles for Education Research, 2002), members of the committee described three types of research questions that might be asked: What is happening? Is there a systematic effect? Why or how is it happening?

Descriptive or correlational research designs often are used to address questions related to what is happening. In the context of an early childhood program, for example, researchers might work with staff and families to examine relationships between (a) teacher, program, and child characteristics and (b) child outcomes. This type of evidence might be used to help inform program modifications such as teacher training initiatives or class size. Qualitative methods might be used to address questions related to why something is happening in the early childhood program. Suppose a causal study demonstrated improved social and cognitive outcomes, on average, for children enrolled in preschool classes with student–teacher ratios of 8:1 compared with children enrolled in preschool classes with ratios of 12:1. Additional research might be conducted to understand the processes or mechanisms by which reduced class size resulted in improved child outcomes. For example, an ethnographic study might reveal qualitatively different teacher–child interactions across the two types of classrooms, which could support theoretical expectations that the quality of teacher–child interactions also relate to child outcomes.

All three forms of evidence (descriptive, causal, process or mechanism) should "count" as legitimate evidence to help inform evidence-based practice decisions. Research that produces evidence, however, should be evaluated against scientifically valid research standards that are appropriate for the particular design used. In addition, as they engage in evidence-based practice, researchers and consumers of research should recognize the types of inferences that can be drawn from the available evidence (e.g., descriptive designs do not permit causal inferences).

INFLUENCES OF THE EVIDENCE-BASED PRACTICE MOVEMENT ON EARLY CHILDHOOD RESEARCH INITIATIVES AND PRIORITIES

The evidence-based practice movement has affected and will continue to influence research initiatives and priorities in early childhood. Efforts to accumulate and synthesize the best available research evidence in early childhood, including initiatives such as the DEC recommended practices (Sandall, et al., 2005), the What Works Clearinghouse (www.w-w-c.org), the Research and Training Center on Early Childhood Development (www.researchtopractice.info) as well as work being conducted by the Center for Evidence-Based Practice: Young Children with Challenging Behavior (http://challengingbehavior.fmhi.usf.edu/) and the Center on the Social and Emotional Foundations of Early Learning (http://csefel.uiuc.edu/), will help to identify what is known empirically about various early childhood interventions and practices. These initiatives also are likely to inform future research funding priorities from various federal agencies and foundations as gaps in the scientific knowledge base are identified.

The evidence-based practice movement also has promoted the use of scientific evidence to inform the development of preschool standards, the selection of preschool curricula, and the use of "certified" programs in early education and care contexts. For example, the Institute for Education Sciences (IES) has funded a Preschool Curriculum Evaluation Research Program (http://pcer.rti.org/Index.htm) to gather evidence about selected preschool curricula. This program is designed to learn more about which preschool curricula are most effective for which children, primarily by using randomized controlled trial research designs.

The curriculum evaluation research program and other research priorities proposed by the IES related to early education (e.g., beginning reading interventions) reflect a growing emphasis for the field of early education to use research evidence to inform practice. Few would argue with the importance of having research help inform practice rather than relying on "cycles of fad and fancy" (Whitehurst, 2001, p. 9). From an evidence-based practice perspective, however, practice-based decisions must be guided not only by research evidence but also by knowledge gained through experience and consumer values. Attention to local circumstances and priorities must also be considered when evaluating research evidence.

Demand for evidence-based practice in early childhood programs also is generating vigorous discussion about what research evidence should be used to inform the overall design of those programs. For example, leading scholars in the field have debated (a) whether Head Start should become an academically oriented early reading program because of research evidence that demonstrates the importance of early exposure to reading to later school success or (b) whether Head Start should continue its comprehensive approach to promoting school readiness. Those who support a greater focus on academically oriented early reading have cited discouraging evidence that the average child exiting Head Start is able to name only one letter of the alphabet (Whitehurst, 2001). Conversely, those who support a comprehensive approach highlight the importance of promoting children's social competence and well-being in addition to their cognitive and language abilities. Shonkoff (2003) noted, "If we really want to enhance children's readiness for school, then we must pay as much attention to their social competence and emotional well-being as we do to their cognitive and language abilities—and we must strengthen the ability of both their parents and early childhood program staff to promote their healthy development" (pp. 2–3). Shonkoff based his position on evidence that he and others reviewed under the auspices of the National Research Council and the Institute of Medicine. This evidence is summarized in the seminal report *From Neurons to Neighborhoods: The Science of Early Childhood Development* (National Research Council & Institute of Medicine, 2000).

Of significance for both positions is the assertion put forth in the National Research Council report (National Research Council & Institute of Medicine, 2000) that a large gap exists between what we know from the science of early childhood development (i.e., knowledge accumulation) and what practitioners do in their day-to-day interactions with young children and their families (i.e., knowledge utilization). Given this recognized gap, the evidence-based practice movement is also stimulating focused research on knowledge utilization. In their testimony to the President's Commission on Excellence in Special Education, Wolery and Bailey (2002) noted that "support is needed to study and use procedures for transferring research knowledge into ongoing practice of existing early intervention providers" (p. 97). Recognizing the importance of knowledge utilization within an evidence-based practice framework, recent requests for proposals from the Institute of Education Sciences and the Office of Special Education programs in the U.S. Department of Education have emphasized conducting scientifically valid research in typical practice settings and research focused on model demonstration and "scale-up" of effective practices.

Researchers have important roles to play in helping to translate research evidence and in ensuring its effective utilization in applied contexts. The participatory action research approach and other participative approaches to inquiry, such as communities of practice described in chapter 3, offer promise for helping to bridge the research-to-practice gap. However, as with other strategies for knowledge accumulation and utilization, empirical evidence that supports the effectiveness of these approaches is needed.

Given the increased emphasis on accountability, data-driven decision making, and use of data to assess local needs and make decisions, early childhood practitioners and consumers will likely increase their demands to have access to the best available research evidence. A descriptive study conducted by Rogers and Holm (1994) found that consumers expect or value at least five key elements when they seek health or rehabilitation interventions. First, they expect the choice of interventions provided to them be based on science or at least on the consensus of experts. Second, they assume the clinician or educator is competent and is using up-to-date techniques and technology. Third, they want an intervention that is designed for and consistent with their individual goals. Fourth, they anticipate that the intervention will be consistent with recognized standards (if standards exist). Finally, they hope the treatment will be effective. Might these findings generalize and also represent the expectations and values of consumers of early childhood services and supports?

Asserting that early childhood education and care programs are research based will require both the conduct of research that informs practice and practice that informs the types of applied research questions that need to be answered. Perhaps more than ever before, research in early education and care must become a transactional, participatory process. The evidence-based practice movement offers the opportunity to enhance the rigor, relevancy, transparency, and social validity of the "best available" research evidence in early education and care. As initiatives focused on generating, compiling, and disseminating the "best available" research evidence continue, however, several key points addressed in this chapter might be relevant.

First, policymakers, researchers, and consumers should not equate evidence-based practice solely with empirically supported interventions or, even more restrictively, with randomized controlled trials. Those who assert that evidence-based practice is simply about research evidence or randomized controlled trials do not understand its history and evolution. Evidence-based practice is a decision-making *process* that integrates the best available research evidence with family and professional knowledge and values. Generating research evidence is a necessary but not sufficient part of evidence-based practice. Second, prolonged debates about whether randomized controlled trials produce superior forms of evidence should be avoided. Randomized controlled trials alone do not produce definitive evidence in the ways that some have claimed, nor are they the solution for every research question of interest. Randomized controlled trials do have a place (as do other research designs) in the context of evidence-based practice and should be recognized, like other forms of scientific inquiry, for their strengths and limitations. Position on a level-of-evidence hierarchy is not the only thing to consider when evaluating the strength of research evidence. Third, laments such as "randomized controlled trials are the only valued research approach" or "we are limited to conducting randomized controlled trials in applied contexts" are naive and do little to advance the implementation of appropriate and relevant scientific research in early childhood education and care. Research questions should drive the choice of research methodologies. Because not all research questions are causal, other forms of data, beyond data generated in randomized controlled trials, will contribute to the best available research evidence (Westen et al., 2005). Finally, and perhaps more important, rather than lament about randomized controlled trials, those in the field should focus attention on initiatives that (a) systematically build research evidence, (b) integrate different forms of evidence, and (c) encourage collaborative inquiry among researchers, practitioners, and consumers.

What are the alternatives to evidence-based early education and care? A *Skeptic's Medical Dictionary* suggests eminence-based practice as an alternative (O'Donnell, 1997). When describing eminence-based practice, the author lightheartedly asserts that experience is worth any amount of evidence and defines experience as "making the same mistakes with increasing confidence over an impressive number of years." As the science of early childhood education continues to evolve, the expectation is that we will thoughtfully and appropriately blend scientifically valid evidence with experiences and values to engage in evidence-based practice for the ultimate benefit of children, families, and society.

REFERENCES

AACPDM Treatment Outcomes Committee Editorial Review Panel. (2002, March). *AACPDM evidence report: Effects of neurodevelopmental treatment (NDT) for cerebral palsy.* Retrieved November 15, 2004, from http://www.aacpdm.org/resources/NDTEvidence.pdf

Agency for Healthcare Research and Quality. (2002, March). Systems to rate the strength of scientific evidence. *Evidence Report/Technology Assessment, 47,* 1–11.

Boruch, R., de Moya, D., & Snyder, B. (2002). The importance of randomized field trials in education and related areas. In F. Mosteller & R. Boruch (Eds.), *Evidence matters: Randomized trials in education research* (pp. 50–79). Washington, DC: Brookings Institution Press.

Bredekamp, S., & Copple, C. (Eds.). (1997). *Developmentally appropriate practice in early childhood programs.* Washington, DC: National Association for the Education of Young Children.

Butler, C., & Darrah, J. (2001). AACPDM evidence report: Effects of neurodevelopmental treatment (NDT) for cerebral palsy. *Developmental Medicine and Child Neurology, 43,* 778–790.

Cabana, M. D., Rand, C. S., Powe, N. R., Wu, A. W., Wilson, M. H., Abboud, P.-A. C., et al. (1999). Why don't physicians follow clinical practice guidelines? A framework for improvement. *Journal of the American Medical Association, 282,* 1458–1465.

Chambless, D. L., Baker, M. J., Baucom, D. H., Beutler, L. E., Calhoun, K. S., Crits-Christoph, P., et al. (1998). Update on empirically validated therapies. II. *The Clinical Psychologist, 51,* 3–15.

Christenson, S. L., Carlson, C., & Valdez, C. R. (2002). Evidence-based interventions in school psychology: Opportunities, challenges, and cautions. *School Psychology Quarterly, 17,* 466–474.

Des Jarlais, D. C., Lyles, C., Crepaz, N., & the TREND group. (2004). Improving the reporting quality of nonrandomized evaluations of behavioral and public health interventions: The TREND statement. *American Journal of Public Health, 94,* 361–366.

Dunst, C. J., Trivette, C., & Cutspec, P. A. (2002, September). Toward an operational definition of evidence-based practices. *Centerscope, 1*(1), 1–10.

Education Sciences Reform Act of 2002, Pub. L. 107-229, Title I-B, 20 U.S.C. §§ 9533, 9562.

Evidence-based education in early childhood. (2002, Fall). *ERIC/EECE Newsletter, 14*(2), 1–6.

Feuer, M., & Towne, L. (2002, February). *The logic and basic principles of scientifically based research.* Paper presented at the U.S. Department of Education working group conference, The Use of Scientifically Based Research in Education (S. B. Neuman, Chair), Barnard Auditorium, Washington, DC.

Gersten, R., Fuchs, L, Compton, D., Coyne, M., Greenwood, C., & Innocenti, M. (2005). Quality indicators for group experimental and quasi-experimental research in special education. *Exceptional Children, 71,* 149–164.

Hayward, R. (1997). Clinical practice guidelines on trial. *Canadian Medical Association Journal, 156,* 1725–1727.

Institute of Education Sciences. (2003, December). *Identifying and implementing educational practices supported by rigorous evidence: A user friendly guide.* Washington, DC: U.S. Department of Education.

Institute of Medicine. (2001). *Crossing the quality chasm: A new health system for the 21st century.* Washington, DC: National Academy Press.

Kazdin, A. E. (1977). Assessing the clinical or applied importance of behavior change through social validation. *Behavior Modification, 1,* 427–452.

Kratochwill, T. R., & Stoiber, K. C. (2002). Evidence-based interventions in school psychology: Conceptual foundations of the *Procedural and Coding Manual* of Division 16 and the Society for the Study of School Psychology Task Force. *School Psychology Quarterly, 17*, 341–389.

Law, M. (2000). Strategies for implementing evidence-based practice in early intervention. *Infants and Young Children, 13*(2), 32–40.

Levin, J. R. (2002). How to evaluate the evidence of evidence-based interventions. *School Psychology Quarterly, 17*, 483–492.

Lomas, J., Anderson, G. M., & Domnick-Pierre, K., Vayda, E., Enkin, M. W., & Hannah, W. J. (1989). Do practice guidelines guide practice? The effect of a consensus statement on the practice of physicians. *New England Journal of Medicine, 321*, 1306–1311.

McCabe, O. L. (2004). Crossing the quality chasm in behavioral health care: The role of evidence-based practice. *Professional Psychology: Research and Practice, 35*, 571–579.

Mosteller, F., & Boruch, R. (Eds.). (2002). *Evidence matters: Randomized trials in education research.* Washington, DC: Brookings Institution Press.

National Research Council Committee on Research in Education. (2004). *Implementing randomized field trials in education: Report of a workshop.* Washington, DC: The National Academy Press.

National Research Council Committee on Research in Education. (2005). *Advancing scientific research in education.* Washington, DC: The National Academy Press.

National Research Council Committee on Scientific Principles for Education Research. (2002). *Scientific research in education.* Washington, DC: National Academy Press.

National Research Council, & Institute of Medicine. (2000). *From neurons to neighborhoods: The science of early childhood development* (J. P. Shonkoff & D. A. Phillips, Eds.). Committee on Integrating the Science of Early Childhood Development; Board on Children, Youth, and Families; Commission on Behavioral and Social Sciences and Education. Washington, DC: National Academy Press.

No Child Left Behind Act of 2001, Pub. L. 107-110, 115 Stat. 1425 (2002).

Odom, S. L., Brantlinger, E., Gersten, R., Horner, R. H., Thompson, B., & Harris, K. R. (2005). Research in special education: Scientific methods and evidence-based practices. *Exceptional Children, 71*, 137–148.

Odom, S. L., & McLean, M. E. (1993). Establishing recommended practices for programs for infants and young children with special needs and their families. In S. L. Odom & M.E. McLean (Eds.), *DEC recommended practices: Indicators of quality in programs for infants and young children with special needs and their families* (pp. 1–10). Reston, VA: Council for Exceptional Children.

O'Donnell, M. (1997). *A skeptic's medical dictionary.* London: BMJ Publishing Group.

Peters, M. T., & Heron, T. E. (1993). When the best is not good enough: An examination of best practice. *Journal of Special Education, 26*, 371–385.

Philibert, D. B., Snyder, P., Judd, D., & Windsor, M. M. (2003). Practitioners' reading patterns, attitudes, and use of research reported in occupational therapy journals. *American Journal of Occupational Therapy, 57*, 450–458.

Portney, L. G., & Watkins, M. P. (2000). *Foundations of clinical research: Applications to practice* (2nd ed.). Upper Saddle River, NJ: Prentice Hall Health.

Reyna, V. (2002, February). *What is scientifically based evidence? What is its logic?* Paper presented at the U.S. Department of Education working group conference, The Use of Scientifically Based Research in Education (S. B. Neuman, Chair), Barnard Auditorium, Washington, DC.

Rogers, J. C., & Holm, M. B. (1994). Accepting the challenge of outcome research: Examining the effectiveness of occupational therapy practice. *American Journal of Occupational Therapy, 48*, 871–876.

Sackett, D. L., Rosenberg, W., Muir Gray, J. A., Haynes, R. B., & Richardson, W. S. (1996). Evidence based medicine: What it is and what it isn't. *British Medical Journal, 312*, 71–72.

Sackett, D. L., Straus, S. E., Richardson, S. R., Rosenberg, W., & Haynes, R. B. (2000). *Evidence-based medicine: How to practice and teach EBM* (2nd ed.). London: Churchill Livingstone.

Sandall, S., Hemmeter, M. L., Smith, B. J., & McLean, M. E. (2005). *DEC recommended practices: A comprehensive guide for practical application in early intervention/early childhood special education.* Longmont, CO: Sopris West.

Sandall, S., Smith, B. J., Snyder, P., & McLean, M. E. (2006). *Using focus groups to help identify recommended practices in early intervention/early childhood special education.* Manuscript submitted for publication.

Shernoff, E. S., Kratochwill, T. R., & Stoiber, K. C. (2002). Evidence-based interventions in school psychology: An illustration of task force coding criteria using single-participant research design. *School Psychology Quarterly, 17,* 390–422.

Shonkoff, J. P. (2003, January). *Reauthorizing Head Start: The need for a comprehensive approach to school readiness.* Retrieved April 2, 2005, from http://www.nhsa.org/download/research/shonkoff.doc

Smith, B. J., McLean, M. E., Sandall, S. E., Snyder, P., & Ramsey, A. B. (2005). DEC recommended practices: The procedures and evidence base used to establish them. In S. Sandall, M. L. Hemmeter, B. J. Smith, & M. E. McLean (Eds.), *DEC recommended practices: A comprehensive guide for practical application in early intervention/early childhood special education* (pp. 27–39). Longmont, CO: Sopris West.

Stokes, D. E. (1997). *Pasteur's quadrant: Basic science and technological innovation.* Washington, DC: Brookings Institution Press.

Thompson, B. (1989). The place of qualitative research in contemporary social science: The importance of post-paradigmatic though. *Advances in Social Science Methodology, 1,* 1–42.

Westen, D., Novotny, C. M., & Thompson-Brenner, H. (2005). EBP ≠ EST: Reply to Crits-Christoph et al. (2005) and Weisz et al. (2005). *Psychological Bulletin, 131,* 427–433.

Whitehurst, G. J. (2001, Summer). *Response to* Much Too Early *by D. Elkind.* Retrieved April 19, 2005, from the Education Next Web site http://www.educationnext.org/20012/8elkind.htm

Whitehurst, G. J. (2002, October). *Evidence-based education*. Presentation at the Student Achievement and School Accountability Conference. Retrieved June 23, 2004, from www.ed.gov/offices/about/list/ies/director.html

Whitehurst, G. J. (2003, April). *The Institute of Education Sciences: New wine, new bottles*. Paper presented at the meeting of the American Educational Research Association Conference, San Diego, CA.

Wolery, M., & Bailey, D. B. (2002). Early childhood special education research. *Journal of Early Intervention, 25*, 88–99.

Wolf, M. M. (1978). Social validity: The case for subjective measurement or how behavior analysis is finding its heart. *Journal of Applied Behavior Analysis, 11*, 203–214.

Woolf, S. H. (1993). Practice guidelines: A new reality in medicine. III. Impact on patient care. *Archives of Internal Medicine, 153*, 2646–2655.

CHAPTER 3

THE EVIDENCE-BASED PRACTICE MOVEMENT AND ITS EFFECT ON KNOWLEDGE UTILIZATION

Pamela J. Winton

The evidence-based practice movement is, in part, a response to the persistent concern that practitioners are not using high-quality educational research to inform and shape their practices. Yet critics complain that the evidence-based practice movement provides little guidance for how to implement evidence-based practices once they are identified (Rothman, 2005). Consider a situation that characterizes the implementation dilemma noted by critics. The director of a child-care program has attended a 2-day workshop on emergent literacy based on the latest research on the topic. On the following Monday morning, she was eager to talk with her teaching staff about the possibilities of making some changes in the literacy practices in her program. The concerns of her staff were immediate and multiple. How could they find time for one-on-one or small-group storybook reading activities within their crowded classroom schedule? How could they manage the class if they focused so much time on individual children? How could the ideas for extending these activities outside of the classroom possibly work with their families?

Will the evidence-based practice movement help the director in her desire to improve her program practices? As suggested in the short vignette, identifying and sharing evidence is only a small part of the gap between research and practice. The literature on knowledge utilization provides a theoretical framework for examining the many factors that must be addressed to support this motivated, but frustrated, child-care director in making changes in her program's literacy practices.

Figure 3.1. Components and Tasks of Knowledge Utilization

The primary purpose of this chapter is to identify how the literature on knowledge utilization can inform and support the evidence-based practice movement's goal of decreasing the gap between research and practice. The first section defines the concept of knowledge utilization as consisting of three components (see Figure 3.1): (a) knowledge generation (how knowledge gets created), (b) knowledge organization and translation (how knowledge gets summarized and interpreted), and (c) knowledge mediation and application (how knowledge gets shared, taught, and used). Current models of knowledge utilization suggest that the more the activities associated with these three components are integrated in a seamless fashion, the more research and practice will be aligned.

The second section of the chapter highlights four promising models for accomplishing this integration: consultation, coaching, mentoring, and lesson study. The third section of the chapter focuses on recommendations for supporting the evidence-based practice movement's goal of decreasing the gap between research and practice.

DEFINITIONS OF KNOWLEDGE DISSEMINATION AND UTILIZATION

A large body of literature exists on the topic of the relationship between research and practice. Different terms such as *dissemination, diffusion, technol-*

ogy transfer, and *knowledge utilization* are used, sometimes interchangeably and sometimes with great distinctions, in the discussions of this topic. The terminology used and the meanings articulated vary depending on the perspective of the authors. A review article by Hutchinson and Huberman (1993) chronicled the evolution in thinking on this topic over the last 50 years. Originally, the focus was simply on disseminating or spreading information. Under this paradigm, knowledge is moved in a linear fashion from one place to another, and the place where knowledge is generated is far from the place where it is used. From this perspective, knowledge is objective, easy to understand, and easy to communicate.

A pivotal study done by the Rand Corporation of dissemination efforts around large-scale, federally sponsored innovations (Berman & McLaughlin, 1978) led to a growing recognition that just because knowledge has arrived at a destination does not necessarily mean it will be used in any meaningful or effective way. These researchers found that even when desired changes in educational practices were made, they were not often sustained. A variety of factors such as changes in key personnel, lack of resources, and lack of ongoing support for teachers contributed to the lack of sustainability (Berman & McLaughlin, 1978).

Current models (Hiebert, Gallimore, & Stigler, 2002; Hood, 2002; Omamo, 2004) take into account the multiple factors identified in the Rand study. They define knowledge utilization as a dynamic process based on a constructivist paradigm whereby learners must be active participants and co-constructors of their own learning. Knowledge generation and use are jointly located and intimately connected. The current paradigm is compatible with the definition of evidence-based practices promoted in this book That is, three sources of knowledge—best available research evidence, family and professional wisdom, and family and professional values—are identified as contributing to decisions about practices. These more complex paradigms for understanding knowledge utilization reflect the challenges the child-care director faces after attending the workshop, as she attempts to implement new ideas in her workplace. Because of daily demands and the absence of additional support, incentives, reinforcement, and facilitation that address the contextual and situational factors unique to her child-care program, she is unable to implement the new knowledge she acquired.

COMPONENTS OF KNOWLEDGE UTILIZATION

Three components related to knowledge utilization include knowledge generation, knowledge organization and translation, and knowledge mediation and application. Issues, promising strategies, contributions of the evidence-based practice movement, and unresolved questions are addressed here in terms of each of these three components.

Knowledge Generation Issues

Traditionally, the generation of educational knowledge has been the domain of researchers and academics. By establishing principles of scientific inquiry and criteria for evaluating the quality of research, the evidence-based practice movement seeks to raise the bar for all educational researchers and bolster the quality of all research. The corollary to this approach is that there will be more high-quality research available to be consumed by practitioners and families, thus enhancing the credibility of the scientific community and the quality of the decisions made by research consumers. Although these efforts to raise the quality of educational research have value, they sidestep one of several long-standing issues related to knowledge utilization—that practitioners generally do not turn to research to answer pressing practical questions. Practitioners usually judge the quality of research by a different rubric than the one being advanced by the evidence-based practice movement; they judge on the basis of whether the results are practical, easy to understand, and congruent with teachers' real-world experience (Honig & Coburn, 2005). The source of information may be more important to users than the research quality (Lamb-Parker, Greenfield, Fantuzzo, Clark, & Coolahan, 2002; Southwest Educational Development Laboratory, 1996). As stated in chapter 1, the source that seems to be highly valued by teachers and early educators is their own professional experience or "craft knowledge," which has been described as concrete and contextually rich with real-world experiences (Hiebert, et al., 2002). This kind of knowledge is often based on tacit understandings, including deeply held beliefs, values, and insights, rather than more explicit knowledge derived from systematic investigations (Nutley, Walter, & Davies, 2002). Research from the allied health literature mirrors these assertions (Philibert, Snyder, Judd, & Windsor, 2003; Rappolt

& Tassone, 2002). The findings indicate that practitioners are more likely to trust and use knowledge that is based on their own and their colleagues' experiences rather than on information from research studies.

These findings relate to the second major issue—how to integrate practitioners' experiences and deeply held beliefs with research findings in a way that informs decisions. Current models of knowledge utilization emphasize the importance of researchers and practitioners jointly striving for knowledge convergence. In a critical appraisal of the evidence-based practice movement in the United Kingdom, a movement that has evolved in multiple disciplines over the last 10 years, Trinder (2000a) stated that even after a decade of concentrated effort on evidence-based practice "comparatively little attention has yet been given the questions of how to combine evidence with clinical experience or consumer perspectives" (p. 214). That task will demand attention, discussion, experimentation, and rigorous research in our own country that builds on models tried and tested in the United Kingdom and elsewhere.

In the early childhood field, the efforts to integrate knowledge are made all the more complicated by the fact that multiple agencies and individuals fund and operate early care and education programs, which means that a huge variety of stakeholders are involved in educational decision making. Included among these stakeholders are the families of young children—a group whose wisdom and values often are not included in discussions about evidence-based practice. For the most part, the tensions between practitioners and researchers are the focus of discussions about reconciling stakeholder values, beliefs, and experiences. Families are the first and foremost teachers in young children's lives and are critical partners in decisions about practices. In fact, families whose children are eligible for early intervention or special education services are mandated by the Individuals With Disabilities Education Act of 1997 to be participants in decision making about services and programs for their children. As the evidence-based practice movement evolves within the early childhood context, some families will expect to be part of discussions about improving programs and practices. Perhaps the involvement of U.S. families in explorations of the evidence-based decision-making process will prevent the decade-long challenges related to the integration of knowledge from different sources experienced in the United

Kingdom. Strategies to involve families meaningfully will need to be developed and implemented for this integration to happen.

Promising Strategies in Knowledge Generation

Constituent participation in research has been described as an effective tool for bridging the gap between research and practice (Turnbull, Friesen, & Ramirez, 1998) and is an approach to research that is in keeping with a new system of knowledge proposed by Hiebert et al. (2002) in which practitioner knowledge is the starting point for building a professional knowledge base. Various approaches to involving constituents have been described in the literature, including participatory action research (Turnbull et al., 1998), teacher research (Mohr, Rogers, Sanford, Nocerino, MacLean, & Clawson, 2004), and action research (Rapoport, 1985). These approaches start from different ideological perspectives and emphasize different aspects of practice; however, they are similar in that practitioners play an active role in all aspects of the research process. Unlike traditional research whereby teachers, children, and families are the subjects of research, the interests and needs of the traditional subjects provide the catalyst for research questions. Teachers and families may, in fact, be co-researchers.

An example of this approach is the evaluation of Parent-to-Parent Support programs undertaken by the Beach Center at the University of Kansas (Singer et al., 1999). Parent leaders and researchers co-constructed the design of the evaluation study and participated as partners in data collection, interpretation, and dissemination of findings. Interest in this approach has grown over the last decade because of the belief that involving constituents, or the intended beneficiaries of research, in all phases of the research process is an effective way of increasing knowledge utilization (Southwest Educational Development Laboratory, 1996). In fact, attention to this approach in the field of early childhood is strong enough that the National Association for the Education of Young Children has created a new online journal called *Voices of Practitioners: Teacher Research in Early Childhood Education* (for information about this journal, see http://www.journal.naeyc.org/btj/vp/). If meaningful partnerships among researchers, practitioners, and families are established, then the constituency-oriented approaches hold promise as a way of generating new knowledge by building on existing research as well as on professional and family wisdom and values. However, research has not evaluated whether engaging in these approaches affects classroom practices (Grossman, 2005). Studies are needed to examine this question.

Contributions of the Evidence-Based Practice Movement to Knowledge Generation

There is little evidence that the evidence-based practice movement supports the kind of sustained interactions between researchers and consumers around knowledge generation that have been described as the best predictor of knowledge use (Hutchinson & Huberman, 1993). The National Research Council Committee on Scientific Principles for Education Research report (2002) implies an openness to relationships with users or an "inclusive view of the science of education" by saying that researchers should consider "alternative paradigms" and a "diversity of perspectives." However, the definition of "diversity" in this statement is not clear. It likely means being open to perspectives of researchers from diverse disciplines and methodological traditions rather than including the perspectives of families and practitioners in knowledge generation.

Unresolved Questions About Knowledge Generation

Still unresolved are the following questions about how the evidence-based practice movement is shaping the content of research and the process by which knowledge is generated, which in turn influences the extent to which the knowledge is trusted and used.

- Does the movement encourage researchers' interests toward populations that are more easily assessed and studied with existing tools and measures and, thus, bring about the exclusion of certain populations?

- How can researchers align funding priorities with the needs of the community, especially if the needs of the community involve complex problems and diverse populations?

- How does one integrate the perspectives, experiences, and skills of researchers, practitioners, and families to conduct research that meets the needs and expectations of all groups?

This last question is perhaps the most pressing. Good integration is not likely to happen without careful planning and infrastructure support. Multiple barriers (institutional, psychological, sociological) make it difficult for researchers and research institutions to change the traditional perspective that those who are specifically trained in research methods and who hold advanced degrees are the only legitimate sources of evidence about effective practices.

Knowledge Organization and Translation Issues

The first component of knowledge utilization is knowledge generation; the second is the organization and translation of research. The big issue related to this second component is the long-standing complaint that researchers do not synthesize findings in ways that are useful to practitioners and parents. From the perspectives of practitioners and parents, researchers most frequently communicate their findings with other researchers, and rarely do they transform their findings into products or training materials that could assist practitioners and families in making changes (Southwest Educational Development Laboratory, 1996; Winton & Turnbull, 1982). Research reports emphasize the abstract rather than the concrete, use technical language, and are too lengthy to be read by busy administrators (Honig & Coburn, 2005). Some researchers legitimately counter these criticisms by stating that they were not trained to translate their work for practitioners and that others are better suited for this task. They also are concerned about the oversimplification of their findings or the possibilities that they or others might overstate the implications that can be drawn from a single study. They sometimes feel the tension between wanting to provide practical guidelines and needing to acknowledge and honor the limits of their data.

Not content to let researchers off the hook, Shonkoff (2003) called for the creation of "publicly literate scientists" (p. 2) who have the skills and motivation to communicate with users in targeted and effective ways. He advocates using techniques from the field of social marketing to hone language and messages in ways that resonate with intended audiences. Social marketing as a tool for creating behavior change based on evidence-based practices is heavily used in the field of health promotion and prevention (Institute of

Medicine, 2002). Social marketing models view consumers as experts whose values, beliefs, and interests enter heavily into how research is organized, translated, and presented. Smoking cessation and "Back to Sleep" (promoting babies sleeping on their backs) campaigns are examples of widely known social marketing approaches to behavior change.

Clearly not every research finding should be widely disseminated or publicized. Evaluating the quality and importance of research findings is one of the roles of peer review and research syntheses. However, researchers interested in heeding Shonkoff's (2003) recommendation need support and partnerships with those who have specialized training in educational writing, media, curriculum development, and social marketing to ensure that the reviewed research findings reach and benefit intended audiences.

Promising Strategies in Knowledge Organization and Translation

Practice guidelines developed by professional organizations traditionally have played an important role in organizing and translating research. For example, the most recent version of the recommended practices in early intervention and early childhood special education of the Division of Early Childhood of the Council for Exceptional Children (Sandall, Hemmeter, Smith, & McLean, 2005) was developed through a process that involved examining the best available research evidence on intervention and teaching strategies as well as professional experiences gathered through focus groups and field validation. This document includes concrete, specific examples of strategies for enacting each recommended practice as a way of helping practitioners envision how to implement the guidelines.

Learning outcomes for children developed by states and by agencies such as Head Start are another means for organizing and translating research. The outcomes are being promoted as a way of helping teachers focus their teaching and intervention efforts. The *Head Start Child Outcomes Framework* (Head Start Bureau, 2001), including *Head Start Performance Standards*, was produced in 1998. Prompted by the federal Good Start, Grow Smart initiative of 2002, 43 states have developed early learning standards with a remaining 7 states still working on them as of 2005 (Neuman & Roskos, 2005).

The evidence-based practice movement is also promoting the organization and translation of research by creating centralized structures within the U.S. Department of Education for translating research into research syntheses on specific educational practices. The approach taken is to examine and evaluate all available research on an intervention topic using "levels of evidence" standards described in chapter 2. Research studies that meet quality standards are synthesized and distilled into reports that are shared on the U.S. Department of Education's What Works Clearinghouse Web site (www.w-w-c.org). The desired outcome of this activity is that teachers who are overwhelmed by the amount of information about effective practices, some of it contradictory, will have a trusted source of valid and reliable information on intervention practices that work. Unfortunately, the clearinghouse currently has no early childhood syntheses.

Other initiatives and projects, some wholly or partially funded by the U.S. Department of Education, have taken the cue from the evidence-based practice movement and have created their own versions of online research syntheses. These online resources are described in this chapter's appendix.

An important first step to maximizing the use of this growing number of research syntheses is to inform practitioners and families about them, and the second step is to provide strategies or structures that support their use in decision making. The Evidence-Based Practice Decision-Making Framework (see Figure 3.2) is an example of the kind of structure that can be helpful in this regard. It was developed by the author for a workshop activity related to evidence-based practices and has been used in the following way. A small group of participants (optimally a mix of practitioners, specialists, administrators, and families) are given a practice dilemma requiring a decision and a set of research syntheses related to the content of the dilemma. They are asked to read the syntheses and discuss the dilemma in a way that includes three sources of knowledge: best available research evidence, family and professional wisdom, and family and professional values. Their goal is to agree on a recommendation. The Decision-Making Framework provides workshop participants with a way to capture information from the discussion and ensures that all three sources of knowledge are included in their decision about a recommendation.

Figure 3.2. Evidence-Based Practice Decision-Making Framework

What is the practice dilemma? _____
Key questions(s): _____
_____

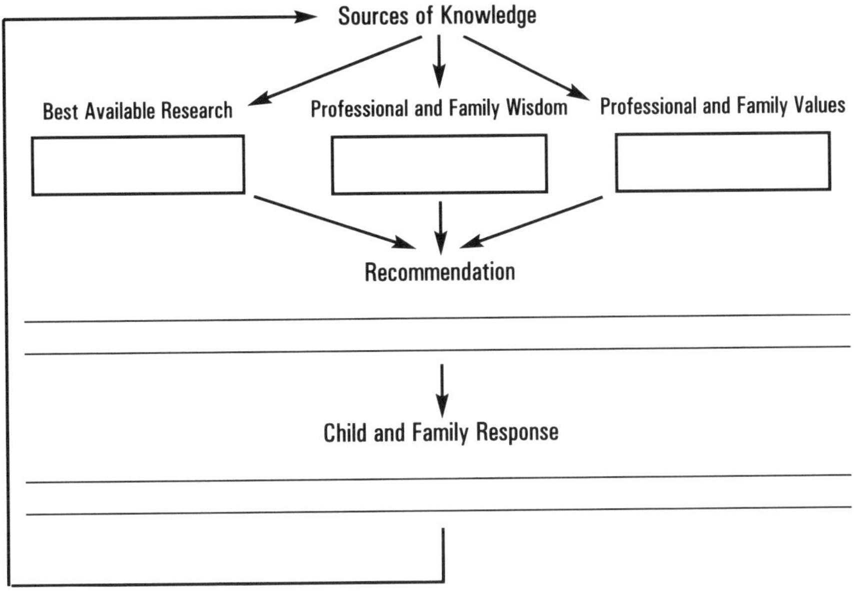

Sources of Knowledge

Best Available Research   Professional and Family Wisdom   Professional and Family Values

Recommendation

_____
_____

Child and Family Response

_____
_____

Contributions of the Evidence-Based Practice Movement to Knowledge Organization and Translation

The evidence-based practice movement has influenced a number of projects and initiatives focused on organizing and translating research information. Even though the What Works Clearinghouse has not yet been a resource to early childhood (thus far, the focus has been K–12 research), there are plans for it to be a resource in the future. In addition, the evidence-based practice movement has served as a catalyst for projects that are creating early childhood research syntheses. Of particular note is the way in which some projects (e.g., Research and Training Center on Early Childhood Development and the Center for Social Emotional Foundations for Early Learning) have attended to the "user-friendliness" (i.e., ease with which one can read, understand, and access) of their syntheses.

Unresolved Questions About Knowledge Organization and Translation

Although these initiatives are promising, chapter 2 mentions some of the caveats and questions associated with them, and they are described more fully here. First of all, the criteria and approaches to evaluating the quality of the research included in the syntheses vary across the different initiatives and projects. Consequently, we must ask several questions. Are the different briefs, reports, and syntheses that purport to be evidence-based of equal quality? How do families and practitioners evaluate the quality of the research syntheses or the relevance of the research to the children and families in their communities? What standards or guidelines should be used to appraise the merits of the various Web sites described in the appendix? Should there be multiple evidence-based practice Web sites on educational topics to navigate, or should there be one official Web site such as the Cochrane Collaborative in the field of medicine (see chapter 2)?

Another question relates to the amount of time it is taking to create the research syntheses and the small number that have been created. The What Works Clearinghouse was created in conjunction with the No Child Left Behind Act of 2001, and there are currently (as of 2006) no research syntheses on the early childhood component of the Web site. It is "under construction." The Center for Social Emotional Foundations for Early Learning has published 16 "What Works Briefs" to date with an exclusive focus on challenging behavior and mental health challenges, and the Research and Training Center on Early Childhood Development has conducted syntheses on 21 practices. Practitioners face a host of intervention and practice dilemmas on a daily basis for which there are no research syntheses to guide decision making. How can practitioners find and evaluate research findings on these topics?

A related question relates to the longevity of these project-based Web sites whose existence is based on short-term grants. Once the grants end, what will become of the Web sites? It should also be noted that the What Works Clearinghouse is the only official U.S. Department of Education clearinghouse for evidence-based practices. Even though other Web sites might use the term *evidence-based practice* in their titles or might receive funding from the U.S. Department of Education, one cannot presume that their products reflect the opinion or endorsement of the U.S. Department of Education.

Another question relates to the fact that we do not know the extent to which these different products, guides, tools, mechanisms, and initiatives actually help practitioners, families, and policymakers understand and use effective practices. As described in the appendix, the Research and Training Center on Effective Practices has created a series of products that range from complex (with links to original source material) to simple and practical, as a way of giving practitioners options for getting access to research. The Center for Social Emotional Foundations for Early Learning has created briefs that combine vignettes, strategies, and research information in a succinct format to assist practitioners with application. Other products have been developed to assist consumers of research in conducting assessments of the quality of individual studies in cases where syntheses are not available (see appendix). These efforts are designed to bridge the research-to-practice and research-to-policy gaps, but are they successful? To date, there are few studies that document the extent to which that bridging happens.

A notable exception is a study by Dunst and Raab (2005) at the Research and Training Center on Early Childhood Development in which they evaluated the effectiveness of an evidence-based practice guide for increasing preschoolers' prosocial interactive behavior with peers. The practice guide consisted of the information from the series of products *Bridges* (see Raab, 2003), *Bottomlines* (see Roberts, 2003), and *If It Fits* on the use of social toys available from the center's Web site. Twenty-eight preschool teachers participated in the study by using the practice guide accompanied by a short written explanation of how to implement the practices. They agreed to use the guide over a 20-day period. The results of data collected on teacher usage of the guide and teacher ratings of children's behavior at the end of the 20-day period indicated a positive correlation between the degree to which the teacher used the practice guide and the teachers' rating of prosocial child behavior in their classrooms. The findings, which included a social validity rating of the guide, also provided preliminary evidence that teachers value practice guides of the sort developed by the Center for Effective Practices.

The study by Dunst and Raab (2005) raises many interesting questions about the role of knowledge organization and translation. First of all, this study could be viewed as support for the linear "dissemination paradigm" of knowledge utilization described earlier whereby the research-to-practice gap could be solved if teachers are simply given clear, easy to understand information. The authors noted that the findings "provide credence to our contention that interventions do not need to be complex to be effective" (Dunst & Raab, 2005, p. 5). If the practice guidelines and the short written explanation are all that teachers needed to change practices, then do the more complex, dynamic, transformative models of knowledge utilization bring complexity where none is needed? How important is the fact that the practice guide was based on valid research? According to literature reviewed earlier in this chapter, teachers pay more attention to the relevance and practicality of recommendations than they do to the quality of the research backing them. Are we underestimating the powers of practice-based journals such as *Young Children, Young Exceptional Children,* and *Zero to Three?* If one undertook a study to evaluate the effect of teachers reading articles in these practice-oriented journals, would one find similar results?

To further consider these unresolved questions related to knowledge translation, we need to look also at the questions not addressed by the Dunst and Raab (2005) study. A certain percentage of teachers did not use the practice guide (low users) or used it only partially (medium users). What contributed to these teachers' reluctance or inability to use the guide? One might speculate that they did not have the resources, time, or motivation to follow the guidelines. The study does not provide information about the pathways to the changes in the teachers' rating of child behavior. One could surmise that the toy-based strategies promoted in the guide perhaps raised the overall quality of the social climate in the classrooms where the guide was used, and that dynamic led to teachers' ratings of more prosocial behavior in their classrooms. Alternatively, perhaps the toys created more positive relationships between teachers and children and between children and children, or perhaps teachers were able to use teaching practices associated with the toys. The literature suggests that these components (i.e., positive peer and teacher–child relationships, high-quality environments, and effective teaching strategies) promote social skills and emotional development in children (Grisham-Brown, Hemmeter, & Pretti-Frontczak, 2005). None of these variables were directly measured in the study but could be assessed in future research with the guide. It is also probable that there were individual children in those classrooms who needed more intensive and individualized interventions (Grisham-Brown et al., 2005). Teachers were asked to rate the interactive behavior of children in their classroom as a totality. They did not rate individual children. Were there children for whom the toy strategies were ineffective? Where did teachers find information for those children? What else informed decisions they made about how to support children's prosocial behaviors?

With respect to the question posed earlier about whether the Dunst and Raab (2005) study refuted the need for complex models of knowledge dissemination, I suggest it does not. Clearly, different levels of intervention and professional development are needed based on the level of effect desired. It is hopeful and encouraging that an intervention as simple as providing written information can be helpful in supporting teachers' use of social toys, which in turn is associated with teachers' positive ratings of children's behavior. However, we need to plan carefully different levels of intervention intensity in relation to the kinds of changes we are trying to achieve. To ensure that research briefs are maximally useful, we need to consider ways in which research syntheses can be linked with curriculum and classroom practices as well as with professional development systems that support increasingly deep levels of effect.

Knowledge utilization is more than helping people find and use research syntheses. Trinder (2000a) observed in her assessment of the evidence-based practice movement in the United Kingdom that "the initial assumption that providing better and more digestible information would change practice has proven unrealistic" (p. 236). Indeed, the second component of knowledge utilization—organization and translation—can accomplish only a certain amount in decreasing the gap between research and practice.

Knowledge Mediation and Application Issues

The third component of knowledge utilization is knowledge mediation and application. There are two important questions to ask about this component: (a) What do we know about evidence-based professional development strategies for delivering early childhood content to others? and (b) Do knowledge mediators (i.e., those who help mediate the transfer and application of knowledge through professional development) have and use this information, and do they also have a solid knowledge base of evidence-based practices in key early childhood content areas? These two questions will be addressed by examining relevant literature in preservice education, defined as the professional body of knowledge imparted through institutions of higher education, and inservice education, defined as continuing education and on-the-job support. Ideally, inservice training and preservice education are integrated into a seamless system of professional development. In reality, this integration rarely happens and they exist as parallel and often disconnected systems with separate literature bases. Therefore, issues and promising practices will be reviewed within these two domains.

Preservice education. One might assume that institutions of higher education are leading the field in terms of infusing new research into practices. Standards for early childhood teacher preparation programs have been developed by the National Association for the Education of Young Children (Hyson, 2003), the Division for Early Childhood of the Council for Exceptional Children (Stayton, Miller, & Dinnebeil, 2003), and the National Council for Accreditation of Teacher Education (2002) to guide faculty teaching practices. Research has demonstrated links between the formal education of early childhood teachers and the quality of early childhood programs (Cost, Quality, Outcomes Study Team, 1995; Tout, Zaslow, & Berry, 2006). Given the important role that teacher preparation programs play, surprisingly little is known about the context and content of programs or the needs and practices of faculty. Dr. Grover Whitehurst, director of the Institute of Education Sciences at the U.S. Department of Education, stated that "research on teacher preparation and professional development is a long way from the stage of converging evidence and professional consensus" (Whitehurst, 2002, para. 8). Cochran-Smith and Zeichner (2005) concurred with that assessment. In a comprehensive report based on the work of the American Educational Research Association's Panel on Research and Teacher Education, they stated that the body of teacher education research that "directly addresses desirable pupil and other outcomes and the conditions and contexts within which these outcomes are likely to occur is relatively small and inconclusive" (p. 5).

The lack of solid research about teacher preparation programs should not preclude the possibility that faculty adopt evidence-based practices as they plan and conduct personnel preparation. Unfortunately, two sources of information challenge that assumption. First, a recent study of early intervention university faculty (Bruder & Dunst, 2005) indicated that content and recommended practices introduced to the field 15 years ago still are not fully embedded across the personnel preparation programs in the early intervention disciplines. The second source of evidence is the finding that early childhood faculty have large class sizes and large numbers of students for which they have responsibility (Early & Winton, 2001), which means less time available for updating coursework and keeping abreast of emerging knowledge. On average, early childhood faculty are teaching 60% more students than their counterparts in other departments within their college and university (Early & Winton, 2001). In addition, course coverage in key content areas such as educating and working with children with disabilities is inadequate (Chang, Early, & Winton, 2005).

The Early and Winton survey (2001) did not directly address the quality of the faculty or professional development strategies, nor did it address the effectiveness of early childhood teacher preparation programs either in building teacher knowledge or skills or in effecting child outcomes. As is the case in the K–12 literature (Cochran-Smith & Zeichner, 2005; Whitehurst, 2002), there is little early childhood research on this topic (Bredekamp, 1996; Maxwell, Feild, & Clifford, 2006).

A recent addition to the sparse body of research on effective personnel preparation practices is a synthesis of the literature by the Research and Training Center on Early Childhood Development (Trivette, 2005) on a promising instructional strategy called *guided design*. First developed for engineering students, the term guided design refers to an instructional method with the following components: (a) a sequential process of mastering course content; (b) a team or small group processing component; (c) the provision of verbal or written feedback from an instructor who, as a professional in the field, has expertise concerning the content; and (d) the use of realistic problems to be solved. The approach has been used across a wide variety of disciplines, predominantly in BA programs. Trivette (2005) reviewed 35 studies, the majority focusing on one-semester courses. Because a variety of outcomes were examined across the studies, Trivette organized the following five outcome constructs for examining the data: (a) mastery of course content, (b) student satisfaction with the guided design process, (c) general critical-thinking skills, (d) student ability to apply the knowledge to realistic situations, and (e) student perceptions of personal competence and confidence in the course content area. She concluded in her synthesis that the guided design learning strategy is associated with increased ability to retain particular information, ability to apply the content to solve realistic problems, and confidence in ability to find information to solve problems. This recent synthesis provides needed guidance to faculty and trainers on effective strategies for delivering content in courses or workshops.

Inservice training. There has been a long-standing lament that knowledge mediators working in inservice contexts are not effective in changing practices. In a review of the literature, Guskey (1986) reported that virtually every major study in the last 30 years has emphasized the lack of effectiveness of staff development efforts. Recent surveys suggest that there has been little improvement since Guskey's review (Farkas, Johnson, & Duffett, 2003; Sunderman, Tracey, Kim, & Orfield, 2004).

Unfortunately, the literature on how to make inservice training more effective is not robust. There are certain themes related to effective professional development that are described in much of the literature (Birman, Desimone, Porter & Garet, 2000; Bowman, Donovan, & Burns, 2001; Brownell, Ross, Colon, & McCallum, 2003; Epstein, 1993; Garet et al., 2001). These include the following: a focus on specific content rather than general teaching strategies; opportunities to apply knowledge; team-based or collective participation by groups who work together; and coherence (extent to which there is an integrated program of teacher learning linked to outcomes, standards, infrastructure, and policy). However, in Whitehurst's (2002) review of the literature, he stated that the recommendations made in the literature for more intense, content-focused training experiences and for opportunities for peer collaboration are based on anecdotal evidence, inferences based on adult learning theories, or survey data related to teacher satisfaction. He concluded that "although literature on professional development is voluminous, there are only a few high quality studies relating professional development experiences to student outcomes" (Intensive and focused inservice training section, para. 1).

Promising Strategies in Knowledge Mediation and Application

An exception to the absence of rigorous research on professional development strategies noted by Whitehurst (2002) is research by Cohen and Hill (1998, 2000) on a statewide math education reform initiative in California. It is reviewed in some detail here because of the attention it received in the Whitehurst review.

The reform effort was multifaceted and included an overall statewide curriculum framework with accompanying teaching modules, a student achievement test aligned with the framework, and various workshops and meetings for preparing teachers to adopt the new practices. The findings from the evaluation study indicated that the more time teachers spent learning about the reform, the more their classroom practices changed consistent with the reform and the better the outcomes were for their students (Cohen & Hill, 2000). Unfortunately, the study does not provide any information about characteristics of the workshop facilitators or the pedagogical strategies they used.

These findings from the California reform effort are intriguing and make sense in many ways. If program planners start with specific child outcomes that can be measured reliably and validly, have a curriculum that focuses directly and effectively on teaching those outcomes in ways that meet the learning needs of all students, and know and use professional development strategies that directly teach teachers to use that curriculum, then it seems likely that the test results for children will improve.

Guskey (2003) recommended just such an approach in a recent article on staff development. He suggested reversing the traditional ways of planning professional development where the starting point is usually what teachers need to know and how professional development leaders (e.g., faculty, consultants) are going to impart these skills and knowledge to teachers (by means of study groups, workshops, etc.). He suggested starting instead with improved student outcomes and mapping backwards from there. In his article, he recommended specific steps for planning effective professional development, which involve identifying the following in this particular order: (a) student outcomes and how those will be measured, (b) instructional practices and policies that will most effectively and efficiently produce the desired results, (c) aspects of organizational support that must be in place for the practices and policies to be implemented, (d) knowledge and skills that the participating professionals must have to implement the practices and policies, and (e) strategies and sets of experiences that provide participants with opportunities to acquire the needed knowledge and skills. Guskey's ideas are promising and reflect the findings of Cohen and Hill (1998, 2000). However, the devil is in the implementation details, as will be described in the section on unresolved questions.

Contributions of the Evidence-Based Practice Movement to Knowledge Mediation and Application

As stated in the introduction this chapter, the evidence-based practice movement provides little direction or guidance about how to initiate or sustain evidence-based practices. Perhaps the lack of guidance is because of the sketchy knowledge base related to knowledge mediation and application, with a few exceptions (e.g., the study of California reform, Cohen & Hill,

Table 3.1. IES Research Goals (2005)

Goal One	Identify existing programs, practices, and policies that may have an impact on student outcomes and the factors that may mediate or moderate the effects of these programs, practices, and policies
Goal Two	Develop programs, practices, and policies that are potentially effective for improving outcomes
Goal Three	Establish the efficacy of fully developed programs, practices, or policies that either have evidence of potential efficacy or are widely used but have not been rigorously evaluated
Goal Four	Provide evidence on the effectiveness of programs, practices, and policies implemented at scale
Goal Five	Develop or validate data and measurement systems and tools

Note: From Institute of Education Sciences Request for Applications NCER-06-08, June 27, 2005 (CFDA 84.305). http://www.ed.gov/about/offices/list/ies/programs.html

1998, 2000, and the synthesis on "guided design," Trivette, 2005). In that respect, a contribution of the evidence-based practice movement is heightened awareness that well-designed research on professional development, change, and reforms is sorely needed.

A second contribution is a framework developed by the Institute of Education Sciences (IES) of the U.S. Department of Education (one of the promoters of the evidence-based practice movement) for research grants that could support a developmental approach to the study of professional development. Five goals focused on the kinds of research that IES funded in their 2005 priorities are outlined in the framework (see Table 3.1 for a list and summary of the goals). This structure with opportunities to engage in a developmental sequence of studies makes it possible to get federal research funding without necessarily having to conduct randomized clinical trials as the only methodological option. It provides a much needed opportunity to study under what circumstances and how professional development can promote evidence-based early childhood practices in key content areas such as literacy, numeracy, social–emotional development, and instruction to children who are English-language learners.

What is missing in the research goals and priorities of the IES is encouragement to use strategies for ensuring that the research is practical and relevant for consumers. Nowhere in the priorities or text of the current (2005) request for proposals can one find guidance or statements that relate to this important aspect of the research process or to sources of knowledge related to family and professional wisdom and values.

Unresolved Questions About Knowledge Mediation and Application

In spite of the support from the IES research funding structure, there are many questions related to developing, implementing, and evaluating a professional development intervention. The step-by-step process to planning professional development interventions proposed by Guskey (2003) assumes a logical, well-defined process and a knowledge base that is agreed on and objective. Within each step, there are many challenges. When one does research that attempts to demonstrate causal links between the steps, the challenges are multiplied.

Questions and issues that must be resolved include the following. Are there agreed on outcomes for children? As mentioned earlier, 43 states have developed early learning standards; however, a review of these efforts by Scott-Little, Kagan, and Frelow (2003) indicated that there is tremendous variability across states in terms of content areas emphasized. If one accepts the notion that research is objective and apolitical, one might question the extent to which the standards are research based.

A related question is whether there are valid and reliable measures associated with the desired outcomes. For example, it is interesting to note that the math achievement test developed as part of the California reform effort and aligned so carefully with the reform curriculum was abandoned after 2 years for various political and methodological reasons (Cohen & Hill, 2000). It is indeed challenging to develop reliable, valid, and agreed-on measures of outcome.

Is there a curriculum or set of prescribed teaching strategies for building the child's skills in a designated outcome area? Again, using the California reform as an example, the curriculum framework that was developed was only an advisory document designed to encourage local districts to use the innovative practices. Attempts to use textbook adoption as a tool for policy change led to rancor and disagreement and, ultimately, was abandoned; hence, the development of the curriculum modules that could be used flexibly in tandem with textbooks. Identifying one effective curriculum for every learning context is a difficult if not impossible task. Attempts to evaluate and identify effective curricula in early childhood have been challenging and inconclusive (Farran, Landry, Klein, Starkey, & Vernon-Feagans, 2005).

Are teachers able to secure the materials, time, and support to implement the practices? Given the complexity of current models of knowledge utilization, attending to this step is critical.

Are there a set of teacher competencies related to the classroom practices? As mentioned earlier, professional organizations such as the National Association for the Education of Young Children and Division of Early Childhood of the Council for Exceptional Children have developed sets of recommended practices. The extent to which these recommendations are routinely linked to professional development efforts is subject to speculation.

Summary of Knowledge Utilization Components

This first section of the chapter has identified various unresolved challenges related to knowledge utilization. Of particular importance is that practitioners do not base decisions solely on research findings. Practitioner values, beliefs, and experiences are valued sources of evidence that weigh heavily in decision making. Strategies for helping key stakeholders (e.g., families, researchers, practitioners) integrate knowledge from these three sources exist, but they are not necessarily supported by the current evidence-based practice movement. A major focus of the evidence-based practice movement is the development of research syntheses based on the best available research evidence; however, little attention is being paid to how these syntheses might be integrated with wisdom and values and how they might be linked with practice guidelines, existing curricula, and professional development systems. A related challenge is the lack of empirical data about professional development strategies that are effective in supporting teachers' use of evidence-based practices. What we do know suggests that sustained and complex models of knowledge utilization that link child outcomes, assessments, curricula, and broader reform efforts with professional development strategies are likely to be effective.

MODELS THAT PROMOTE CHANGE

The second section of this chapter focuses on five approaches to supporting the professional growth of practitioners that are designed specifically to bring about changes or reforms to existing practices. They are considered promising because they offer a way of potentially integrating best available research with wisdom and values in ways that shape and change practices within the framework of a complex model of knowledge utilization. However, like most of the professional development strategies mentioned in this chapter, there is limited empirical evidence of the effectiveness of these five approaches in the early childhood field. In some cases, current studies are being conducted or research syntheses are being developed that are addressing the efficacy of these approaches. Four of these approaches—consultation, coaching, mentoring, and a strategy developed in Japan called lesson study—will be briefly described in this section of the chapter. A fifth approach, communities of practice, will be described in chapter 4.

Consultation

Consultation has been described in the early childhood literature as a way of achieving changes through collaborative problem solving between a consultant and a consultee who willingly enter a relationship for the purpose of ultimately benefiting the children and families served by programs or organizations (Buysse & Wesley, 2005; Dinnebeil, Buysse, Rush, & Eggbeer, in press; Wesley, 1994). This approach is relatively new to early childhood, having been developed and used in general education contexts and adopted in early childhood during the last decade. General steps to the consultation process include the following:

- Introducing participants and forming relationships
- Gathering information
- Identifying goals and activities (developing a plan)
- Selecting strategies
- Implementing goals and plans
- Evaluating and arriving at closure

There is a professional support aspect to the consultation process in that the consultant brings extensive knowledge and expertise to the relationship that can be drawn on through the teaching and modeling of effective practices. Likewise, the wisdom and experience of the consultee shape the process and inform the consultant. The process also provides the opportunity through problem solving to consider practitioners' experience and values as well as contextual issues that affect change. All of these elements contribute to a plan of action that guides the change process. The change might focus on a teacher's behavior, on the learning environment, or on both. Whatever the focus, the ultimate beneficiaries are the children and families served by the teacher. A book by Buysse and Wesley (2005) provides tools, strategies, and detailed information on the consultation process and its application to early childhood settings.

A few small early childhood studies demonstrate the positive effects of consultation on child-care quality (Campbell, Milbourne, Silverman, & Feller, 2005; Kontos, Howes, & Galinsky, 1996; Palsha & Wesley, 1998; Wesley, 1994). A randomized study of the Partnerships for Inclusion model of the consultation used in the Palsha and Wesley study is now being conducted in five states through funding from the Child Care Bureau. For more information about this study, see www.fpg.unc.edu/~quince.

Coaching

Coaching is similar to consultation in that it usually involves two individuals (learner and coach) who agree to work together over time so the learner can refine existing practices and develop new skills with the ultimate goal of better serving children and families (Dinnebeil et al., in press). Coaching evolved first from athletic models to supervision and staff development with educators. Gallacher (1997) described a number of different models of coaching, including expert, peer, team, technical, collegial, reflective, cognitive, and challenge coaching. The major differences among the models include the primary reason for coaching, who defines the focus of the coaching, the coach's role, the degree of structure in the coaching process, and whether the coaching involves a dyad or a group. Wolfe (1994) suggested that regardless of the model, coaching is most successful when it is voluntary, is separated from supervision, is ongoing, and is based on trust. The model most often used in early childhood seems to fall under the description of cognitive coaching, described by Gallacher as a model designed to stimulate teachers' thinking and reflection about (a) their instructional decisions and (b) problem solving about how to make improvements. Steps in the coaching process that are common across models include the following:

- Developing initial interest or initiation
- Planning
- Gathering information through observation or review
- Taking action
- Reflecting
- Reviewing or evaluating

Gersten and Woodward (1992) conducted a small study of a coaching intervention that they designed, implemented, and evaluated in a large inner city elementary school. One of their conclusions from the study was the observation that "coaches' intuitions, experience and biases seemed to determine which research findings were emphasized and which were ignored" (p. 212). This comment mirrors what has been said earlier about the importance of values and beliefs in decision making about practices. Knowledge mediators play an especially important role as "gatekeepers" of knowledge in that they are often entrusted to impart or share best available research findings and facilitate the integration of that knowledge with wisdom and values.

The coaching model has been implemented in a number of different early childhood contexts as described by Gallacher (1997) and Hanft, Rush, and Shelden (2004). Hanft et al. have written a guidebook for early interventionists who want to participate in a coaching process with professional colleagues, families, or both. The Research and Training Center on Early Childhood Development (see the appendix) currently is preparing a research synthesis on the efficacy of coaching.

Mentoring

Mentoring has been defined as a caring and supportive interpersonal relationship between an experienced, more knowledgeable practitioner (the mentor) and a less experienced individual (the mentee), which is designed to facilitate the transfer of knowledge, skills, attitudes, beliefs, and values between mentor and mentee. Again, the similarities among consultation, coaching, and mentoring are strong. The steps in a mentoring relationship, as identified by Gallacher (1997), include the following:

- Initiating the relationship
- Identifying the mentee's interests and needs
- Developing a plan
- Providing assistance to the mentee as the plan is executed
- Evaluating effectiveness

Fenichel (1992) identified three essential features to the mentoring process: reflection, collaboration, and regularity. Mentoring has its roots in the mental health field (Dinnebeil et al., in press). It has been used as part of induction programs for new teachers (Finance Project & Public Education Network, 2004) but is being used increasingly in early childhood contexts (Dinnebeil et al.).

According to Whitehurst (2002), the research on the efficacy of mentoring as a professional development approach is weak and is based primarily on anecdotal evidence or survey data. The same criticism could be made about the body of literature on mentoring in early childhood.

Lesson Study

Lesson study is a strategy used for many years by Japanese educators with small groups of teachers as a means for reflecting on and improving their practices (NEA Foundation for the Improvement of Education, 2003). Study groups occur a few hours a week and are organized around curriculum topics such as math, science, or reading (Greene, 2004). Lewis (2004), an American who has observed and written about Japanese lesson planning, identified the following four features as central to its implementation: agreement among teachers of a broad, shared, long-term goal; focus on a particular content area within the broad goal; careful study on student learning and development; and live observation of the lesson. The heart of lesson study is the collection of, reflection on, and analysis of data gathered from observations that teachers conduct of one another's teaching (Lewis, 2004; NEA Foundation for the Improvement of Education). This recursive cycle of observation, reflection, discussion, analysis, and experimentation has been identified in Japan as a promising strategy that is gaining favor in the United States (Lewis, 2002; NEA Foundation for the Improvement of Education). Lewis (2002) has published a book on lesson study for teachers and administrators in the United States, which includes step-by-step guidelines for conducting lesson study in a school setting. It should be noted that the research base for lesson study is extremely limited in Japan and in the United States.

A Vision for the Future of Professional Development

In 2000, I was asked to write an article for the journal *Topics in Early Childhood Special Education* outlining a vision for the future on the topic of personnel preparation (Winton, 2000). In that article, I stated that my vision was for "learning communities" whereby professional development was part of the "ongoing fabric of daily work." Specific features of the vision included the following:

- Professional development is guided by collaboratively created personnel development plans, with the responsibility for implementing and evaluating the plans being shared across agencies and institutions.

- Preservice and inservice are intimately linked rather than operating as they currently do as parallel and disconnected programs.

- A variety of models and strategies for professional development are available and accessible for meeting the needs of individuals and programs at different levels of effect.

- Emphasis is on learning in teams and through relationships.

- Structures (career ladders) and incentives (increased salaries) support staff participation in professional development.

- The links between child outcomes, teacher practices, and professional development are the heart of evaluation, which includes individual, program, and community level variables.

- Families are given options for being meaningfully involved in all aspects of the process of making improvements in programs and practices.

If communities had a professional development infrastructure of this sort in place, the chances of implementing new ideas or evidence-based practices would be greatly increased for the child-care director we met in the introduction.

RECOMMENDATIONS FOR NEXT STEPS

Two major recommendations for early childhood professionals are made here. The first is to engage stakeholders in discussions about evidence-based practice. The second is to implement and evaluate evidence-based professional development interventions.

Recommendation 1: Engage All Stakeholders in Discussions About Evidence-Based Practice

This chapter began with a question about the extent to which the evidence-based practice movement will accomplish one of its primary reasons for being, that is, to lessen the gap between research and practice. I conclude that it is too early to tell. It depends on how the movement evolves and whether that evolution incorporates what is known about knowledge utilization. The movement is helping to decrease the gap between research and practice in the following ways:

- The evidence-based practice movement has raised awareness about the need to think about the varying quality of research in the professional journals and in professional presentations. Consumers of research are beginning to be aware that not everything found in print, included in a peer-reviewed journal, or presented at a professional conference is of equal quality.

- The evidence-based practice movement has been a catalyst for the production of new research-based resources for practitioners (user-friendly briefs and Web sites). Issues abound with how to ensure that these resources are relevant and of high quality, but they have potential for serving a need in the field.

- The evidence-based practice movement helped focus the attention of the field of early childhood education on the "so what" question; that is, does a particular professional development intervention make a difference for children and families? For many years, we have been content with evaluating professional development on the basis of whether teachers liked it or felt they learned something. We are challenged now to make and evaluate changes at deeper levels—the levels of teacher practices and child outcomes. Although difficult, this effort is creating a needed paradigm shift in how professional development is being conceptualized, implemented, and evaluated.

- The evidence-based practice movement has raised awareness about the challenges and dearth of quality research on professional development.

The many unresolved questions about the evidence-based practice movement point to areas for continued dialogue about evidence-based practice among all stakeholders. The questions that need to be addressed in those discussions include the following:

- Does the focus on what makes a difference for children include the whole child or only that part of the child that is easily assessed?

- Does the focus on what makes a difference include all children? What about those with significant disabilities or non-English speakers for whom standardized tests are not appropriate?

- Does the focus on what makes a difference include families? They are critical partners in decisions about learning and teaching, and their role in the evidence-based practice movement has not been addressed.

- In general, is the evidence-based practice movement restricting the research agenda to small, narrow issues that are removed from the realities of communities, families, and practitioners?

- Is the evidence-based practice movement being enacted with an appreciation for the complexities of change and of paradigms related to knowledge utilization? Will time and attention be paid to the challenges of how to integrate different knowledge from different sources?

- Will the evidence-based practice movement be inclusive of diverse voices and partners (practitioners, parents, administrators, institutions of

> higher education, multiple agencies) to deal with the organizational,
> institutional, and political factors that affect changes in early childhood
> practices?

The evidence-based practice movement has the potential for being a positive and galvanizing force for the early childhood field. Its evolution depends on leadership in the field being willing to address the above questions. Efforts to engage stakeholders in learning with and from one another about this topic should start immediately. In many instances, I hear concerns about the negative impact of No Child Left Behind and the evidence-based practice movement. Editorials and news stories recount teachers' complaints that they are not getting the support, information, and resources they need to meet high standards and expectations and that their unique context is not considered in the U.S. Department of Education's quest for better outcomes for all children. Having constructive discussions about evidence-based practices may help U.S. educators avoid what apparently happened in the United Kingdom (Trinder, 2000b)—groups became polarized into camps of those for and those against evidence-based practice. As stated above, it is important to find ways to inform and engage diverse perspectives including those of both critics and proponents of evidence-based practice in dialogue. Taking cues from the United Kingdom, we must help the champions of evidence-based practice recognize that evidence-based practice is not the only factor that affects decision making. Equally, the critics will need to recognize the contributions of the knowledge provided by the evidence-based practice movement to the development of practice. We need to recognize the limitations of the evidence-based practice movement, in and of itself, to solve the research to practice gap. That effort is a massive undertaking that will require much more than productions of syntheses and Web sites. Even after a decade of effort, the United Kingdom is still struggling.

Recommendation 2: Implement and Evaluate Evidence-Based Professional Development Interventions

The need to develop, implement, and evaluate high-quality professional development interventions, based on what we know from the literature on knowledge utilization and the best available research on professional development, is critical and must become part of the research agenda for early childhood. Multiple efforts are needed.

First, professional development about evidence-based practice (its definition, components, issues, and questions) is needed. This undertaking includes creating structures for conversations around the questions, as stated in the first recommendation.

Second, the fact that the evidence base is dynamic and ever-changing and must always be interpreted within the broader context of culture and community reinforces the important role of knowledge mediators. Knowledge mediators need guidance in how to integrate what is known about professional development into their work. Guidelines for how those involved in professional development might adopt evidence-based practices in their teaching and training are provided in Table 3.2.

Third, professional development interventions must be planned from an evidence-based practice perspective. Heeding the advice of Guskey (2003) and the lessons learned from the California reform effort (Cohen & Hill, 2000), those engaged in these efforts must align curricula, assessments, standards, and professional development strategies in ways that ensure that effect not only occurs but also is measured at the level of child outcomes and teacher practices. We need in-depth longitudinal studies of teacher preparation programs to examine issues related to quality and the relationships among different characteristics of students, faculty, and pedagogy as they affect the use of classroom practices and the outcomes for children being served by the newly graduated teachers. These studies could be done in high-priority content areas such as literacy, social–emotional development, and teaching English-language learners. The effort will not be easy, as indicated by the unresolved questions that have been identified in the first part of this chapter. Much preliminary work would need to be done before conducting these types of studies, including reaching consensus on child outcomes, common language, tools and measures, and approaches to research that recognize and accommodate the complexities of variables and relationships that are involved.

It is important to note that the early childhood context only adds to the complexity involved in designing and evaluating a professional development intervention model, given the many organizational and structural issues that need to be addressed. These include the multiple agencies and organizations

Table 3.2. Guidelines for Faculty and Trainers:
Evidence-Based Professional Development

Topic	Guidelines
Content	• What are the outcomes for children (e.g., your state's early learning standards or Head Start Child Outcomes Framework and Performance Standards), recommended practices from professional organizations (e.g., DEC Recommended Practices) and research base (e.g., research syntheses or research articles) related to the content covered in your coursework or workshop? Do your syllabus, textbook, and supplemental materials (e.g., readings, Web sites) reflect best available research knowledge? • Are you involving colleagues, families, practitioners, and potential participants in helping plan your course or workshop? Are their needs, values, and wisdom included in how you define the evidence that needs to be conveyed to course participants? • Is information about the evidence-based practice movement part of the course content? Are you preparing participants to find and appraise research findings and syntheses and to consider the broader meaning of evidence-based practice?
Process	• Are the strategies and activities you are using designed to have an effect on participants at multiple levels: knowledge, attitudes, and practices? • Are the professional development strategies you are using to relay content and make an effect based on best available research? Have you considered approaches such as "guided design" (Trivette, 2005) that have some research to support their efficacy? • Are you considering ways to engage key stakeholders (e.g., teachers, families, administrators, and researchers) in sharing their wisdom and values with course participants? • Are you providing participants with opportunities to explore the meaning and application of evidence-based practices in class simulations or in real-life situations through practica or field experiences? • How will you ensure that participants have ongoing support for using evidence-based practices?
Evaluation	• How might you evaluate the effect of your course or workshop at levels deeper than satisfaction, knowledge, and attitude changes? Are there ways you could document changes in practices and effect on children's outcomes? • Will other stakeholders (e.g., parents, colleagues) with whom you or the course participants have had contact during the coursework or workshop be involved in evaluating the course or workshop?

that teach and serve young children, the low salary structures and high turnover rates for most early childhood teachers, and the general fragmentation of what is often called "a nonsystem." Cochran-Smith and Zeichner (2005) contended that research on teacher education is not at the point where randomized field trials are appropriate. Preliminary theoretical and empirical work needs to be done first. If this point is true for K–12 education, then the imperative is even greater in early childhood education.

CONCLUSION

We need to recognize that professional development will not solve, and research will not answer, every question related to how the director of the child-care program we met in the introduction can enact changes in her program. The nature of change is such that there will always be elements of chance and the unexpected lurking beneath and interfering with our desire to know and to shape human actions. The challenge in this era of evidence-based practice is to ensure that as we use an evidence-based approach to inform and change practice, we do not limit ourselves to only those outcomes that are measured easily.

We need to continually remind ourselves of our ultimate goal in attempting to decrease the gap between research and practice, that is, to ensure that teachers and parents have the support they need to engage in the relationships, create the environments, and implement the practices that promote children's optimal development within the unique context of culture and community. The child-care director needs not only support for integrating research findings with the values and wisdom of staff and families but also the resources and support to implement, evaluate, and sustain the changes that her staff and families agree are desired. This recursive sequence of activities whereby knowledge generation, translation, and application are seamless needs to be part of program routines. There need to be multiple opportunities to share what is being learned with other programs, policymakers, faculty, consultants, and researchers so research is constantly informing practice and vice versa. Within this kind of scenario, each one of us (teacher, parent, faculty, researcher, or administrator) has the capacity to be a partner in an integrated process of teaching, learning, and researching. When this approach is supported by federal policies and becomes common practice in the field of early childhood, then the evidence-based practice movement will have accomplished the goal of decreasing the research to practice gap.

REFERENCES

Berman, P., & McLaughlin, M. (1978). *Federal programs supporting educational change* (Vol. 3). Santa Monica, CA: Rand Corporation.

Birman, B. F., Desimone, L., Porter, A. C., & Garet, M. S. (2000). Designing professional development that works. *Educational Leadership, 57*(8), 28–33.

Bredekamp, S. (1996). Early childhood education. In J. Sikula, T. Buttery, & E. Grayton (Eds.), *Handbook of research on teacher education* (2nd ed., pp. 323–347). New York: Simon & Schuster Macmillan.

Brownell, M. T., Ross, D. R., Colón, E. P., & McCallum, C. L. (2003). *Critical features of special education teacher preparation: A comparison with exemplary practices in general teacher education* (Executive summary). COPSSE document number RS-4E. Gainesville: University of Florida, Center on Personnel Studies in Special Education.

Bruder, M. B., & Dunst, C. J. (2005). Personnel preparation in recommended early intervention practices: Degree of emphasis across disciplines. *Topics in Early Childhood Special Education, 25*(1), 25–33.

Buysse, V., & Wesley, P. W. (2005). *Consultation in early childhood settings.* Baltimore: Brookes.

Campbell, P., Milbourne, S., Silverman, C., & Feller, N. (2005). Promoting inclusion by improving child care quality in inner city programs. *Journal of Early Intervention, 28*(1), 65–79.

Chang, F., Early, D., & Winton, P. (2005). Early childhood teacher preparation in special education at 2- and 4-year institutions of higher education. *Journal of Early Intervention, 27,* 110–124.

Cochran-Smith, M., & Zeichner, K. (2005). Executive summary. In M. Cochran-Smith & K. M. Zeichner (Eds.), *Studying teacher education:*

The report of the AERA panel on research and teacher education (pp. 1–36). Mahwah, NJ: Erlbaum.

Cohen, D. K., & Hill, H. C. (1998, January). *State policy and classroom performance: Mathematics reform in California.* CPRE Policy Briefs. Philadelphia: Consortium for Policy Research in Education, University of Pennsylvania.

Cohen, D. K., & Hill, H. C. (2000). Instructional policy and classroom performance: The mathematics reform in California. *Teachers College Record, 102,* 294–343.

Cost, Quality, and Child Outcomes Study Team. (1995). *Cost, quality, and child outcomes in child care centers: Public report.* Denver: Economics Department, University of Colorado–Denver.

Dinnebeil, L., Buysse, V., Rush, D., & Eggbeer, L. (in press). Teaching skills for effective collaboration. In P. J. Winton, J. McCollum, & C. Catlett (Eds.), *Preparing effective professionals: Evidence and applications in early childhood and early intervention.* Washington, DC: ZERO TO THREE Press.

Dunst, C. J., & Raab, M. (2005, February). Evaluation of an evidence-based practice guide for increasing preschoolers' prosocial peer interactions. *Centerscope, 4*(1), 1–7. Retrieved from http://www.evidencebasedpractices.org/centerscope/centerscopevol4no1.pdf

Early, D., & Winton, P. (2001). Preparing the workforce: Early childhood teacher preparation at 2- and 4-year institutes of higher education. *Early Childhood Research Quarterly, 16,* 285–306.

Epstein, A. S. (1993). *Training for quality: Improving early childhood programs through systematic inservice training.* (Monographs of the High/Scope Educational Research Foundation No. 9). Ypsilanti, MI: High/Scope Press.

Farkas, S., Johnson, J., & Duffett, A. (2003). *Stand by me: What teachers really think about unions, merit pay and other professional matters.* Retrieved September 14, 2005, from http://www.broadfoundation.org/med-pubs/Stand_By_Me.pdf

Farran, D., Landry, S., Klein, A., Starkey, P., & Vernon-Feagans, L. (2005, April). *Curricula as intervention: Results from randomized control trials.*

Presentation at a meeting of the Society for Research in Child Development, Atlanta, GA.

Fenichel. D. (Ed.). (1992). *Learning through supervision and mentorship to support the development of infants, toddlers and their families: A source book.* Arlington, VA: ZERO TO THREE: National Center for Clinical Infant Programs.

Finance Project, & Public Education Network. (2004). *Teacher professional development: A primer for parents and community members.* Retrieved December 14, 2004, from http://www.publiceducation.org/ Teacher_Prof_Dev/message.asp

Gallacher, K. K. (1997). Supervision, mentoring, and coaching. In P. J. Winton, J. A. McCollum, & C. Catlett (Eds.), *Reforming personnel preparation in early intervention: Issues, models, and practical strategies* (pp. 191–214). Retrieved September 13, 2005, from http://www.fpg.unc.edu/~scpp/ pdfs/Reforming/08-191_214.pdf

Garet, M. S., Birman, B. F., Porter, A. C., Desimone, L., Herman, R. & Yoon, K. (1999). *Designing effective professional development: Lessons from the Eisenhower Program.* Washington, DC: American Institutes for Research.

Gersten, R., & Woodward, J. (1992). The quest to translate research into classroom practice: Strategies for assisting classroom teachers' work with at-risk students and students with disabilities. In D. Carnine & E. Kameenui (Eds.), *Higher cognitive functioning for all students* (pp. 201–218). Austin, TX: Pro-Ed.

Greene, K. M. (2004). *Professional development in inclusive early childhood settings: Can we create communities of practice through lesson study?* Unpublished doctoral dissertation, University of North Carolina at Chapel Hill.

Grisham-Brown, J. G., Hemmeter, M. L., & Pretti-Frontczak, K. (2005). *Blended practices for teaching young children in inclusive settings.* Baltimore: Brookes.

Grossman, P. (2005). Research on pedagogical approaches in teacher education. In M. Cochran-Smith & K. M. Zeichner (Eds.), *Studying teacher education: The report of the AERA panel on research and teacher education* (pp. 425–476). Mahwah, NJ: Erlbaum.

Guskey, T. R. (1986). Staff development and the process of teacher change. *Educational Researcher, 15*(5), 5–12.

Guskey, T. R. (2003, Fall). Scooping up meaningful evidence. *Journal of Staff Development, 24*(4). Retrieved April 23, 2004, from http://www.nsdc.org/library/publications/jsd/guskey244.cfm

Hanft, B. E., Rush, D. D., & Shelden, M. L. (2004). *Coaching families and colleagues in early childhood.* Baltimore: Brookes.

Head Start Bureau. (2001). Head Start child outcomes framework. *Head Start Bulletin, 70,* 44–50. Retrieved from http://www.headstartinfo.org/publications/hsbulletin70/hsb70_15.htm

Hiebert, J., Gallimore, R., & Stigler, W. (2002). A knowledge base for the teaching profession: What would it look like and how can we get one? *Educational Researcher, 31*(5), 3–15.

Honig, M. I., & Coburn, C. E. (2005). When districts use evidence to improve instruction: What do we know and where do we go from here? *Voices in Urban Education, 6*(Winter). Retrieved March 10, 2005, from http://www.annenberginstitute.org/VUE/winter05/Honig.html

Hood, P. (2002). *Perspectives on knowledge utilization in education.* San Francisco: WestEd. Available online at http://www.wested.org/online pubs/perspectives.pdf

Hutchinson, J., & Huberman, M. (1993). *Knowledge dissemination and use in science and mathematics education: A literature review.* Washington, DC: National Science Foundation.

Hyson, M. (2003). *Preparing early childhood professionals:* NAEYC's standards for programs. Washington, DC: National Association for the Education of Young Children.

Individuals with Disabilities Education Act Reauthorization of 1997, Pub. L. 105-17, 20 U.S.C. §1400 *et seq.*

Institute of Medicine. (2002). *Speaking of health: Assessing health communication strategies for diverse populations.* Washington, DC: National Academy Press.

Kontos, S., Howes, C., & Galinsky, E. (1996). Does training make a difference to quality in family child care? *Early Childhood Research Quarterly, 11,* 427–445.

Lamb-Parker, F., Greenfield, D. B., Fantuzzo, J. W., Clark, C., & Coolahan, K. C. (2002). Shared decision making in early childhood research: A foundation for successful community-university partnerships. *NHSA (National Head Start Association) Dialog, 5*(2&3), 356–377.

Lauer, P. A. (2004). *A policymaker's primer on education research: How to understand, evaluate and use it.* Aurora, CO: Mid-continent Research for Education and Learning.

Lewis, C. (2002). *Lesson study: A handbook of teacher-led instructional change.* Philadelphia: Research for Better Schools.

Lewis, C. (2004). Does lesson study have a future in the United States? *Journal of Social Science Education, 2004-1.* Retrieved September 21, 2005, from http://www.jsse.org/2004-1/lesson_lewis.htm

Maxwell, K. L., Feild, C. C., & Clifford, R. M. (2006). Defining and measuring professional development in early childhood research. In M. Zaslow & I. Martinez-Beck, Eds., *Critical issues in early childhood professional development.* Baltimore: Brookes.

Mohr, M. M., Rogers, C., Sanford, B., Nocerino, M. A., MacLean, M. S., & Clawson, S. (2004). *Teacher research for better schools.* New York: Teachers College Press.

National Council for Accreditation of Teacher Education. (2002). *Professional standards for the accreditation of schools, colleges, and departments of education.* Washington, DC: Author.

National Research Council. (2001). B. T. Bowman, M. S. Donovan, & M. S. Burns, Eds.). *Eager to learn: Educating our preschoolers.* Committee on Early Childhood Pedagogy, Washington, DC: National Academy Press.

National Research Council Committee on Scientific Principles for Education Research. (2002). *Scientific research in education.* Washington, DC: National Academy Press.

NEA Foundation for the Improvement of Education. (2003, Issue Brief No. 5). *Using data about classroom practice and student work to improve professional development for educators*. Washington, DC: Author.

Neuman, S. B., & Roskos, K. (2005). The state of state pre-kindergarten standards. *Early Childhood Research Quarterly, 20,* 125–145.

No Child Left Behind Act of 2001, Pub. L. 107-110, 115 Stat. 1425 (2002). Retrieved from http://www.ed.gov/policy/elsec/leg/esea02/107-110.pdf

Nutley, S., Walter, I., & Davies, H. (2002). *From knowing to doing: A framework for understanding the evidence-into-practice agenda.* Discussion paper 1. St. Andrews, Fife, Scotland, UK: University of St. Andrews, Department of Management.

Omamo, S. W. (2004). *Bridging research, policy, and practice in African agriculture.* DSGD Development Strategy and Governance Division, Discussion Paper 10. Washington, DC: International Food Policy Research Institute.

Palsha, S., & Wesley, P. (1998). Improving quality in early childhood environments through on-site consultation. *Topics in Early Childhood Special Education, 18*(4), 243–253.

Philibert, D. B., Snyder, P., Judd, D., & Windsor, M. M. (2003). Practitioners' reading patterns, attitudes, and use of research reported in occupational therapy journals. *American Journal of Occupational Therapy, 57,* 450–458.

Raab, M. (2003). Relationship between types of toys and young children's social behavior. *Bridges, 1*(5), 1–13. Retrieved from http://www.evidencebasedpractices.org/bridges/bridges_vol1_no5.pdf

Rapoport, R. N. (1985). Reconsidering action-research. In R. Rapoport (Ed.), *Children, youth, and families: The action-research relationship* (pp. 266–289). New York: Cambridge University Press.

Rappolt, S., & Tassone, M. (2002). How rehabilitation therapists gather, evaluate, and implement new knowledge. *The Journal of Continuing Education in the Health Professions, 22,* 170–180.

Roberts, K. (2003). Is it time for a toy tune-up? *Bottomlines, 1*(5), 1–2. Retrieved from http://www.evidencebasedpractices.org/bottomlines/bottomlines_vol1_no5.pdf

Rothman, R. (2005). A fad or the real thing? Making evidence-based practice work. *Voices in Urban Education*, 6(Winter). Retrieved on March 10, 2005, from http://annenberginstitute.org/VUE/winter05/Rothman.html

Sandall, S., Hemmeter, M. L., Smith, B. J., & McLean, M. E. (2005). *DEC recommended practices: A comprehensive guide for practical application in early intervention/early childhood special education.* Longmont, CO: Sopris West.

Scott-Little, C., Kagan, S. L., & Frelow, V. (2003). *Standards for preschool children's learning and development: Who has standards, how were they developed and how are they used.* Greensboro: University of North Carolina at Greensboro, Southeastern Regional Vision for Education.

Shonkoff, J. P. (2003). *Closing the science-policy gap: A conversation with Council Chair Jack Shonkoff.* Retrieved September 13, 2005, from http://www.developingchild.net/papers/article_1.pdf

Simmons, W. (2005). Evidence-based practice: Building capacity for informed professional judgment. *Voices in Urban Education*, 6(Winter 2005). Retrieved March 10, 2005, from http://www.annenberginstitute.org/VUE/winter05/Simmons.html

Singer, G., Marquis, J. G., Powers, L. K., Blanchard, L., DiVenere, N., Santelli, B., Ainbinder, J., & Sharp, M. (1999). A multi-site evaluation of Parent to Parent programs for parents of children with disabilities. *Journal of Early Intervention, 22*(3), 217–229.

Southwest Educational Development Laboratory (SEDL). (1996, July). *A review of the literature on dissemination and knowledge utilization.* Austin, TX: Southwest Educational Development Laboratory (SEDL) and National Center for the Dissemination of Disability Research (NCDDR).

Stayton, V. D., Miller, P. S., & Dinnebeil, L. A. (Eds.). (2003). *DEC personnel preparation in early childhood special education: Implementing the DEC recommended practices.* Denver, CO: Sopris West.

Sunderman, G. L., Tracey, C. A., Kim, J., & Orfield, G. (2004). *Listening to teachers: Classroom realities and No Child Left Behind.* Retrieved August 10, 2005, from http://www.civilrightsproject.harvard.edu/research/esea/nclbteach.php

Tout, K., Zaslow, M. & Berry, D. (2006). Quality and qualifications: Links between professional development and quality in early care and education settings. In M. Zaslow & I. Martinez-Beck (Eds.), *Critical issues in early childhood professional development.* Baltimore: Brookes.

Trinder, L. (2000a). A critical appraisal of evidence-based practice. In L. Trinder & S. Reynolds (Eds.), *Evidence-based practice: A critical appraisal* (pp. 212–241). Oxford, UK: Blackwell.

Trinder, L. (2000b). Introduction: The context of evidence-based practice. In L. Trinder & S. Reynolds (Eds.), *Evidence-based practice: A critical appraisal* (pp. 1–16). Oxford, UK: Blackwell.

Trivette, C. M. (2005). Effectiveness of guided design learning strategy on the acquisition of adult problem-solving skills. *Bridges, 3*(1), 1–18.

Turnbull, A. P., Friesen, B. J., & Ramirez, C. (1998). Participatory action research as a model of conducting family research. *Journal of the Association of Persons with Severe Handicaps, 23*(3), 178–188.

U.S. Department of Education, Institute of Education Sciences. (2003). *Identifying and implementing educational practices supported by rigorous evidence: A user friendly guide.* Retrieved September 1, 2005, from http://www.ed.gov/rschstat/research/pubs/rigorousevid/guide_pg4.html#intro

U.S. Department of Health and Human Services. (2005). *Head Start impact study: First year findings.* Retrieved September 13, 2005, from http://www.acf.hhs.gov/programs/opre/hs/impact_study/reports/first_yr_finds/first_yr_finds.pdf

Wesley, P. (1994). Providing on-site consultation to promote quality in integrated child care programs. *Journal of Early Intervention, 18*(4), 391–402.

Whitehurst, G. J. (2002, March 5). *Research of teacher preparation and professional development.* Address to White House Conference on Preparing Tomorrow's Teachers. Retrieved April 26, 2005, from http://www.ed.gov/admins/tchrqual/learn/preparingteachersconference/whitehurst.html

Winton, P. J. (2000). Early childhood intervention personnel preparation: Backward mapping for future planning. *Topics in Early Childhood Special Education, 20*(2), 87–94.

Winton, P. J., & Turnbull, A. (1982). Dissemination of research to parents. *The Exceptional Parent, 12*(4), 32–36.

Wolfe, B. (1994). *Coaching as follow up to training.* Unpublished manuscript, Eau Claire, WI: Portage Project, Region V Resource Access Project.

APPENDIX

WEB SITES RELATED TO EVIDENCE-BASED PRACTICE

• **The Research and Training Center on Early Childhood Development** (http://www.researchtopractice.info) at the Olena Puckett Institute has produced a number of documents and research syntheses focused on various intervention approaches or practices in 11 domains in the area of early childhood, one of which is knowledge utilization. These domains include documents at different levels of technical detail and conceptual focus. The standards of evidence used are somewhat different than those used by the U.S. Department of Education What Works Clearinghouse, which appraises the quality of a study's research design. The approach taken is to examine the relationships between interventions or practices and outcomes and then evaluate research on the basis of the strength of those relationships. Products specifically of interest to practitioners are *Bridges*, which are research syntheses; *Bottomlines*, which are one- to two-page summaries of the syntheses; *Solution Tool Kits*, which include methods and strategies for enacting the practices; and *If It Fits*, which are short newsletters about the practices. These products provide interested consumers with several options. Some consumers might be solely interested in getting information at a very practical and applied level. Others might want to delve deeper into a topic by examining the technical details and conceptual frameworks related to the research being synthesized.

• **The Center on the Social Emotional Foundations for Early Learning (CSEFEL)** (http://csefel.uiuc.edu/) publishes *What Works Briefs*, summaries of effective practices for supporting children's social–emotional development and preventing challenging behaviors. The *Briefs* describe practical strategies, provide references to more information about the practice, and include a one-page handout that highlights the major points of the *Brief*. The summaries do not explicitly state the standards of evidence they use for including research studies in their syntheses. Nor do they appraise the quality of the research design. However, they do report on the kinds of children and settings that were studied in the research they synthesize. The scope of the *What Works Briefs* is limited to prevention and intervention practices in the social–emotional domain for children ages 2 through 5. The *Briefs* also include policies and procedural and administrative practices needed to support the use of evidence-based practices.

- **The Promising Practices Network (PPN)** (http://www.promisingprac-tices.net/) Web site summarizes research and is a repository for reports that highlight programs and practices that research indicates are effective in improving outcomes for children, youth, and families. The summaries do not mention criteria or standards used for appraising the quality of the research. The information offered is organized around three major areas: Proven and Promising Programs, Research in Brief, and Strengthening Service Delivery. The information pertains to children from the prenatal period to age 18 as well as to the families and communities in which they live. The report titled *Head Start Impact Study: First Year Findings* (U.S. Department of Health and Human Services, 2005) is an example of the kind of study available on the PPN Web site.

- **The Campbell Collaboration (C2)** (http://www.campbellcollabor-ation.org/) is an international nonprofit organization started in 1999 to prepare, maintain, and disseminate systematic reviews of studies of inter-ventions focusing on social, behavioral, and educational topics. The C2 links to the Database of Abstracts of Reviews of Effects (DARE) of The Centre for Reviews and Dissemination (CRD). DARE contains sum-maries of systematic reviews that have met strict quality criteria (i.e., ran-dom assignment of study participants to controlled trials or consensus among experienced experts in the field). Included reviews have to be about the effects of interventions. Each summary also provides a critical commentary on the quality of the review.

- **The Pathways Mapping Initiative** (http://www.pathwaystoout comes.org/index.cfm) Web site has a wide array of information from a variety of sources organized in terms of two broad areas: School Readiness and Family Economic Success. Within each of these areas, information is provided on goals or intended outcomes, actions that can be taken locally to contribute to outcomes, ingredients of effectiveness, indicators of progress, rationale, evidence, and examples related to actions. The Web site is best suited for policymakers, intervention planners, administrators, and grant writers.

- **Identifying and Implementing Educational Practices Supported by Rigorous Evidence: A User Friendly Guide** (http://www.ed.gov/rschstat/ research/pubs/rigorousevid/guide_pg4.html#intro) was developed by the U.S. Department of Education, Institute of Education Sciences (IES) to provide practitioners with tools to distinguish practices supported by rigorous evidence, as defined by IES, from those that are not (U.S. Department of Education, Institute of Education Sciences, 2003). This guide could be used in cases when research syntheses are not available and practitioners need to identify, assess, and synthesize research on their own. The guide is fairly lengthy and does not provide a summary assessment tool.

- **A Policymaker's Primer on Education Research** (http://www.ecs.org/ html/educationIssues/Research/primer/index.asp) (Lauer, 2004), created for policymakers by the Mid-continent Research for Education & Learning (McRel) and Education Commission for the States, is designed to help policymakers understand and evaluate research reports. It includes a two-page assessment tool for applying information from the primer to individual research reports.

- *Evidence & Policy*, (https://www.policypress.org.uk/journals/evidence_ policy/) a journal begun by the Policy Press in 2005, is an additional resource for policymakers that is entirely devoted to the relationship between research and decision making.

CHAPTER 4

MAKING THE CASE FOR
EVIDENCE-BASED POLICY

Patricia W. Wesley and Virginia Buysse

The disconnect between research and policy, which often is upstaged by the gap between research and practice, may have equally far-reaching implications. Competition for funding in times of limited resources has brought not only a new emphasis on how priorities are determined but also increased pressure on policymakers to deliver affordable, effective policies. At question in the discussions about the relationship between research and policy is the extent to which policymakers use science to improve their decision making and the extent to which policy drives research. One symptom of the gap is the fact that the success or failure of policy often is measured by whether its stated goals are attained rather than by whether those goals were appropriate to achieve the desired outcomes (Loveless, 1998). Evidence is needed to illuminate the links between intended outcomes and policy objectives and to tie those links to strategic directions so policymakers can see the connection between what they intend to do and what they are doing now (Shaxson, 2005).

In contrast with practitioners who do not turn routinely to science for answers to their practical problems (Hiebert, Gallimore, & Stigler, 2002; Richardson & Placier, 2001), federal and state policymakers appear to be committed to the idea that research studies are an important tool to examine the effectiveness of a program or intervention (Weiss, 1989). Accessing, understanding, appraising, and applying research findings to sometimes overwhelming social dilemmas have not been easy, though. Compounding the challenge is the fact that the early childhood field is a complex and rapidly changing one requiring policy action to address multiple issues such as safety and health, poverty, the needs of young children for nurturing and stimulating experiences, and the child-care needs of working parents. Even with the belief that research can improve decision making, researchers and policymakers have neither communicated clearly about the availability and quality of existing evidence nor been able to appraise the likely effects of various policy options as a way to choose among them (Shaxson, 2005). As a result, policymakers use research more to help them think about issues and the scope of a problem than to dictate specific solutions (Garrett & Islam, 1998). Now, with the advent of evidence-based practice, a new wedge has been driven between research and policy, bringing with it the perspective that only those studies using an experimental design should be considered legitimate sources of evidence about program effectiveness.

What sources of evidence are available and legitimate? What weight should policymakers give to different types of evidence? What frameworks exist for integrating scientific evidence as well as ethical and practical concerns in a policymaking process? This chapter reviews the meaning of evidence-based policy and explores not only the conditions that support it but also the tensions that challenge it. We examine briefly the development of selected policies affecting young children and families to understand the influence of theory, research, and stakeholder wisdom and values. Finally, we consider the methods by which policymakers can integrate evidence from multiple sources in making social policy decisions.

CURRENT ASSUMPTIONS ABOUT POLICY

Just as there has been a traditional separation between knowledge makers and knowledge users (including policymakers), there also has been a gap between policymakers and policy users. People outside the policy arena may assume that policy is already evidence-based, that the evidence supporting a practice is what turned the practice into policy (Zussman, 2003). They may assume that policy decisions are based on empirical science and that although professionals at the local level may not have the resources to access and understand the latest research findings, policy institutions make this connection regularly. The recent push to link policy and outcomes, especially the explicit objective to reward only those programs that are delivering positive outcomes, may suggest to the public that policy and science are coupled effectively. When the requirement for hard-number accountability is publicized under the slogan of No Child Left Behind, for example, the assumption is that policymakers are indeed using a scientific process to ensure that our children get the best possible education. Carrying this assumption one step further, agency administrators may be tempted to include policies as one source of evidence in their decision making because policies by virtue of their existence are equated with evidence-based practice. For example, state policy establishing a 50–50 ratio of children with and without special needs in state-funded developmental centers may be interpreted to mean that research promotes this ratio as optimal when, in fact, no research exists to support this ratio.

In contrast, other people may feel that research is misused by policymakers who pluck findings selectively to support their positions on issues. Or, they may assume that policymaking is all about politics and power, that decisions are not informed so much by facts as by other influences such as special interests, crises, social trends, or even a focus on re-election. Although sometimes hidden from view, interests and values are assumed to be powerful determinants of policy and practice, and for that matter, of evidence (Levitt, 2003).

The reality is that policies are made in all of these ways—sometimes with scientific evidence at the forefront of decision making; sometimes with consumer preferences, cost effectiveness, ideology, or other influences in play; and often through a process that considers all of these types of information and more. The problem is that the early childhood field has not come to agreement about what it means to make policy decisions based on evidence. Although the evidence-based practice movement in the United States includes government-sponsored Web sites, documents, and coalitions that promote randomized controlled trials as the gold standard for obtaining evidence of program effectiveness, scholars in the United Kingdom and other countries conclude that policy decisions cannot be made on the basis of empirical science alone (see, e.g., Davies & Nutley, 2001; Dobrow, Goel, & Upshur, 2004; Marston & Watts, 2003). Their conclusion is based on two fundamental understandings. First, various research methodologies are needed to address the complex issues affecting policy development. Second, the policymaking process itself is complicated and often subjected to short-term pressures and timelines that defy waiting for the results of empirical science. In these cases and in others, policymakers must consider the best available evidence, including the experiences, perspectives, and values of stakeholders.

POLICYMAKERS AND PROCESSES

It is important to consider the effect of evidence on both the development and implementation of policy. Although we are warned in a popular quote that "to respect sausages and laws, one must not watch them in the making" (attributed to 19th-century German Chancellor Otto von Bismarck), a review of the processes through which policies are developed and implemented may be helpful.

Definitions of policy vary somewhat according to whether they describe a process at the community, municipal, regional, state, or national levels. In the governmental arena, the term *policy* generally is taken to mean the rules and standards governing the allocation of public resources to meet social needs (Gallagher, 1994). Policy is made at multiple administrative levels by a few people and typically is implemented at locations often distant from the policymakers. For the purposes of this discussion, the policymakers we have in mind are federal and state legislators and agency representatives engaged in government, administration, and regulation. The policy implementers are professionals, families, and other stakeholders who are the recipients of these policies in the early childhood field. Because decisions about policy are made in a variety of ways that reflect varying degrees of formality and structure, let us consider the broad steps of developing policy within government.

The politicians and bureaucrats who make policy generally do so after much communication with many government actors, lobbyists, advocates, and other members of interest groups or the general public. The information they use to inform their decisions about any given policy may come from multiple agencies and disciplines reflecting diverse ideologies and agendas. That information may be commissioned specifically for a particular issue or drawn from an archive that is maintained by staff (Garrett & Islam, 1998). But policymaking is not necessarily a linear process that involves focusing on a social need or problem; figuring out what additional information is needed to understand the issue and identify possible solutions; canvassing, evaluating, and comparing options to address the problem in terms of their social, political, and economic costs and benefits; and then choosing one to implement. That rational model of policymaking, however, has been the dominant conceptualization of how research enters into policy processes (Neilson, 2001). It frames policymaking as a balanced and analytical process of solving problems in which expert opinion and evidence are critical, suggesting a natural partnership between researchers and policymakers (Omamo, 2004).

Other schools of thought with respect to policy processes are less clear, but more realistic, and emphasize features such as the assessment of research effect, the interplay of tacit and explicit knowledge, the diffusion of innovation, and the role of uncertainty (Omamo, 2004). They have in common a description of a decision-making process that is more convoluted, contentious, and likely to incorporate science in a haphazard way. In the policy literature, a question that often is raised is whether a unified framework for organizing and explaining policy processes will ever emerge, or is even appropriate, given the socially embedded nature of knowledge and the importance of context (Caplan, 1979; Levitt, 2003; Marston & Watts, 2003; Neilson, 2001; Nutley, Walter, & Davies, 2002; Omamo, 2004).

WHAT IS EVIDENCE-BASED POLICY?

It is difficult to find a definition of evidence-based policy. In much of the literature, the term is assumed to be self-explanatory. At the time of this writing, our review of 11 peer-reviewed journals in the early childhood field over the past 5 years yielded only 12 articles with the words evidence-based in their titles (several of them described the No Child Left Behind legislation) and none on evidence-based policy. The mission of the Coalition for Evidence-Based Policy, which has worked with the U.S. Education Department since 2001, is "to promote government policy making based on rigorous evidence of program effectiveness" (Coalition for Evidence-Based Policy, 2002, p. 1). The coalition urges the use of evidence-based policy in education to correct the government's tendency to implement programs "costing billions of dollars yet failing to address critical needs of our society" (Coalition for Evidence-Based Policy, 2002, p. 1). Their documents and Web site (www.excel.gov.org/evidence) make clear that what is meant by evidence-based policy is policy that promotes only those practices in education that have been shown to be effective through randomized controlled trials. Prepared by the Coalition for the Institute of Education Services, the manual *Identifying and Implementing Educational Practices Supported by Rigorous Evidence: A User Friendly Guide* (Coalition for Evidence-Based Policy, 2003) states that if interventions are not backed by randomized controlled trials (and, in limited cases, other group design studies in which the intervention and comparison groups are closely matched on key variables) that meet criteria specified in the Guide for "strong" or "possible" evidence, then "one may conclude that the intervention is not supported by meaningful evidence" (p. v). Ironically, the methodology used in a recent independent evaluation of the coalition's effectiveness was "telephone conversations with personnel in several federal agencies that the Coalition had worked with, some members of the Coalition's Board of Advisors, and others with knowledge of the Coalition's activities at the Federal and State levels" (Martin, 2004, p. 1).

The Urban Institute, a nonpartisan institute that investigates and analyzes U.S. social and economic problems, offers the following definition of evidence-based policy:

> Evidence-based policy is a rigorous approach that draws on careful data collection, experimentation, and both quantitative and qualitative analysis to answer three questions: What exactly is the problem? What are the possible ways to address the problem? And what are the probable impacts of each? A fourth question that figures into all public policy decisions—What political and social values do the proposed options reflect?—is largely outside the scope of evidence-based policy. (The Urban Institute, 2003, p. 1)

Boaz and Ashby (2003) provide a similar definition in their description of evidence-based policy as policy that is informed by reliable, valid, replicable, and fit-for-purpose evidence. Such evidence identifies and possibly explains the links between causes and effects or correlations between significant variables. Perhaps the definition provided by Davies (as referenced in Shaxson, 2005) comes closest to our definition of evidence-based practice presented in chapter 1. He refers to evidence-based policy as "the integration of experience, judgement [sic], and expertise with the best available evidence from systematic research" (p. 102). Building on these thoughts, we suggest that evidence-based policymaking refers to a process that systematically integrates reliable, valid, and relevant scientific research with the wisdom and values of professionals, families, and other stakeholders to decide what programs and actions to implement for the good of society. The inclusion of "other stakeholders" in this definition recognizes the function of policymaking to intervene in social affairs to effect change and acknowledges that a broad range of input can and should contribute to the evidence pool.

Although much of the evidence-based policy discourse has focused on research quality and what other types of evidence are needed, less attention has been paid to the process for integrating different types of information from various sources. In the early childhood field, it is not hard to envision the ways in which the wisdom and values of stakeholders influence the policy process; a history of grassroots advocacy provides numerous illustrations. Consider, for example, the groundswell of support from families and other advocates for establishing services for young children with special needs. Because of the strength and the breadth of their commitments to people with disabilities, advocates successfully urged Congress to end discrimination on the basis of disability and to fund early intervention. To begin to see the relationship of research to policy, we first must understand the complexity of the policy process.

Levitt (2003) described seven elements of policymaking to illustrate the dynamic interactions involved in the process, which we have amplified to foreshadow the challenges of using research to influence the policy decisions:

1. *The design of the policy process itself*—How the decision-making process is orchestrated and managed will determine when, where, and how research can be influential. For example, the design may include both formal and informal opportunities for input from stakeholders, researchers, and lobbyists.

2. *The scope of the decision*—The interplay of surface issues (e.g., case-by-case or regulatory concerns) and deeper issues (e.g., long-range effects on a population) will determine the types of evidence that are relevant and the extent to which research may be used to help policymakers define the problems, identify possible responses, predict their potential impact, and evaluate the effects of the decision once it is made.

3. *The stance of government*—The government's disposition on the issues related to the policy will affect the selection of issues about which they commission additional information, whether or not they turn to science, and the sources of information they use.

4. *The timing of the policy decision*—The time frame for decision making may be imposed from within or outside the policymaking body, depending on the nature of the problem. Time lines may or may not be related to the readiness of the evidence, and much at play is the policymakers' ability to predict the need for research. Indeed, one of the most important questions is what type of evidence can support policymaking in response to short-term pressures (Shaxson, 2005).

5. *Expectations*—The anticipatory hopes, assumptions, and projections that people bring to the table can become a seemingly reasonable basis for comparison with research findings, evaluation results, and other outcomes.

6. *Information and ideology*—Policymakers obtain their information from interactions with their staff or consultants, from reports and briefs, from the media, through conversations with their fellow policymakers, by means of conferences, and through public dialogue. Research is but one source (Garrett & Islam, 1998). The amount of information people have about research and their experiences and beliefs about science affect their view of the benefits of research. The policymaker's view of research will affect whether his or her use of research findings is deliberate, haphazard, or even present at all.

7. *The adequacy of the evidence*—Policymakers, researchers, and stakeholders may have different standards for determining whether evidence is adequate to be used in making decisions about policy.

In addition to the seven elements above, another factor that complicates the policymaking process is that decisions about policy are likely to depend on information from various strands that may not be linked together (Levitt, 2003). Research reflecting different disciplines, methodologies, and reporting time lines make it difficult for policymakers to analyze the information within an overarching framework. For example, in making decisions about young children and their families, policymakers might review evidence pertaining to numerous fields including medicine and allied health, genetics, psychology, special education and early intervention, nutrition, social work, and child development, to name a few. They could receive input of special interest groups, public opinion, legal counsel, policy analysts, and governmental committees. Add to this panoply of information economic projections and the history and status of related policies with which the new policy must interact, and the task of analyzing the situation as a whole becomes daunting.

Current efforts to bring brain research into play in public policy illustrate the complexity of the policy process. In this example, policymakers are not so much trying to identify solutions to a specific problem as they are attempting to integrate sweeping new research into their policymaking process. Knowing the benefits of nurturing and stimulating early childhood experiences does not tell them how to make those experiences available to children and families. Where should policymakers begin their discussion of how the new knowledge about children's brain development should affect their decision making?

Already at play in this discussion is a continued distinction between childcare and early education, an issue that has been on the agenda of early childhood advocacy groups and professional organizations for years. This discussion in the policy arena has led to debate about whether to extend formal education to children younger than age 5. The Michigan in Brief Web site's report on children's early education and care (Michigan in Brief, n.d.) provides a description of how this dialogue has unfolded in that state, and their concerns mirror the national debate. Some Michigan policymakers believe that because young children spend their time in a variety of settings, including family, relative, and community care, then attention and resources should be given to all these settings. Others conclude that children who are most at risk for school failure should be the first priority. Still others argue that universal preschool should be available to all children. Responding to the same new knowledge about children's brain development, some legislators suggest that it would be more effective to reduce poverty through strategies such as expanding the early income tax credit and making it easier for people to work part time so they can spend more time with their children. Others doubt that current research about how the brain develops provides a sufficient reason for detailing new policies; still others question whether more investment in early childhood services will make any difference at all. Among those legislators who support more funding for early childhood education, a major consideration is the balance between federal and state funding and the assignment of agency role. In Michigan, public opinion polls show strong support for improving access to high-quality child care and for paid parental leave; taxpayers also would rather provide access to early childhood programs such as Head Start and after-school programs than take a tax cut (Michigan in Brief, n.d.)

Where would one begin to use gold-standard research to sort out this complicated array of views? What other types of research would be helpful? What should be the role of public sentiment? These questions cannot be answered in this chapter or this book (and probably not in the next decade), but we raise them here to illustrate the hazards of narrow conceptualizations of evidence and decision-making processes informed by evidence. The next section highlights the way various types of evidence have influenced policy development affecting young children and families over the past couple of decades.

A Brief Look at the Development of Policies Affecting Young Children and Families

The needs of children and families began to appear on the social and policy agenda nearly a century ago as child development became a focus of psychology, child welfare became a domain within the judicial and social work arenas, and pediatrics became a specialization in medicine (National Research Council, 1981, 1982, as cited in National Research Council & Institute of Medicine, 2000). The past several decades have seen an array of policies addressing the health, economic security, and education of children and families. They also have witnessed the power of advocacy groups, including families, practitioners, and researchers, who have pressed forward to influence legislation. The following sections contrast the evolution of three areas of policy affecting young children and their families: (a) the federal policy to establish services for young children with disabilities and those considered at risk for disabilities, (b) the movement of states to create rated licenses for child-care facilities that are linked to indicators of program quality, and (c) current federal and state efforts to develop early learning standards. The first two examples are of policies that are in effect already in many states, whereas the last example is a current policy initiative across the nation. In each section, we describe the policies themselves and comment on the way various strands of evidence were used or are being considered in the policymaking process. In the section describing early learning standards, we also include recommendations for continued policy development in this area.

Policies Promoting Intervention and Education for Children With or At Risk for Disabilities

Just 3 years after the creation of Head Start in 1965, the passage of the Handicapped Children's Early Education Assistance Act (Pub. L. 90-538) was perhaps the single most powerful force in establishing early childhood special education as a field (McCollum & Maude, 1993). That act, based on research findings that intervention at an early age was effective and that early development and experience had a lasting effect on the child, established the Handicapped Children's Early Education Program (HCEEP) with the Bureau of Education for the Handicapped, which funded experimental and demonstration preschools across the country (McCollum & Maude, 1993; Shonkoff & Meisels, 1993). Nearly two decades later, the federal government again recognized the needs of children with disabilities in the passage of the Education for All Handicapped Children Act of 1975 (Pub. L. 94-142), which mandated free and appropriate public education for all school-age children with special needs, but left services for children ages 3 through 5 and young adults 18 to 21 at the discretion of the states. Services for young children 3 through 5 under this law were inconsistent because not all states took advantage of the incentives to serve preschoolers under the preschool grants program (Smith, 1984). When services were provided, they were fragmented across poorly coordinated health, education, and social policies, thus constraining knowledge and emerging best practice (McCollum & Maude, 1993). Through intensive and well-organized grassroots efforts of families and practitioners pressing for legislation more in line with current understandings of family systems and effective intervention practices, the Education for All Handicapped Children Act Amendments of 1986 (Pub. L. 99-457) amended Public Law 94-142 and strengthened incentives to serve 3–5-year-olds with special needs while providing discretionary funding for early intervention services for children younger than 3 years. The name of this legislation was changed to the Individuals With Disabilities Education Act (IDEA) and it later was amended to establish a comprehensive system of services to infants, toddlers, and their families. At its reauthorization in 1997, IDEA amendments made clear the preference for inclusion by stating that, to the maximum extent possible, early intervention services were to be provided in inclusive or natural environments.

What is interesting about the history of policy development in this area is the influence of both research findings and advocacy. Although the early legislation was launched in the wake of key findings by prominent scientists about early learning and development, the civil rights movement also helped to set the stage for society's concern for the needs of minority groups (Bailey & Wolery, 1984). During this period, a nascent early intervention field was building its knowledge base, in large part through the flourishing interactions between the researchers and program developers involved in the early HCEEP projects (Shonkoff & Meisels, 1993). The amendments and new acts that followed the 1968 legislation were passed largely in response not only to the sentiments and values (and lawsuits) of parents but also to the persistence of practitioners who believed strongly in children's rights to and the benefits of comprehensive, coordinated early intervention services for infants, toddlers, and preschoolers, even without the affirmation of gold-standard research. Also worth noting is the decision of many states not to develop legislation and policy for young children with special needs during the 1960s and 1970s. This decision came in spite of the child development research mentioned above, the social recognition of the rights and needs of minority groups, the federal legislation offering incentives to serve preschool children, and the War on Poverty's emphasis on education as an antidote to poverty. Clearly for these states, concerns about cost, agency role, other implementation challenges, or the social policy climate at the time outweighed the evidence supporting a decision to serve young children.

State Policies to Link Child-Care Licensure to Program Quality

In response to the significant numbers of children in child care, changes in federal welfare programs requiring mothers to work, national concern about school readiness, and studies affirming the connections between children's early experiences and later development, lawmakers in many states are focusing on policies to enhance the quality of child care. The majority of states and the District of Columbia have implemented one or more of the following strategies through a tiered system: tiered reimbursement for child-care programs, a quality rating system, rated child-care licensing, or a combination of these approaches (Clemens, Poppe, & Clothier, 2004).

North Carolina was one of the first states to establish a rated child-care license. Before the rated license system, two types of licenses were awarded to child-care centers in North Carolina, an "A" license for meeting minimum mandatory standards and an "AA" license for meeting slightly higher standards for group size, staff-to-child ratio, program policies, and space and activities. Family child-care home providers registered with the state but were not licensed or rated in any way. The system created in 1999 changed the way child-care centers and homes are regulated and shifted the approach to licensing from one of establishing minimum health and safety standards so child care will "do no harm" (Morgan, 1996) to one of promoting high-quality programs that nurture children's development and learning. North Carolina's initiative in this area was a direct reaction to the Cost, Quality, and Child Outcomes Study (Cost, Quality, and Child Outcomes Study Team, 1995), a national study that reported that the quality of care in North Carolina was dismal, with only 10% of the state's child-care programs providing developmentally appropriate care. Child-care programs participate voluntarily in the rated system and can earn one to five stars on their license, depending on the criteria they choose to meet. For each star, there is a sequentially higher level of standards to be met in areas that have been shown through research to be linked to quality. Increases in child-care subsidy also are provided with increases in stars. Currently, 90% of child-care programs in North Carolina have received some level of star ratings (North Carolina Division of Child Development, n.d.).

Because North Carolina was one of the first states to legislate a tiered licensing system, lawmakers did not have the advantage of considering the structure, benefits, and challenges of tiered systems in other states. Research findings documenting the poor quality of child care nationwide and its effect on young children were recent at that time, and dissemination to the general public was still under way. North Carolina legislators and the state's Child

Care Commission faced vocal opposition to the tiered license from some child-care providers who were concerned about costs and from some faith-based groups who decried government's involvement in regulating child care. Early childhood professional organizations, advocates, and many parents weighed in, favoring tighter regulations, whereas other parents expressed concerns about the new standards leading to higher child-care fees.

For policymakers, research led the way. State policymakers had positive relationships with several of the researchers of the national Cost, Quality, and Child Outcomes Study (1995) who lived and worked in North Carolina. Especially powerful were the study's findings that in the majority of settings, child-care conditions for infants and toddlers actually threatened their health and safety. These findings confirmed state leaders' belief that quality was poor. They knew that staff-to-child ratios were higher than recommended, for example, but they lacked specific information about other indicators (P. Ball, personal communication, August 30, 2005). The study, however, did not provide a solution to the problem. The original components of the rated license were chosen for different reasons—some because of supporting research (e.g., staff education), some because of demographics (e.g., North Carolina's early childhood credential became the base requirement for education because so many child-care providers already had it), and some because of politics (e.g., compliance history; P. Ball, personal communication, August 30, 2005). The decision to establish a system of incrementally higher, *voluntary* levels of licensure, however, was a response to the challenge of improving quality without significantly increasing costs to families (Ash Institute for Democratic Governance and Innovation, 2004).

Current Policies Related to Early Learning Standards

In recent years, the early childhood field has embraced wholeheartedly the standards movement in education. Efforts to define early learning standards for very young children have been prompted in part by research showing the critical importance of brain development and early learning as well as research suggesting that many children enter kindergarten ill-prepared to succeed in school (Rimm-Kaufman, Pianta, & Cox, 2000). But, undoubtedly, it was the Good Start, Grow Smart Initiative of 2002 described in chapter 1 that was most influential in encouraging states to develop state early learning standards that focused on pre-academic skills and that aligned with state K–12 standards. Forty-three states now have early learning standards, and the remaining states are in the process of developing descriptions of desired results, outcomes, and expectations with respect to what children should know and be able to do before beginning kindergarten (Neuman & Roskos, 2005).

The early learning standards movement is part of the larger accountability movement in which federal and state programs are required to show measurable results for the services they provide to children and families. As mentioned in chapter 1, state policymakers have been hampered in their efforts to build accountability systems in early childhood by the fragmentation of accountability initiatives, the lack of frameworks or models on which to build such systems, and the difficulty of gaining consensus among stakeholders about which outcomes should be measured (Harbin, Rous, & McLean, 2005). There is also confusion about the terminology that is used to discuss children's learning standards. Table 4.1 provides definitions of the most common terms related to the standards movement.

Table 4.1. Definition of Terms Related to the Standards Movement

Standards	Broad expectations for student learning
Early learning standards	Expectations for the learning and development of young children before beginning kindergarten
Content standards	Descriptions of what students should know and be able to do within a particular discipline or content area
Benchmarks	Descriptions of specific knowledge or skills that students should acquire by a particular point in their development or schooling—usually tied to a grade or age level
Program standards	Expectations for the characteristics or quality of schools, child-care programs, and other educational settings
Performance standards	Expectations for the characteristics or quality of Head Start programs

Source: National Association for the Education of Young Children (NAEYC) and National Association of Early Childhood Specialists in State Departments of Education (NAECS/SDE), 2002.

Note that although the terms *standards* and *outcomes* often are used interchangeably, these concepts have different origins and different meanings. Standards are associated with the educational accountability movement and are used primarily in public schools to focus on learning expectations for typically developing students. Outcomes are associated with program evaluation and are used primarily to describe the results of services and interventions targeting specialized populations such as children with disabilities. Within the program evaluation tradition, *outcome* has been defined as a statement of measurable changes, whereas *indicator* (a term that corresponds to benchmarks in the standards tradition) refers to the metrics used to quantify the extent to which an outcome has been met (Harbin et al., 2005).

In developing national or state early learning standards, policymakers generally have relied either on one of the following approaches or on a combination of these approaches (B. Rous, personal communication, August 22, 2005): (a) follow the lead of the National Education Goals Panel and frame learning expectations around children's developmental domains, (b) implement a downward extension of learning standards designed for kindergarten students with an emphasis on academic content areas, or (c) look to other state systems as models for developing their own state's early learning standards. Table 4.2 summarizes several national systems of early learning standards or outcomes and examples of two state systems (Kentucky and North Carolina; see Neuman & Roskos, 2005, for a more comprehensive review of how states are organizing early learning standards and benchmarks and the extent to which these reflect developmentally appropriate expectations for young learners). An examination of these systems reveals similarities and differences in these approaches to describing children's expectations for learning. The three national systems (National Goals Panel, Head Start, and Early Childhood Outcomes Center) all emphasize the same common core of developmental domains, although some have been embedded within much broader outcomes, as in the case of the Early Childhood Outcomes system, or have been combined with federally mandated content areas (e.g., literacy, mathematics, science), as in the case of Head Start. The Kentucky system divides learning standards according to age group, relying on the developmental domain framework for children from birth to the age of 3 years and focusing on academic content areas for 3- and 4-year-olds, whereas the North Carolina system relies on developmental domains for 3–4-year-olds with pre-academic content embedded within these broad domains. A standard on approaches to learning appears in all systems, with the exception of the Kentucky system.

Although policymakers may be too busy with the demands of actually developing prekindergarten standards to reflect on the effect of this policy, it is helpful to consider the implications of marching in lockstep with policies and practices that promote learning standards for older children. A joint position statement by the National Association for the Education of Young Children and the National Association of Early Childhood Specialists in State Departments of Education (NAEYC & NAECS/SDE, 2002) reminds us that early childhood is a distinct period of life in which children's learning is highly dependent on family relationships and environments that are embedded within a wide range of sociocultural contexts. Moreover, assessing progress in meeting early learning standards must take into account that young children's development varies widely and is connected across domains—more so than at any other stage of human development—with progress in one area being strongly influenced by other domains. All of these factors make it more difficult to create a set of generalized learning expectations for children enrolled in early education programs than it is for older children.

The NAEYC and NAECS/SDE (2002) position statement also identifies some of the potential risks and benefits of using early learning standards to measure the results of early childhood programs and services. The risks include the potential negative consequences for children who fail to meet learning standards (e.g., delaying entry into kindergarten) or the creation of standards that are too narrowly defined, rigid, or culturally inappropriate. Conversely, standards that are well conceived and developmentally appropriate hold the potential (a) to build consensus with families and communities with respect to appropriate early learning expectations and experiences, (b) to promote continuity between early childhood programs and K–12 schools, and (c) to stimulate investments that lead to improvements in program quality and children's school readiness.

Table 4.2. National and State Systems of Early Learning Standards and Outcomes

National Education Goals Panel Dimensions of School Readiness	Head Start Child Outcomes Framework	Early Childhood Outcomes Center (Part C Infant – Toddler and Part B Preschool)	Kentucky Early Childhood Standards	North Carolina Early Learning Standards
1. Physical and motor development	1. Language development	1. Children have positive social relationships	Birth–3 yrs.: 1. Communication 2. Cognitive 3. Social–Emotional 4. Motor 5. Creative expression	1. Approaches to learning
2. Social and emotional development	2. Literacy	2. Children acquire and use knowledge and skills	3–4 yrs.: 1. Language arts 2. Mathematics 3. Science 4. Social studies 5. Health education 6. Physical education 7. Arts and humanities	2. Emotional and social development
3. Approaches to learning	3. Mathematics	3. Children take appropriate action to meet their needs		3. Health and physical development

Continued

Table 4.2. National and State Systems of Early Learning Standards and Outcomes *continued*

National Education Goals Panel Dimensions of School Readiness	Head Start Child Outcomes Framework	Early Childhood Outcomes Center (Part C Infant–Toddler and Part B Preschool)	Kentucky Early Childhood Standards	North Carolina Early Learning Standards
4. Language	4. Science			4. Language development and communication
5. Cognition	5. Creative Arts			
6. General knowledge	6. Social and emotional development			
	7. Approaches to learning			
	8. Physical health and development			

Sources: The national education goals report, by National Education Goals Panel, 1991, Washington, DC: Author; *Head start child outcomes framework,* by Head Start, 2000, retrieved August 21, 2005 from: http://www.kaplanco.com/includes/content/classroom/UGCOF.pdf; *Family and child outcomes for early intervention and early childhood special education,* by Early Childhood Outcomes Center, 2005, retrieved August 20, 2005, from http://www.fpg.unc.edu/~eco/index.cfm; *Building a strong foundation for school success series: Kentucky's early childhood standards,* by Kentucky Department of Education, 2003, retrieved on August 21, 2005, from http://www.kidsnow.ky.gov; *Foundations: Early learning standards for North Carolina preschoolers and strategies for guiding their success,* by North Carolina State Board of Education, 2005, retrieved August 20, 2005, from http://www.ncpublicschools.org/success/

Recommendations About Current Policies Related to Early Learning Standards

An evidence-based practice framework could guide future efforts to create or revise existing early learning standards for children enrolled in early education programs. The role of research in developing these standards, for example, is notably absent (Neuman & Roskos, 2005; Shore, Bodrova, & Leong, 2004). Yet longitudinal research is needed to determine whether specific early learning benchmarks or indicators actually predict later academic success and positive developmental outcomes. Specific expectations of early learning (e.g., recognizing certain phonemes, counting to a particular number) that are found to be unrelated to subsequent learning may not be valid measures of early education effectiveness and may need to be eliminated or revised.

Policymakers must consider sources of knowledge other than those already mentioned in establishing the evidence base for early learning standards. They must determine, for example, whether early learning standards will apply broadly to all young children, including children with disabilities and those from diverse cultural and linguistic backgrounds, or whether separate standards developed specifically for these populations will apply (McConnell, McEvoy, & Priest, 2002). Hebbeler (2004) cautioned policymakers against potential misuses of outcome data, for example, focusing on a narrow set of outcomes or expecting all children with disabilities to function like typically developing children. These are complex policy issues requiring multiple sources of knowledge, professional wisdom, and broad-based stakeholder participation. A recent national study that identified and validated state preschool accountability systems using a modified Delphi approach (Rous, LoBianco, Moffett, & Lund, 2005) could serve as a model in this regard. Policymakers also must consider the multiple systems and settings in which young children receive early education and intervention services as well as the multiple levels of accountability in existence to evaluate the effect of these services (Harbin et al., 2005).

The absence of research evidence in developing early learning standards suggests that policymakers should avoid a strict downward extension of school-age content areas and focus instead on broad-based learning goals and expectations grounded within a developmental framework that includes pre-academic areas. Establishing the linkages between learning that occurs in early education (e.g., vocabulary development, self-regulatory behaviors) and learning that occurs in K–12 grades (e.g., reading skills) promotes a more unified approach to education. Standards related to social–emotional development and approaches to learning are particularly important during the early childhood period because these appear to be strong predictors of later learning (National Research Council & Institute of Medicine, 2000; Rimm-Kaufman et al., 2000) Finally, policymakers must consider how early learning standards align with program standards and support appropriate and high-quality curriculum and assessment practices.

NAEYC and NAECS/SDE (2002) offer the following recommendations with respect to the development of early learning standards (p. 4):

1. Effective early learning standards emphasize significant developmentally appropriate content and outcomes;

2. Effective early learning standards are developed and reviewed through informed, inclusive processes;

3. Early learning standards gain their effectiveness through implementation and assessment practices that support all children's development in ethical, appropriate ways;

4. Early learning standards require a foundation of support for early childhood programs, professionals, and families.

The above examples illustrate the complex relationship between research and policy. Much as a teacher who needs particular information often struggles amid competing demands to fill some gap in her knowledge, policymakers often struggle to attend to the many factors that compete for their attention: implementation costs, benefits, risk analysis, degree to which policy fits public values, tension between individual responsibility and role of government, expert advice from policy analysts, tight time frames for decision making, and more. We can say with certainty that the process of integrating multiple concerns will have to meet the needs of many different policymaking bodies concerned with diverse and changing priorities. In the following section, we propose several conditions that are likely to promote a climate supportive of evidence-based policy.

FAVORABLE CONDITIONS FOR EVIDENCE-BASED POLICYMAKING

What conditions need to be present for policymakers to use an evidence-based policy process rather than opinion-based decision making? In other words, how do we establish a systematic, step-by-step process for considering research and the wisdom and values of stakeholders? The answer to this question has implications for policymakers, researchers, and the evidence itself.

Implications for Policymakers

From the start, policymakers must know how to manage the wide array of information, people, advice, and argument that build the evidence. They must be able to analyze different types of information to then sort, accept, and reject it as appropriate. In addition, they need to determine whether research is trustworthy and should be used to guide policy decisions (Lauer, 2004). At the same time, policymakers need to recognize that the standard set forth by some definitions of evidence-based policy to accept only those data that are produced through randomized controlled trials may result in a reality that is too narrow to serve as the foundation for decisions involving broad-scope policy issues.

Successful implementation may depend on evidence from many different sources. When commissioning research or reviewing research sponsored by others, policymakers should consider the sources carefully in terms of whether their organizational affiliations lie inside the policy arena (e.g., a governmental policy research unit) or outside it (e.g., a university). They should also consider the research sponsors, for example, whether it was funded by a backer with a vested interest in the policy outcome. Weiss (1991) predicted that one result of an increased influence of systematic empirical analysis on public policymaking may be an increase in the establishment and use of policy research units such as the Heritage Foundation and the Cato Institute that reflect different political leanings in terms of conservative or liberal dispositions. Such a development would underscore the importance (a) of screening research for its high methodological quality and relevance and (b) of ensuring that the full body of evidence is presented.

Policymakers may want to consider the extent to which they rely on professional journals, magazines, newspapers, books, television, radio, and other sources external to government for scientific information. Is the information they gather from informal sources such as these the result of deliberate search or accident? Finally, although a much discussed strategy to close the research-to-policy gap is to develop ongoing communication between policymakers and researchers, how can policymakers remove their values, ideologies, and political preferences from their analysis of data?

Although clearly a challenge, the policymaking process should make clear the purposes for which policymakers need evidence. At what level and on how broad an audience will the decisions they are making have an effect? What is the time frame for the particular decision to be made? Shonkoff (2004) distinguished between knowledge for understanding and knowledge for advocacy. *Knowledge for understanding* refers to scholarship or science that, in the early childhood field, serves to identify and explain the multiple influences on child development outcomes. Knowledge for understanding is all about finding out what is not already known, and thus, represents a relatively low-stakes endeavor. The primary use of *knowledge for advocacy* is to affect policy and service delivery. It is a high-stakes enterprise that lobbies to prove a point and focuses on how much we do know. Research on program evaluation, for example, serves to provide knowledge for advocacy. When policymakers have long-range visions and resources to enact them in thoughtful ways, then research in both areas can be ongoing and both types of knowledge are likely to inform decision making.

Implications for Researchers

Researchers must understand that in the political world of policymakers, research interacts with values (including the policymakers') and vested interests to determine policy outcomes. Such understanding dispels expectations that there is any typically linear progression from evidence to policy (Marston & Watts, 2003). Weiss (1991) suggested that the effect of research on policy is indirect. As new concepts are introduced over time, policymakers may alter the language they use to reflect the generalizations yielded by data. Glimpses of new ideas and approaches gained from research and elsewhere may influence their perceptions and understanding of issues incrementally.

We agree that the role of researchers is to provide empirical evidence, but researchers should recognize the limits of a one-time, one-way flow of information to policymakers. Weiss (1991) hypothesized that research can be used as data, ideas, and argument by policymakers, and she set forth conditions in which each use is likely. For example, data can clarify the parameters of a problem or, if designed to test specific alternatives, indicate which are best. Research as a springboard for ideas is likely to be used in the early stages of policy discussion and when separate policymaking bodies are involved in a policy decision; often an idea can gain acceptance faster than detailed data. When conflict is high, for example in legislatures where ideological and interest-based differences are aired, research as argument is likely to be influential. This likelihood also comes into play after decisions are made. Using research to legitimize a policy outcome may speed implementation.

These different types of use create many opportunities for communication between researchers and policymakers. These communication opportunities should include interactive discussion to promote understanding of research findings and of policymakers' needs. Caplan's (1979) early ideas about the role of the experienced researcher are relevant today:

> ...to formulate judgments on the appropriateness of various types of social science information in relation to policy makers' interests and needs, to make realistic appraisals of the relative merit of diversified social science information, to link persons with relevant expertise to the policy setting, to redefine issues in terms that may make them more amenable to solution or which allow them to be viewed from a different perspective. (p. 467)

With respect to the notion that ongoing discussions between the research and policy communities would increase the influence of scientific research in policy decisions, Caplan (1979) pointed out that such an alliance is not a panacea that will produce relevant research and translate scholarly analysis into terms of practical politics. Researchers already feel the pressure of developing research agendas based on funding priorities. Although reciprocal relationships may result in improved understanding and greater use, they also run the risk of putting pressure on the researcher's role as an objective scientist and call into question the relationship between intellectual property and academic freedom. Marston and Watts (2003) reported that in the United

Kingdom, both politicians and researchers have raised concerns about the practice of government departments amending research reports before publication and requiring researchers to obtain departmental permission before sharing research findings publicly with the media.

Implications for Research

Aspects of the research itself may contribute to the likeliness of its being used by policymakers. Results of a study conducted by Weiss (1980) involving interviews with 255 policymakers indicate that they found research to be useful when it (a) conformed to accepted research standards of excellence, (b) produced findings that fit with their previous knowledge and expectations, (c) offered direct implications for action, and (d) provided new perspectives about existing assumptions, institutional organization, philosophies, or services.

Echoing some of Weiss's points, Davies and Nutley (2001) suggested that attention is more likely to be paid by policymakers to research findings when

- The research is timely, the evidence is clear and relevant, and the methodology uncontested.
- Results support existing ideologies, are convenient, and uncontentious to the powerful.
- Policymakers believe in evidence as an important counterbalance to expert opinion, and act accordingly.
- The research findings have strong advocates.
- Research users are partners in the generation of evidence.
- The results are robust in implementation.
- Implementation is reversible if need be (p. 94).

CHALLENGES IN IMPLEMENTING EVIDENCE-BASED POLICY

In addition to the favorable conditions for evidence-based policymaking that we have considered, we must also examine the challenges to implementing evidence-based policy. Gallagher and Clifford (2000) described various types of barriers that the implementation of new policies in the early childhood field must overcome: institutional, psychological, sociological, economic, political, and geographic. In this section, we identify some of the specific criticisms that have emerged about evidence-based policy.

Although the push for accountability has created a new demand for a wide array of information, it may create a climate that stifles constructive criticism (Shonkoff, 2004). If funding is at stake, no one wants to talk about what does not work; it is far more prudent to show outcomes that at least preserve the status quo. Similarly, in the policymaking arena with its multiple layers of receiving and processing information, there is the risk that data could be first screened by staff or policy analysts and then shared with key decision makers only if the data support current beliefs about the policy or program. Marmot (2004) suggested that this potential for "policy-based evidence" is unavoidable because, even among policymakers themselves, their willingness to take action in a given area influences their view of the evidence.

Policymakers often are called on to make decisions under challenging circumstances such as short time frames imposed by budget cycles or social problems. Sometimes they are asked to make recommendations based on an estimate of what might happen in the future. Evidence may be unavailable, confusing, contradictory, or inconsistent. In these conditions, policymakers operate in an air of uncertainty as they weigh predictions about effects of policy against the credibility of the sources of those predictions and their own experience (Zussman, 2003). They may not have the time to wait on research or to thoroughly canvass the concerns and advice of stakeholders. Although they may receive numerous analyses from sources inside and outside of government, most information exchanges do not include challenges to empirical claims (Weiss, 1989). Consider also the power of lobbyists who often invest substantial thought and resources in researching effective and persuasive methods for their outreach with policymakers. They know how to package their message so it is understandable, accessible, and convincing. Perhaps most important, they offer certainty in their advice when policymakers most need it (Masch, 2004). They are likely to read legislation and come prepared to tell lawmakers exactly what sections to address and how to change them (Weiss, 1989).

Another challenge to evidence-based policy is the competition between effective versus popular policies. Why should policymakers turn their backs on popular policies, even in the face of otherwise persuasive empirical evidence (Masch, 2004)? Consider North Carolina's position on taxing cigarettes. Facing clear scientific evidence proving the link between smoking and a variety of diseases, legislators nevertheless have been reluctant to take action that could decrease cigarette sales in a state where tobacco has been a leading industry for decades.

Related to this concern is the potential challenge of gaining support for the transparency that evidence-based policy encourages, that is, the need to make explicit "what is done to what effect" across research, practice, policy, and professional development venues (Gambrill, 2003, p. 6; Trinder, 2000). Increased transparency will highlight the uncertainties surrounding a decision, which may concern those policymakers and researchers who want their work to be seen as clear and decisive. Transparency makes it more difficult to claim that recommended strategies are based on relevant empirical research when they are not, which is a decided benefit for all.

Evidence-based policy calls for ongoing communication among policymakers and researchers. This level of communication presents challenges to researchers who do not see dissemination as their strength or role. If they are having a hard time communicating with practitioners (and some do not see it as their job to do the "translation"), will they be willing to face the challenges of communicating regularly with the policy world? The enhanced relationship between research and policy has other implications for the role of researchers. In a climate that promotes the influence of research, and given the likelihood that research is most influential when researchers interface with the policy process at several points, will scientists be able to resist pressure to engage as activists for certain policies? This question was raised in the earlier discussion of the implications of evidence-based policy for researchers, but it bears repeating: Will researchers who engage as activists for certain policies jeopardize the interests of institutional science (Weiss, 1991)?

A serious limitation to evidence-based policy that arises when meaningful evidence is defined only as randomized controlled trials concerns its potential to crush critical inquiry and innovation (Pirrie, 2001). Federal and state policies supporting early childhood inclusion, for example, grew largely from a sense of social justice and moral concern for a group of children and families who had been shut out from the mainstream of life. When the first legislation in support of inclusion was passed in 1975, research did not exist to support the notion that children with and without disabilities could learn alongside each other and benefit from the social contact. Policymakers, educators, families, and other stakeholders took a leap of faith that ultimately was rewarded by more than 30 years of research that proved the efficacy of inclusion. How will innovations such as that one be possible if evidence-based policy is defined too narrowly?

What about innovations in instructional strategy and professional development? The increased numbers of children with disabilities who have been placed in community child-care programs has created the need for a system of itinerant education services, including the need for consultation between early interventionists and child-care providers (Dinnebiel & McInerney, 2000; Wesley & Buysse, 2004). Although only limited research is available on effective early childhood consultation (none of which used randomized controlled trials), technical assistance is on the rise across the country, with some states now considering establishing a system of tiered qualifications that would certify consultants. Should the field not deliver consultation to child-care providers until its efficacy has been established through empirical science? Should we consider evidence of its effectiveness with school-age children in public schools? Is it premature to consider a way to standardize the consultation process and certify those who provide the service? In the most conservative view of evidence-based practice and policy, how would new ideas be cultivated? Is it reasonable to expect research to anticipate and keep up with the ever-changing needs of practice and policy?

Related to the narrow definition of evidence as randomized controlled trials in the No Child Left Behind legislation is a reduced willingness by schools to participate in experimental studies (Supovitz, 2002). The pressures of meeting expectations for adequate yearly progress preclude the risk of being in a control group, which suggests the ironic possibility that a policy promoting randomized controlled trials as the only source of meaningful evidence decreases the likelihood of that evidence being relevant.

Finally, it is difficult to know to what extent research does or does not inform policy, particularly because the use of research is undefined (Weiss, 1991). Does the use of research mean that policymakers consider it as one source of evidence or does it mean that the research directly affects the policy decision—and that without it a different decision would have been made?

THE BENEFITS OF EVIDENCE-BASED POLICY

Despite its limitations, evidence-based policy provides a favorable prospect for improved early childhood programs and increased accountability to the public. From a general perspective, the evidence-based practice movement has raised awareness about the quality of research at many different levels, including among policymakers. It requires discussion and wise interpretation of data, including an understanding of the limitations of evidence. Researchers and policymakers alike have acknowledged that some of the criticisms with respect to the lack of scientific rigor in research that occurred before the evidence-based practice movement are justified. The movement's focus on results that show what works ultimately may build trust in government.

When evidence-based policy is made through a systematic process of considering the wisdom and values of professionals, families, and other stakeholders along with the findings of scientific research, it has the potential to organize discussion in a way that illuminates the ideologies, theories, values, and science that drive a decision. That kind of process is a clear benefit when compared with traditional political decision making, which lacks a clear mechanism for defining and using evidence effectively (Dobrow et al., 2004). The inclusion of professional and family perspectives reaffirms the value of constituent participation in government by recognizing that families and practitioners have important knowledge to share.

In response to the call for rigorous research and research reviews as a basis for policy decisions, researchers are expected to provide candid descriptions of the limitations of their studies. Although the ethical standard of providing accurate descriptions of limitations predates the evidence-based movement, evidence-based policy increases opportunities for public discussion in this vein. The explosion of strategies (particularly those that are Web based) that have been developed to maximize the flow of accurate information discussed in chapter 3 provides an accessible and transparent trail of evidence that will help families and the general public to make informed decisions not only about services for young children but also in response to government policy.

AN ANALYTICAL FRAMEWORK FOR ACTING ON EVIDENCE IN POLICYMAKING

Given the relatively recent arrival of the evidence-based practice movement, it may seem presumptuous to suggest approaches for implementing evidence-based policy. For this reason, we rely heavily on the literature from the United Kingdom where evidence-based practice had its origin in the mid-1990s and where a few policy researchers have begun to develop frameworks for describing, implementing, and assessing policy processes (see, e.g., Levitt, 2003). In this section, we describe general considerations and promising approaches for building a consensus informed by robust evidence.

Lessons Learned as a Framework for Policy Discussion

A familiar framework for discussions related to program evaluation is one that identifies "lessons learned." Patton and Millett (1998) described characteristics of high-quality lessons that distinguish them from the sometimes trivial and overgeneralized way in which the phrase is used in public discourse. These characteristics provide a good place to start in an attempt to specify what policymakers should consider as they integrate various types of information in decision making. High-quality lessons learned are derived from the following (Patton & Millett, 1998):

- Practitioners' experience and professional wisdom
- Consumers' experience
- Evaluation findings and patterns across programs
- Basic and applied research
- Expert opinion
- Connections and patterns across disciplines
- The assessment of the importance of the lesson learned
- The strength of connection to outcome attainment

More confidence would be given to lessons that have more rigorous supporting evidence, the greater numbers of supporting sources, and the greater triangulation among them (Patton & Millett, 1998). Although policymakers may find the above framework helpful in making sense of the evidence available to inform a decision about whether to continue a particular program, the challenge remains to apply these findings to decisions about future action.

Shaxson's Proportional Approach

In an article described as a tool to help policymakers in government communicate with their advisors, Shaxson (2005) cautioned: "Good evidence-based policymaking is not simply about creating a vast database of everything and then cherry-picking the best, or most accessible or most immediately relevant information" (p. 103). Strategies for managing, analyzing, interpreting, and using evidence must change in response to a dynamic evidence base. Table 4.3 describes Shaxson's (2005) five components of robustness (which she describes as a work in progress) against which policymakers can screen evidence to decide which ones are important for each particular policy question.

Using what Shaxson (2005) called a "proportional approach" (p. 108), policymakers would decide which aspects of robustness are important in which situations and why. The process requires an interdisciplinary approach to the evidence and an understanding that all evidence related to all policies will not be completely robust all of the time. Rather, there will be times in the policymaking process when each characteristic of robustness rises or falls "in proportion to the perceived risk or anticipated impact of a policy" (p. 109).

RECOMMENDATIONS

As policymakers, researchers, practitioners, families, and other stakeholders in the early childhood field embark on a new era of evidence-based policymaking, several directions may prove helpful as next steps. These include recommendations for an overall approach to improved technology, the use of communities of practice to enlighten both the policy processes and decisions, a new type of empowerment for families, and a commitment by policymakers to building the honesty and transparency of evidence.

Given the complexity of policymaking and the analytical frameworks described in this chapter, the policymakers' need for accessible,

Table 4.3. Shaxson's Components of Robustness

Components of robustness	Key questions
Credibility Also referred to as internal validity, credibility relates to the processes of analyzing and synthesizing information.	• Are we confident that these conclusions flow from this evidence? Would others derive the same results? • Does it matter whether a particular piece of evidence comes from expert or lay knowledge? • Does the evidence we are able to collect limit the questions we are able to ask? • Does the evidence make sense to others, including internal and external advisors? • Would involving our critics in gathering and analyzing the evidence deepen its credibility?
Generalizability Also referred to as transferability, this term refers to whether evidence gathered for a specific purpose can be used in a different context, or to answer another question.	• Can the findings be widely applied or are they specific to context? Does this level of applicability have to do with sampling techniques or with broader framing of the issue and policy questions? • Is it possible that the arguments are generalizable even if specific findings are not? Why? • In what ways does the context matter or change the findings?
Reliability For policymaking, this term refers to whether or not the evidence can be used for monitoring, evaluation, or impact assessment. This definition differs from the broader use of the term in the literature to mean consistency.	• Does the evidence provide a sound basis for future monitoring, evaluation, or impact assessment? • Will the way the question is framed initially hold up over time? • What contextual information is needed for continued monitoring? • Is there a clear trail of qualitative evidence?
Objectivity This term refers to an exploration of bias in the evidence base.	• Has bias been removed from the evidence and from the methods of analysis? • Is bias absent from the presentation of options to decision makers and stakeholders? • How certain are we that the findings have been determined by the subjects and context of the inquiry rather than by the biases, agendas, and perspectives of the investigators, policymakers, and stakeholders?

Table 4.3. Shaxson's Components of Robustness (*continued*)

Components of robustness	Key questions
Rootedness This concept addresses the fact that "the relationship between the evidence that is gathered and the conclusions that [are drawn] is inevitably sensitive to the process that is used" (p.108). Rootedness refers to understanding the nuance of the evidence, approaching it with an open mind and a questioning disposition.	• Have all viewpoints among different stakeholders been considered in framing the question and gathering the evidence? • Does the question represent the fullness of the issue? • What is the history of the evidence? • Have the different implications of the evidence been examined by people with different specialist knowledge? • How do the results stimulate action and empower people to act?

Source: "Is Your Evidence Robust Enough? Questions for Policy Makers and Practitioners," by L. Shaxson, 2005, *Evidence & Policy*, 1, pp. 101–111.

cross-disciplinary, and current information is obvious. It would seem, to start, that effective policies are more likely to be made when the policymakers who are engaged in decision-making are reflective about their own practice. Histories of previous policy processes, including data and records of other information that informed the decisions, are archived by the government and easily available to lawmakers and other stakeholders. The development and ongoing cultivation of government intranets that support sharing knowledge across departments and that provide key word access to the documentation, reports, and commissioned reviews of research and policy analyses should be a priority (Amann, 2000). In addition, Amann suggested several other key elements to an overall approach for taking advantage of expanding sources of knowledge. These include high-quality, interactive Web sites built around key policy developments, a directory that identifies experts who can contribute knowledgably to policy discussion and development, and links between government libraries and networks of research and analytical information that draw on research evidence from the wider research community.

Communities of practice, described in chapter 5, hold promise for integrating the knowledge, perspectives, and experiences of families, researchers, practitioners, and other stakeholders (Wesley & Buysse, 2001). Although their potential to close the distance between research and practice, research and policy, and policy and practice is largely untested in the early childhood field, communities of practice are an established approach to shared inquiry and knowledge generation in the policy research literature. Communities of practice create opportunities to navigate and clarify the uncertainties and complex issues related to particular policy issues (e.g., Haas, 1992; Neilson, 2001; Stone, 2001). Such communities consist of professionals from various disciplines who are not formed as a group around a particular profession or discipline but who share a knowledge base and a common enterprise. Their potential to contribute to policy decisions lies in their common understandings of the decision-making process within a specific policy field. In early childhood, for example, a community of practice would include policy experts, families, researchers, practitioners, and policymakers who generate knowledge that assists to clarify policy questions and who generate and analyze the evidence that attempts to answer them.

We recommend that families and other consumers use the increasingly accessible and diverse knowledge produced in evidence-based practice and policy environments to develop critical appraisal skills with respect to early childhood services, research, and policy. They should routinely ask what evidence was used to determine recommended services and question methods that have not been tested in relation to desired outcomes (Gambrill, 2003). Although the task is a daunting challenge for any stakeholder, families should determine whether a strategy or guideline is applicable to their situations.

Finally, policymakers need to become consumers of research themselves as a way of maximizing their understanding of the value of work by experts, both internal and external to their agencies. They should cultivate and make public their commitment in three areas. First, they should sustain a policymaking climate that encourages stakeholders to share all the facts related to an issue, including those that may not support existing policy or stated intentions. Second, they should make the information that informs their decisions available to the public, and third, they should inform researchers about areas of policy and practice that require additional research.

CONCLUSIONS

Policymakers are charged with a huge task. They gather and try to understand all the information relevant to deciding the best course of action for the public good. They strive to mediate the interests of various groups while remaining mindful of their own ideological leanings. Policymakers work in a complex environment in which a high volume of communication with numerous people is ongoing to inform discussions of multiple, simultaneous policy issues. Although it seems rational to rely on science to inform the decision-making process, its influence on policy often is hampered by the inadequacy of research to respond to the timing and scope of decisions and by the likelihood that research findings do not identify solutions to problems. For this reason, and because many policymakers are politicians who have been chosen by constituents to represent their interests, the idea of basing decisions on the wisdom and values of professionals, families, and other stakeholders is not new. The evidence-based practice movement, however, makes clear the expectation that a wide range of evidence, including reliable, valid, and relevant scientific research, should be considered in a systematic way, and it underscores the critical importance of using high-quality research whenever possible to inform decisions. The movement toward evidence-based policy challenges all of us to cultivate a deeper understanding of the interdependence of evidence, policy, and practice.

Although we have not expanded the discussion in this chapter to explore the relationship of policy to practice, it is important to recognize the potential for the policies that ultimately are implemented to be different from what was intended by policymakers. Because of inadequate infrastructure, resources, or expertise, the policy may not survive its reduction to applicable details (Stone, 2001). Tracing the success of implementation is a key focus in policy studies, one of the most rapidly growing subspecialties in this country's political science (Weiss, 1991).

We predict that policy analysis, including interdisciplinary studies, will become increasingly visible in early childhood education. Just as Web-based research catalogs and syntheses seemed to appear almost overnight in response to the evidence-based practice movement, sources of policy analysis also are under way. The increased interest in evidence-based policy will create new opportunities to study policy, not only within universities but also within government as analysts are hired to serve agencies and law-making bodies at the state and federal levels. Researchers particularly will be challenged to maintain their objectivity as they respond to policymakers' increasing interests and needs for research. Policy analysts will be challenged to look outside the boundaries of a single and perhaps favored academic discipline to consider all the types of evidence that help to analyze the problem situation, generate reasonable policy alternatives, and select and test the feasibility of the chosen alternative (Haskins, 2002).

We conclude with a warning articulated so clearly by Levitt (2003), which states that if the definition of evidence-based policy excludes the interests, wisdom, values, and beliefs of policymakers, professionals, and families, then "policy and subsequent practice will risk being inadequate for the task of interpreting what society wants, needs, and will consent to. This will be compounded if admissible evidence is unable to answer the questions that require resolution: in the absence of that evidence, the basis for decision making will be the values of the decision makers" (p. 29).

REFERENCES

Amann, R. (2000, May). Evidence-based policy: Taking the vision forward. *Public Management and Policy Association Review*, 9, 9–11.

Ash Institute for Democratic Governance and Innovation. (2004). *Five-star related license*. Retrieved August 25, 2005, from http://www.ashinstitute.harvard.edu/Ash

Bailey, D. B., & Wolery, M. (1984). *Teaching infants and preschoolers with handicaps*. New York: MacMillan.

Boaz, A., & Ashby, D. (2003). *Fit for purpose? Assessing research quality for evidence based policy and practice* (Working Paper 11). London: Economic and Social Research Council. U.K. Centre for Evidence Based Policy and Practice. Retrieved August 19, 2005, from http://www.evidencenetwork.org

Caplan, N. (1979). The two-communities theory and knowledge utilization. *American Behavioral Scientist, 22*(3), 459–470.

Clemens, B., Poppe, J., & Clothier, S. (2004). Incentives for quality: Tiered strategies in child care. *National Conference of State Legislatures Report, 29*(3), 1–2.

Coalition for Evidence-Based Policy. (2002). *Program description*. Retrieved August 20, 2005, from http://www.excelgov.org/usermedia/images/uploads/PDFs/Coalition_purpose_&_agenda_Jan_05.pdf

Coalition for Evidence-Based Policy. (2003). *Identifying and implementing educational practices supported by rigorous evidence: A user friendly guide*. Retrieved August 20, 2005, from http://www.excelgov.org/evidence

Cost, Quality, and Outcomes Study Team. (1995). *Cost, quality, and child outcomes in child care centers, public report* (3rd ed.). Denver, CO: Economics Department, University of Colorado at Denver.

Davies, H. T. O., & Nutley, S. M. (2001). *Evidence-based policy and practice: Moving from rhetoric to reality* (Discussion Paper 2). University of St. Andrews: Research Unit for Research Utilisation.

Dinnebiel, L. A., & McInerney, W. F. (2000). Supporting inclusion in community-based settings: The role of the "Tuesday morning teacher." *Young Exceptional Children, 4*, 19–26.

Dobrow, M. J., Goel, V., & Upshur, R. E. G. (2004). Evidence-based health policy: Context and utilisation. *Social Science & Medicine, 58*, 207–217.

Early Childhood Outcomes Center. (2005). *Family and child outcomes for early intervention and early childhood special education.* Retrieved August 20, 2005, from http://www.fpg.unc.edu/~eco/index.cfm

Education for All Handicapped Children Act of 1975, Pub. L. 94-142, 20 U.S.C. §§ 1400 *et seq.*

Education for All Handicapped Children Act Amendments of 1986, Pub. L. 99-457, 20 U.S.C. §§ 1400 *et seq.*

Gallagher, J. (1994). Policy designed for diversity: New initiatives for children with disabilities. In D. Bryant & M. Graham (Eds.), *Implementing Early Intervention* (pp. 336–350). New York: Guilford.

Gallagher, J., & Clifford, R. (2000). *The missing support infrastructure in early childhood.* Retrieved August 29, 2005, from http://ecrp.uiuc.edu/v2n1/gallagher.html

Gambrill, E. D. (2003). Evidence-based practice: Sea change or the emperor's new clothes? *Journal of Social Work Education, 39*(1). Retrieved August 16, 2005, from http://www.cswe.org/publications/jswe/03-1editorial.htm

Garrett, J. L., & Islam, Y. (1998). *Policy research and the policy process: Do the twain ever meet?* (Gatekeeper Series 74). London: International Institute for Environment and Development, Sustainable Agriculture and Rural Livelihoods Programme.

Haas, P. M. (1992). Introduction: Epistemic communities and international policy coordination. *International Organization, 46*(1), 1–35.

Hammersley, M. (2005). Is the evidence-based practice movement doing more good than harm? Reflections on Iain Chalmers' case for research-based policy making and practice. *Evidence and Policy, 1*(1), 85–100.

Handicapped Children's Early Education Assistance Act of 1968, Pub. L. 90-538.

Harbin, G. L., Rous, B., & McLean, M. (2005). Issues in designing state accountability systems. *Journal of Early Intervention, 27*(3), 137–164.

Haskins, R. (2002). The application of successful applied research through policy analysis. In D. C. Miller & N. J. Salkind (Eds.), *Handbook of research design and social measurement* (6th ed., pp. 65–71). Thousand Oaks, CA: Sage.

Head Start. (2000). *Head Start child outcomes framework.* Retrieved August 21, 2005, from http://www.kaplanco.com/includes/content/classroom/UGCOF.pdf

Hebbeler, K. (2004). Uses and misuses of data outcomes for young children with disabilities. Early Childhood Outcomes Center. Retrieved September 9, 2005, from http://www.fpg.unc.edu/~eco/index.cfm

Hiebert, J., Gallimore, R., & Stigler, J. W. (2002). A knowledge base for the teaching profession: What would it look like and how can we get one? *Educational Researcher, 31*(5), 3–15.

Individuals With Disabilities Education Act (IDEA) Reauthorization of 1997, Pub. L. 105-17, 20 U.S.C. § 1400 *et seq.*

Kentucky Department of Education. (2003). *Building a strong foundation for school success series: Kentucky's early childhood standards.* Retrieved on August 21, 2005, from http://www.kidsnow.ky.gov

Lauer, P. A. (2004). *A policymaker's primer on education research: How to understand, evaluate, and use it.* Aurora, CO: Mid-continent Research for Education and Learning (McREL), and the Education Commission of the States.

Levitt, R. (2003). GM crops and foods. *Evidence, policy and practice in the UK: A case study* (Working Paper 20). London: Economic and Social Research Council Centre for Evidence Based Policy and Practice.

Loveless, T. (1998). Uneasy allies: The evolving relationship of school and state. *Educational Evaluation and Policy Analysis, 20*(1), 1–8.

Marmot, M. G. (2004). Evidence based policy or policy based evidence? *British Medical Journal, 328,* 906–907. Retrieved August 15, 2005, from http://bmj.bmjjournals.com

Marston, G., & Watts, R. (2003). Tampering with the evidence: A critical appraisal of evidence-based policy-making. *The Drawing Board: An Australian Review of Public Affairs, 3*(3), 143–163.

Martin, B. H. (2004). *The coalition for evidence-based policy: Its impact on policy and practice.* Retrieved August 19, 2005, from http://www.excelgov.org/displaycontent.asp?keyword=prppcHomePage

Masch. V. A. (2004). Return to the "natural" process of decision-making leads to good strategies. *Journal of Evolutionary Economics, 14,* 431–462.

McCollum, J. A., & Maude, S. P. (1993). Portrait of a changing field: Policy and practice in early childhood special education. In B. Spodek (Ed.), *Handbook of research on the education of young children* (pp. 352–370). New York: MacMillan.

McConnell, S. R., McEvoy, M. A., & Priest, J. S. (2002). "Growing" measures for monitoring progress in early childhood education: A research and development process for individual growth and development indicators. *Assessment for Effective Intervention, 27*(4), 3–14.

Michigan in Brief. (n.d.). *Michigan in brief: Children's early education and care.* Retrieved August 20, 2005, from http://www.michiganinbrief.org/edition07/Chapter5/ChildEarlyEd.htm

Morgan, G. (1996). *Regulation and the prevention of harm.* Retrieved August 21, 2005, from www.nara-licensing.org/displaycommon.cfm?an=1&subarticlenbr=28

National Education Goals Panel. (1991).*The national education goals report.* Washington, DC: Author.

National Research Council, & Institute of Medicine. (2000). *From neurons to neighborhoods: The science of early childhood development* (J. P. Shonkoff & D. A. Phillips, Eds.). Committee on Integrating the Science of Early Childhood Development; Board on Children, Youth, and Families; Commission on Behavioral and Social Sciences and Education. Washington, DC: National Academy Press.

Neilson, S. (2001). *Knowledge utilization and public policy processes: A literature review.* Ottawa, Ontario: International Development Center, Evaluation Unit.

Neuman, S. B., & Roskos, K. (2005). The state of state pre-kindergarten standards. *Early Childhood Research Quarterly, 20,* 125–145.

No Child Left Behind Act of 2001, Pub. L. 107-110, 115 Stat. 1425 (2002).

North Carolina Division of Child Development. (n.d.). *Monthly statistical summary.* Retrieved February 12, 2005, from www.ncchildcare.dhhs.state.nc.us

North Carolina State Board of Education. (2005). *Foundations: Early learning standards for North Carolina preschoolers and strategies for guiding their success.* Retrieved August 20, 2005, from http://www.ncpublicschools.org/success/

Nutley, S. M., Walter, I., & Davies, H. T. (2002). From knowing to doing: A framework for understanding the evidence-into-practice agenda (Discussion Paper 2). St. Andrew's, Scotland: University of St. Andrews, Research Unit for Research Utilisation.

Omamo, S. W. (2004). *Bridging research, policy, and practice in African agriculture.* Washington, DC: International Food Policy Research Institute, Development Strategy and Governance Division.

Patton, M. Q., & Millett, R. A. (1998). Lessons learned. *The Evaluation Exchange, 4*(3/4), 14.

Pirrie, A. (2001). Evidence-based practice in education: The best medicine? *British Journal of Educational Studies, 49*(2), 124–136.

Richardson, V., & Placier, P. (2001). Teacher change. In V. Richardson (Ed.), *Handbook of research on teaching* (pp. 905–947). Washington, DC: American Educational Research Association.

Rimm-Kaufman, S. E., Pianta, R. C., & Cox, M. J. (2000). Teachers' judgments of problems in the transition to kindergarten. *Early Childhood Research Quarterly, 15*, 147–166.

Rous, B., LoBianco, T. Moffett, C. L., & Lund, I. (2005). Building preschool accountability systems: Guidelines resulting from a national study. *Journal of Early Intervention 28*(1), 50–64.

Shaxson, L. (2005). Is your evidence robust enough? Questions for policy makers and practitioners. *Evidence & Policy, 1*(1), 101–111.

Shonkoff, J. (2004). Evaluating early childhood services: What's really behind the curtain. *The Evaluation Exchange, 10*(2), 1–4.

Shonkoff, J. P., & Meisels, S. J. (1993). Early childhood intervention: The evolution of a concept. In S. J. Meisels & J. P. Shonkoff (Eds.), *Handbook of early childhood intervention* (pp. 3–31). New York: Cambridge University Press.

Shore, R., Bodrova, E., & Leong, D. (2004). Child outcomes standards in pre-K programs: What are standards; what is needed to make them work? *Preschool Policy Matters, 5*. National Institute for Early Education Research. Retrieved April 28, 2005, from http://www.nieer.org/resources/policybrief/5.pdf

Smith, B. (1984). Expanding the federal role in serving young special needs children. *Topics in Early Childhood Special Education, 4*(1), 33–42.

Stone, D., (2001, July). *Bridging research and policy.* Background paper presented for Bridging Research and Policy International Workshop Funded by the U.K. Department for International Development, Radcliffe House, Warwick University.

Supovitz, J. (2002). *Expert opinion: An evidence-based policy?* Retrieved August 15, 2005, from the Northwest Regional Educational Laboratory Web site, http://www.nwrel.org/nwedu/09-04/expert.php

Trinder, L. (2000). A critical appraisal of evidence-based practice. In L. Trinder & S. Reynolds (Eds.), *Evidence-based practice: A critical appraisal.* Oxford, U.K.: Blackwell Science.

The Urban Institute. (2003). *Beyond ideology, politics, and guesswork: The case for evidence-based policy.* Retrieved August 21, 2005, from http://www.urban.org

Weiss, C. H., with Buculavas, M. J. (1980). *Social science research and decision making.* New York: Columbia University Press.

Weiss, C. H. (1989). Congressional committees as users of analysis. *Journal of Policy Analysis and Management, 8*(3), 411–431.

Weiss, C. H. (1991). Policy research as advocacy: Pro and con. *Knowledge and Policy, 4*(1), 37–55.

Wesley, P. W., & Buysse, V. (2001). Communities of practice: Expanding professional roles to promote reflection and shared inquiry. *Topics in Early Childhood Special Education, 21*(2), 114–123.

Wesley, P., & Buysse, V. (2001). Communities of practice: Expanding professional roles to promote reflection and shared inquiry. *Topics in Early Childhood Special Education, 21*(2), 114–123.

Wesley, P., & Buysse, V. (2004). Consultation as a framework for productive collaboration in early intervention. *Journal of Educational and Psychological Consultation, 15*(2), 127–150.

Zussman, D. (2003, April). *Evidence-based policy making: Some observations on recent Canadian experience.* Paper presented at the Social Policy and Evaluation Conference, Wellington, New Zealand.

CHAPTER 5

BUILDING THE EVIDENCE BASE
THROUGH COMMUNITIES OF PRACTICE

Patricia W. Wesley and Virginia Buysse

Previous chapters in this book have addressed the origin of the evidence-based practice movement and its effect on research, knowledge utilization, and policy in the early care and intervention field. In this chapter, we explore communities of practice as a way of creating opportunities for diverse constituents to study and reflect on these and other dimensions of practice. We also consider the potential outcome of communities of practice to contribute to the knowledge base that guides local practice and the larger professional field as a whole. After we examine the use of similar terms that have been used to describe collaborative inquiry and learning (e.g., professional communities, learning organization, community of learners), we describe the distinguishing characteristics of a community of practice and present three examples of communities of practice in the field of early intervention and education.

EFFORTS TO CLOSE THE GAP BETWEEN
PRACTICE AND RESEARCH

In spite of decades of professional discussions in the field of early intervention and education concerning the extent to which research influences practice, the so-called research-to-practice gap continues. Researchers, practitioners, and policymakers have scrutinized their own and each other's roles in this stalemate and have identified numerous and provocative directions for change. For example, in response to the criticism that researchers operate inside ivory towers that separate them from the real problems and concerns of communities, universities are altering their institutional structures and definitions of scholarship to link theory more closely to practice and to promote faculty–student and university–community co-learning (Boyer, 1990). Initiatives such as these are varied and include, for example, the creation of professional development schools and other field-based partnerships (Book, 1996; Darling-Hammond, 1994; The Holmes Group, 1990; Valli, Cooper, & Frankes, 1997).

In response to recent calls to increase scientific rigor and the quality of educational research, there also has been a rethinking of how to organize research enterprise at the federal and local levels to promote collaboration among researchers, practitioners, and policymakers (Barnett & Frede, 2001; Cousins & Simon, 1996; National Academy of Education, 1999; National Research Council Committee on a Feasibility Study for a Strategic Education Research Program, 1999; National Research Council Committee on Scientific Principles for Education Reasearch, 2002). Researchers are considering the trustworthiness, usability, and accessibility of research in an effort to increase public appreciation of and demand for it (Carnine, 1997), while the field is exploring knowledge management strategies that promote the transfer, use, and reticulation of information, including the use of interactive technology to enhance knowledge and to steward professional competence (Becker, 1991; Hood, 2002; Pea, 1999; Renninger & Shumar, 2002; SEDL, 1996; Willinsky, 2001).

Although professionals share the concern that practices not based on evidence may lead to disappointing child and family outcomes, some explanations of the concern locate the problem's source in the inability of the field to identify what really works. In other words, the issue is not so much about the under-implementation of the knowledge base but, rather, its lack of viability. The belief that child and family programs may be ineffective because practices are not derived from studies involving adequate scientific rigor is at the heart of the evidence-based practice movement. At the other extreme, Gallagher (1998) suggested that we are misguided in our belief that we can explain, predict, and control teaching and learning. She posited that empirical methods in education research will not produce generalizations of any instrumental utility but, rather, at best, will set forth a list of instances in which a strategy has worked. She concluded that failed interventions cannot lead to advances in knowledge because of the difficulty in identifying the sources of failures and feeding them back into the body of knowledge. Like Gallagher, others have recognized the value of using a variety of methods of inquiry, including an interpretive or hermeneutical approach, as a means to understand the complexity of children's learning processes, intervention practices, and educational contexts (Hatton & Smith, 1995; LaBoskey, 1994; Schön, 1987; Wesley & Buysse, 2001).

Swirling between these sharp edges of debate are continued explorations into the nature and value of craft knowledge (Bromme & Tillema, 1995; Hiebert, Gallimore, & Stigler, 2002; Ruthven, 2002; Zeichner, 1994) and the roles of families and practitioners in research (Calhoun, 1994; Cochran-Smith & Lytle, 1993, 1999; Fenstermacher, 1994; Patterson, Santa, Short, & Smith, 1993; Richardson, 1994). These lines of study reflect the priority of eliminating the division of the two separate communities—knowledge generators and knowledge consumers (Fuhrman, 1994; Neilson, 2001; Palincsar, Magnusson, Marano, Ford, & Brown, 1998)—as a way to produce and verify professional knowledge. Heibert and colleagues (2002) envisioned a research and development system that would incorporate the skills and expertise of both teachers and researchers in the field of education:

> Researchers and teachers could work side-by-side as authentic partners in the new system, each gaining from the other's expertise. Teachers, for example, would use the wealth of their experience to test difficult-to-implement but promising new ideas and then, based on their own and the researchers' observations, new hypotheses could be constructed for future tests. Researchers, in turn, would have greater access to investigational contexts and populations, and gain a rich source of new ideas and hypotheses. They would get ideas from teachers that could be turned into testable hypotheses, much as clinicians make discoveries that are exploited by biomedical scientists to create new generalized knowledge. Rather than being made redundant or obsolete, the work of researchers could become more relevant with a system in place to digest and transform their general findings into professional knowledge for teaching. (p. 13)

In early intervention and education, one approach to integrating theory and practice is to create communities of practice that, as in the above description, are based on collective expertise and designed to stimulate a bidirectional flow of knowledge from research to practice and from practice to research

(Buysse, Sparkman, & Wesley, 2003; Buysse, Wesley, & Able-Boone, 2001; Wesley & Buysse, 2001). Communities of practice, first introduced through the work of Lave and Wenger (see, e.g., Lave, 1988, 1991, 1997; Lave & Wenger, 1991; Wenger, 1998), hold particular promise for altering the traditional linear relationships through which knowledge trickles down from those who discover it to those who provide and receive services shaped by it.

WHAT IS A COMMUNITY OF PRACTICE?

Communities of practice build on the theory that learning is a social activity involving participation in the practices of social communities and construction of identities related to those communities (Wenger, 1998). A community of practice emerges from a common desire on the part of its members to improve their practice in a particular area, although members may represent a variety of backgrounds and organizations as well as varying degrees of engagement with the community. A community of practice has been defined as a "set of relations among persons, activity, and world, over time and in relation with other tangential and overlapping communities of practice" (Lave & Wenger, 1991, p. 98). The term was first used to describe the way in which meaning was negotiated and reflected in the practices of specific occupations such as those of architects, physicians, tailors, performing artists, and midwives (Brown & Duguid, 1991; Lave & Wenger, 1991).

In a community of practice, members focus on issues, dilemmas, and ambiguities that emerge from authentic situations in their professional practice. In this way, communities of practice reflect *situated learning*, that is, learning that is derived from and applied to everyday experiences as opposed to learning that occurs as a result of an individual's study of a decontextualized body of knowledge (Barab & Duffy, 2000; Hummel, 1993). Specific activities may vary, but members typically engage in a reflective process of sharing perceptions and observations related to specific work practices and then questioning their assumptions about those practices and the practices themselves. Reflection of this type, defined by Han (1995) as an ongoing process of critically examining past and current practice to facilitate the development of future action, is a central tenet of communities of practice, as is the notion that by improving what and how they learn, members create positive outcomes that extend beyond their own learning (Wesley & Buysse, 2001). For example, community of practice members who focus on a common issue over time (e.g., developing and evaluating consultation strategies, defining school readiness) may develop new processes or products that they share with the broader education community.

Lave and Wenger (1991) suggested that members enter a community at the periphery and move closer to full, legitimate participation over time as they encounter people, tools, and tasks and as they gain knowledge about the community's customs and rituals. As newcomers begin to learn the practice, core members also gain new insights from them that may affect the expertise at the center of the community. In this way, the permeable periphery or boundaries of the community of practice become as important as its core, making the community a dynamic, practice-centered approach to learning in which novices, experts, and those in between are engaged. Characterized by the constant interaction of understanding and experience, communities of practice ultimately result in the development of a common repertoire of language, images, resources, assumptions, roles, and understandings among members (Englert & Tarrant, 1995; Marshall & Hatcher, 1996; Rogoff, 1994; Stamps, 1997). Understood by its members as a joint enterprise that is continually renegotiated, a community of practice is defined by knowledge and not by tasks, and its life cycle is determined by its value to the members (Wenger, 1998).

Wenger (1998) identified three dimensions of a community of practice. In his own words, they are as follows:

1. *Evolving forms of mutual engagement:* discovering how to engage, what helps and what hinders; developing mutual relationships: defining identities, establishing who is who, who is good at what, who knows what, who is easy or hard to get along with.

2. *Understanding and tuning their enterprise:* aligning their engagement with it, and learning to become and hold each other accountable to it; struggling to define the enterprise and reconciling conflicting interpretations of what the enterprise is about.

3. *Developing their repertoire, styles and discourses:* renegotiating the meaning of various elements; producing or adopting tools, artifacts, representations; recording and recalling events; inventing new terms and redefining or abandoning old ones; telling and retelling stories, creating and breaking routines. (p. 95)

These dimensions emphasize the social relationships among members and the balance between commonality and diversity within the group (Eraut, 2002). They also describe the priority placed on reflective inquiry not only about what practice involves but also about how members come to understand this meaning.

Barab and Duffy (2000) further extend our understanding by describing three essential characteristics of communities of practice. First, although members in the community may represent diverse disciplines, expertise, and roles, their membership in the community creates a common cultural and historical heritage through their shared goals and meanings. Second, members recognize their connections not only to the community of practice and to the organizations for which they work but also to the larger field of their professional practice, and they consider the implications of their own experiences, perspectives, and knowledge within this larger arena. Third, every community of practice has an ability to regenerate itself as veterans leave and new members enter, subsequently learning from peers who serve as exemplars of mature practice, and as the focus of concern and activities shift.

Distinguishing Communities of Practice From Similar Terms

Beginning with the work of Lave and Wenger (1991), the literature on communities of practice has led to valuable debates about the context and nature of learning. The emphasis on participation by the learner in a group of other learners is reflected by the use of numerous similar terms such as *professional community* (see, e.g., Hausman & Goldring, 2001), *learning organization* (Senge, 1990; Starkey, 1996), and *community of learners* (see, e.g., Brown & Campione, 1996; Schoenfeld, 2004) to describe a variety of communal endeavors to enhance professional knowledge, practice, and commitment in both academic and entrepreneurial arenas. Wesley and Buysse (2001) contrasted the goals, participants, methods, and outcomes of five models of collaborative inquiry, including learning organizations, action research, learning communities in higher education, professional development schools, and communities of practice. Common to all is the emphasis on increased dialogue among professionals about professional knowledge and practice, with ongoing reflection and active inquiry being core to each approach. The models are different in at least three ways. First, they vary according to their scope, that is, who participates and whether the goal is short term and local or long term and public. Second, they vary in the value placed on diverse views and expertise, with communities of practice promising the most in terms of broad participation that includes families. Finally, the potential effect of the group's work on the field as a whole is different across models.

Borrowing from Eraut's (2002) comparison of activity theory (Engestrom, Miettinen, & Punamaki, 1999) and communities of practice, another distinction between communities of practice and other collaborative models is that, in communities of practice, the emphasis is on participation and relationships among people starting from the *community* end. In other words, participants come from an established common tradition of relating to each other and recognize the link between their mutual engagement and their individual and collective learning, which they want to sustain (and perhaps protect). In contrast, the literature that describes "fostering communities of learners" among teachers and among teachers and students places emphasis on activity that starts from the *practice* end and is more learner centered (see, e.g., the entire issue of the *Journal of Curriculum Studies*, 2004, Vol. 36, No. 2). Joint participation is structured purposefully, typically within schools, to systematize a group focus on pedagogical content knowledge and on similarities and differences in implementing curriculum. In action research, professional development schools, and other researcher–practitioner collaborations initiated by institutions of higher education, participation typically is invited for the purpose of enacting a *research* agenda or improving some aspect of teacher preparation.

Certainly a potential contribution of all of these efforts is the professional development of the participants, and it could be argued that if continued over time, the participants' discourse and reflection could lead to public outcomes that would advance their professional field. Of all of these forms of collaborative inquiry, however, communities of practice may offer the most flexibility and power both in terms of their freedom from institutional protocols or supervision (Wenger & Snyder, 2000) and their emphasis on community as a form of relationships among people rather than as a collection of people (St. Clair, 1998). In the following section, we examine three examples of communities of practice in the early intervention and education field.

Examples of Communities of Practice in Early Intervention and Education

Communities of practice in early intervention and education have been defined loosely as a group of professionals and other stakeholders in pursuit of a shared learning enterprise and commonly focused on a particular topic (Buysse et al., 2003). Although communities of practice are not common and are rarely documented in the literature, they emerge primarily to sustain relationships and improve practice as well as in response to several barriers to professional development, most notably, the isolated nature of providing direct services, the separation of research and practice, weak or poorly articulated theoretical frameworks for embracing specific interventions or educational practices, and the lack of consensus about what constitutes recommended practices in some areas (Buysse et al., 2003; Buysse et al., 2001; Wesley & Buysse, 2001).

This section describes three approaches to conducting communities of practice in early intervention and education. The first examines the use of lesson study to support the development of communities of practice within inclusive early childhood settings. The second traces the evolution of a community of professionals engaged in the delivery of consultation to support early childhood inclusion. Finally, the third approach presents an effort by the Office of Special Education Programs in the U.S. Department of Education to establish communities of practice to address program improvement challenges associated with implementation of the Individuals With Disabilities Education Act. (IDEA).

A feature of all three examples is the intentional inclusion of faculty and staff from institutions of higher education and practitioners in the community of practice in an attempt to create an opportunity for them to identify or develop common frames of reference, assumptions, beliefs, and professional goals, thus closing the gap between the different professional cultures in which they traditionally practice. Another feature of the approaches described below is that although they have different goals and methods, each illustrates an effort to examine and integrate the knowledge guiding professional practice, with one community evolving to contribute knowledge to the field at large. Finally, each community of practice involves diverse members representing various disciplines, experiences, and organizations. Table 5.1 presents similarities and differences in the three approaches.

The Lesson Study Process

In their description of communities of practice, Hanks (1991) as well as Barab and Duffy (2000) emphasized the shift in focus of learning from the individual mind to a participatory process involving a group of people who learn through their own actions and those of other participants. The lesson study method involves this type of professional development process through which teachers engage in systematic and collective examination of their practice with a goal of becoming more effective.

Originated in Japan, the term *lesson study* was first used by Makoto Yoshida to describe groups of teachers within or across schools who met a few hours each week to examine and improve the lessons they created within specific curricular areas such as math, science, and reading (Yoshida, 1999). Japanese lesson study groups often include master teachers or advisors who are considered expert in the content discipline and who also serve to expedite a group's access to information such as theoretical information or recent research findings (Fernandez, 2002).

The lesson study process involves at least four steps: (a) create a lesson and observe its implementation, (b) discuss observations, (c) revise the lesson and teach it again, and (d) agree on the final lesson. First, teachers create a lesson and observe a colleague conducting that lesson while they focus on the effect of the specific teaching practices on students. Their observations may be recorded through video, audio, or written notes. Then the teachers meet to discuss their observations after first hearing the reflections of the teacher who taught the lesson. They consider multiple aspects of the lesson, including the importance of connecting the lesson to prior and future lessons, the development of content within the lesson to maximize student understanding, teacher instruction and facilitation during the lesson, and anticipated and documented student outcomes. The lesson is then revised, based on the discussion, and taught again, perhaps by another member of the group. This cycle is repeated until the lesson study group agrees they are satisfied with the lesson (Lewis, 2002). Lesson study groups with many teachers may divide

Table 5.1. Three Approaches to Communities of Practice (CoP) in Early Intervention and Education

CoP	Core Members	Purpose	Activities						
			Observe members' practice	Use written notes or other data related to practice experiences to guide discussion about practice	Compare current practice with theory, research, policy, and recommended practices guiding the profession	Formulate and test hypotheses concerning individual practice	Participate as a group to conduct research within the broader field of early intervention and education	Share findings outside the CoP through formal presentations, publications, or recommendations	Regenerate membership through systematic and regular communication between meetings that is inclusive of peripheral participants
Lesson study 3 groups: Intervention setting Preschool setting Elementary school	Teachers Parents Service coordinators Therapists Education administrators Researchers	Solve local practice dilemmas related to embedding work on a specific child's special education goals in typical routines and activities	Yes	Yes	No	Yes	No	No	Yes

Consultation	Early intervention and education consultants including therapists, University-based technical assistance providers, Researchers	Engage in peer support and problem solving to improve consultation practice in North Carolina	No	Yes	Yes	Yes	Yes	Yes
OSEP/IDEA 6 groups: Child find, 0–3, Natural environments, 3–5, Least restrictive environments, Exiting Part B, School-age, least restrictive environments, Part B and C data systems	State education agency staff, administrators, Other agency administrators, Parents, State technical assistance providers, University faculty and staff	Improve implementation of IDEA in areas such as accessing, providing, and evaluating early intervention and special education services across the nation	No	Yes	No	No	Yes	No

into subgroups of four to six teachers who stay abreast of each other's work by commenting on their respective lesson plans and by attending one another's lesson demonstrations and follow-up discussions.

In Japan, teachers participating in lesson study produce a report of what their study lessons have taught them with respect to their research question (Fernandez, 2002). These reports are circulated among school administrators and teachers and are often featured at school open houses, regional, and national conferences. Some Japanese study groups publish their writings, making them available through bookstores where teachers can find a variety of publications based on lesson studies from all across Japan. These publications are promoted by the government because all teachers use the same national curriculum, which has in turn been influenced by the research of the lesson study groups. This type of officially sanctioned and facilitated dissemination and the prevalence of lesson study as an ongoing teacher commitment at the preservice and in-service levels create a dynamic system of professional development in Japan. Although the reassignment of teachers to different schools on a regular basis ensures the rotation of both novice and veteran teachers, the fact that many teachers belong to study groups within their own school and across schools in a region enriches each group with the multiple experiences individual teachers in the group may have (Fernandez, 2002).

Now emerging as a promising approach to producing effective teachers in classrooms in the United States, lesson study in this country most often involves elementary and secondary math and science educators (Fernandez, 2002) and is present throughout 22 states (Greene, 2004). Two innovative features of the approach in this country are (a) the inclusion of university faculty to the study groups (Little, 2000) and (b) in the instance of lesson study groups formed to examine strategies for teaching specific children with disabilities in natural environments, the addition of parents, service coordinators, specialized therapists, and education administrators to the group of teachers (Green, 2004). However, compared with the Japanese experience in which lesson study groups have addressed long-term, public goals resulting in continuous educational improvement and reform (Lewis & Tsuchida, 1997), lesson study groups in this country have met many challenges. These challenges include the lack of common curriculum here in the United States and the tradition of teachers working independently rather than collaboratively in spite of an increasing number of teacher learning initiatives that center on teachers carefully examining their own practice (Fernandez, 2002). Although teachers may be reluctant at first to invite their colleagues' observation and feedback, of greater concern is the possibility that they lack the ability to adopt and sustain a view of themselves as researchers (Fernandez, Cannon, & Chokshi, 2003).

Recent attempts to implement lesson study in American schools suggest that teachers need much support throughout the study process to be able to develop and test meaningful hypotheses, to rely on evidence to determine the success of their research, and to generalize findings to other contexts. At the same time, participants perceive lesson study to be effective and are drawn to it because through lesson study they are engaged in addressing problems that are important to them (Fernandez, et al., 2003; Greene, 2004; Lesson Study Research Group, (n.d.); Stepanek, 2001).

Greene (2004) studied three lesson study groups that addressed practice dilemmas related to educating a child with disabilities in early intervention, preschool, and elementary school settings. Each group was composed of a team that worked within a program, school, or agency with established policies supporting the provision of services in natural or inclusive environments. The groups focused on the challenges of embedding early intervention or special education strategies in the typical routines and activities of a specific child with disabilities in an inclusive setting. The individualized family service plan (IFSP) group focused on an 18-month-old child with spina bifida served by multiple therapists in her home. The preschool individualized education program (IEP) group supported a 4-year-old child with Asperger's Syndrome who attended a city-funded child-care program. The second grade IEP group worked with an 8-year-old child with cerebral palsy in a public school classroom.

Each group followed a lesson study process involving four stages. First, the participants collaboratively designed an embedded intervention to address a specific goal of the child with whom they were working. The second stage required one team member to implement the embedded intervention while the other team members observed. In the third stage, members shared their observations, child data, and reflections concerning the intervention to determine whether any revisions in the strategy were needed. Finally, during the fourth stage, the modified intervention was tried, observed, and revised again if necessary until the team was satisfied that the intervention was increasing the child's engagement and worked well in the setting.

Green examined three broad research questions, including (a) how participants changed their practices, beliefs, and discourses as a result of their lesson study participation, (b) whether lesson study supported the development of communities of practice and (c) whether the three lesson study groups varied in their development into communities of practice based on individual, group, and contextual factors. Green concluded that by providing a framework through which participants could work together to develop strategies for embedding children's instruction in their natural routines and activities, the lesson study process promoted interactions among team members' diverse content knowledge and expertise, which in turn created increased individual practice knowledge, skills, and confidence among the participants. In terms of the second question, the IFSP group, especially, demonstrated characteristics and outcomes described in the literature on communities of practice. These included (a) actively seeking and considering the perspectives of newcomers and veterans across disciplines as the group shared reflections and (b) working to understand and improve strategies to support members' engagement with one another. Green speculated that this group's success in these areas and the general positive nature of their communication was related to their prior history as a collaborative community. They profited from the administrative support they received as a lesson study group and from the fact that they began the lesson study process with a shared philosophy about their work, including the values of family-guided practice, inclusion, and embedded interventions.

The three lesson study groups did not publicize their outcomes because they addressed specific interventions with specific children. Like other groups described in the lesson study literature in this country, their contributions appear to be limited to their own practice in their own work settings. Although the preschool IEP group members pledged to continue meeting and discussed implementing lesson study in other classrooms with children who had disabilities, the scope of these lesson study groups was constrained by the short, 4-month period during which they were active.

The Consultation Community of Practice

The consultation community of practice emerged in North Carolina in 1994 as a result of the enthusiasm of several early intervention and education consultants who recently had shared an intensive 6-month consultation training experience and the enthusiasm of their university-based trainers, one of whom is the first author of this chapter. The group committed to meet face-to-face three to four times a year to continue the dialogue about consultation that they had begun during training seminars and that they found to be beneficial. The consultants hoped to sustain the peer support and problem solving they received from their colleagues as they continued to implement newly learned consultation stages and strategies, and the trainers hoped to gain ideas about how to improve the consultation training, which was offered to new groups each year. Several members of the community of practice also saw one another outside their meetings because they worked in the same counties or served on the same committees.

During the next decade, the group experienced four phases of development characterized by different levels of interaction and activities among members, from the initial identification of a shared interest in improving members' consultation practice to the conduct of research to address new questions about consultation. Development throughout these phases was not predicted or orchestrated in any way but, rather, is described now as a way to organize the group's long history of increasingly complex and significant activities.

Phase One. During the first phase, the consultation community of practice defined its membership as well as the tools and routines the group used to address the topic of consultation. Members included primarily early intervention consultants serving children with special needs in inclusive early childhood programs in central North Carolina and child-care resource and referral consultants who were responsible for enhancing global quality in child-care centers in the same region—all newly trained in an on-site model of consultation developed by the Partnerships for Inclusion Project at the FPG Child Development Institute at the University of North Carolina at Chapel Hill. The university-based professionals who had conducted the consultation training, including one researcher, also were members of the community of practice. Group members typically met in the spring, summer, and winter at the university, which was centrally located and offered free meeting space, and they held occasional meetings at community agencies.

Meetings initially were arranged and conducted by the university professionals, who took responsibility for developing meeting agendas jointly with the group, scheduling, and facilitating the meetings. Agendas included an opening session of sharing recent consultation experiences followed by group problem solving around specific challenges that had relevance for the most members. Because members implemented the same on-site consultation model involving administration of environment rating scales as a springboard for developing goals for change (Palsha & Wesley, 1998; Wesley, 1994), they were able to share common tools, including self-assessments of consultation skills, environment rating scale scoring sheets and other assessment instruments, action plans, and implementation resources. Some consultants presented their own consultation case studies and brought photos of the consultation sites to illustrate changes made during the consultation process. Continuing an activity introduced during the formal training, members engaged in brainstorming answers to "What If" scenarios designed to help them anticipate and plan for difficult consultation situations. Sometimes, members decided to focus their discussion on a particular stage of consultation (e.g., entry, goal and strategy selection, implementation), its related skills, and lessons learned. Members also reviewed Web sites and children's books related to high-quality child care and early childhood inclusion. Other than regular meeting notices, including an opportunity for members to contribute items to the agenda, communication outside of meeting time was infrequent.

Toward the end of the second year, the leadership role began to rotate as various community-based members took interest in leading discussions. The role of the university-based members changed to simply reserving the meeting room; identifying additional educational resources related to consultation in general or the particular topic of concentration; and whenever possible, making links between the discussion and research on other models of consultation such as the behavioral and mental health approaches. By the end of the first phase, membership seemed fairly stable, with 10–15 people attending each meeting, occasionally including consultees who came with the consultants with whom they were working. In addition, many members shared phone calls and e-mails between meetings.

Phase Two. In the second phase, outsiders were invited to attend meetings for the purpose of providing training that was identified as needed by members and, as a result, the group raised new questions about consultation practice. Visitors to the community of practice included a researcher who discussed his work in the area of integrating therapies for children with special needs into the typical routines of the preschool classroom and a speaker who addressed promoting child engagement through other activity-based interventions. After these presentations and the members' own experiences and discussions of local barriers and supports to early childhood inclusion, the group began not only to discuss their challenges in providing consultation in different programs with varying approaches to inclusion but also to wonder about the comfort of child-care providers with inclusion, some of whom were serving children with disabilities for the first time. The latter concern became the basis for a research study conducted by one of the university-based community of practice members and colleagues (see Buysse, Wesley, Keyes, & Bailey, 1996). Members of the consultation community of practice assisted in conducting interviews with child-care providers about factors affecting their comfort with inclusion and, in turn, played a role in disseminating the study's findings through their ongoing communication with child-care providers. Subsequent discussions within the community of practice examined how the new knowledge about factors affecting child-care providers' comfort would affect future consultation with the consultees.

By this time, about 5 years into the development of the community of practice, some of the members had changed jobs and had stopped attending. Others had entered as newcomers to the group because they had just been hired in a consulting role and had heard about the group from colleagues or because they had completed the university-sponsored consultation training, which was offered annually. There were no criteria, per se, for group membership other than an interest in consultation, and consultants sometimes simply showed up at meetings and introduced themselves for the first time. Members worked out informal strategies for orienting newcomers, including contact with them between meetings to share the group's history of activities and recent topics of discussion. As new members began to share their experiences and views related to their professional practice from the periphery of the group, opportunities arose for the community of practice to revisit its collective view of consultation and early childhood inclusion. One way in which new members' experiences influenced the group was to expand the focus to include consultation in family child-care homes. By the end of phase two and largely as a result of information provided by the university-based members, the community of practice also began to share an understanding of key literature and principles related to consultation, and in so doing, they learned how lacking the body of scholarly knowledge was in terms of addressing consultation in early childhood settings.

Phase Three. As discussions continued about the resources and skills needed to be an effective consultant, the community of practice's third phase of development brought the formulation of questions related to the consultants' own comfort working with different types of consultees in a variety of settings. Was there a type of early childhood program or consultee that seemed most receptive to consultation (e.g., historically inclusive versus newly inclusive program, novice versus experienced consultee)? With respect to what types of children did the consultants feel most comfortable providing consultation? Building on the findings of the previous research on child factors affecting child-care provider comfort with inclusion, two authors of the previous study (one of whom continued as a member of the community of practice) proposed a plan to determine the comfort level of early childhood special education consultants in their role of providing consultation. The study, which was endorsed by the community of practice and in which some members participated, was conducted throughout an 18-month period during which the community of practice continued to meet. In addition to continuing their examination of consultation challenges and solutions, the members also engaged in discussions about barriers and facilitators to quality in inclusive and noninclusive programs, and they identified several types of new educational products that would be helpful to them as they promoted early childhood inclusion. One of those products was described as a resource kit of succinct and easy-to-read information about issues related to high-quality inclusive child care that consultants could share with child-care providers. Two members of the community of practice subsequently developed such a resource with a colleague and published the product through a national press (Wesley, Dennis, & Tyndall, 1999).

Phase Four. The fourth and current phase of the community of practice's development is characterized by activities related to continued production and dissemination of consultation knowledge in the spirit of contributing to a knowledge base that is public, shared, and integrated (Heibert et al., 2002). Two journal articles were published that reported findings from the comfort zone study involving early childhood consultants (Wesley, Buysse, & Keyes, 2000; Wesley, Buysse, & Skinner, 2001). Several members of the community of practice participated in conducting sessions at state and national conferences related to the outcomes of consultation to promote global program quality, the stages and strategies of the on-site consultation model they practiced, and strategies for child-care providers working with consultants in the classroom for the first time. Other members have played important roles in supporting and recruiting consultants for a new national project funded by the U.S. Child Care Bureau and the Administration on Children and Families to export North Carolina's on-site consultation model to improve global program quality to four other states and to assess changes in child outcomes as part of its evaluation. At the same time, the community of practice has sustained its focus on current, authentic practice situations and has continued the reflective cycle of questioning and improving practices. Members also have identified a shared new interest in the effect of state and national school readiness policies on consultation, and some members have participated not only in conducting a statewide study to determine the perspectives of parents, preschool teachers, kindergarten teachers, and elementary school principals about school readiness (Wesley & Buysse, 2003) but also in reporting its findings at state meetings and conferences. In the meantime, the membership of the consultation community of practice continues to evolve, retaining some of its original stakeholders and welcoming others as the workforce of consultants in North Carolina continues to expand and develop.

Unlike the lesson study experiences studied by Greene (2004), the consulta-tion community of practice described above not only has shared and expanded practice knowledge at the individual and local levels but also has contributed to the evidence base that guides the professional field at large. Two obvious reasons for the scope of this community's effect are the long-standing relationships among practitioners and researchers in the community and the longevity of the group as a whole. We could speculate about possible differences between members of this community and those of the lesson study groups in terms of their dispositions toward their own learning and toward collaborative inquiry, given that the consultation community emerged on its own over time and the lesson study groups were created by a researcher who modified existing team structures and tasks for the purposes of conducting a study.

The Office of Special Education Programs Technical Assistance Communities of Practice

The U.S. Department of Education has documented the need for improve-ment across Part B and Part C provisions of the Individuals With Disabilities Education Act (IDEA), including areas such as accessing, providing, and evaluating early intervention and special education services across the nation. To help address these challenges, the Office of Special Education Programs introduced a new technical assistance (TA) initiative that they refer to as "communities of practice." Facilitated by the National Early Childhood Technical Assistance Center, the TA communities of practice have the following goals:

- To increase the use of high-quality research-based information and effective policies and practices related to the IDEA
- To identify solutions to key implementation issues and challenges
- To enhance shared inquiry and learning
- To prevent duplication of effort
- To facilitate connections and collaboration among many stakeholders
- To develop new service system special education capacities
- To implement the IDEA better and improve results (Trohanis, 2004).

Members include administrators and staff of state educational agencies, parents and family members, educators and early interventionists, administrators, state TA providers, and university faculty and staff. As many as six TA communities have been formed to address the following IDEA implementation challenges: child identification; providing services in natural environments; expanding opportunities for children ages 3–5 years to be included with typically developing peers in community settings; developing least restrictive environments for school-age children with disabilities; and improving data collection, analysis, and use.

The TA communities use an electronic forum, which is a special Web site designed to support the entire community of practice effort, as their primary tool for supporting a community experience. To achieve their goals of engaging members, sharing expertise, and solving problems together, the communities rely on teleconferences, listservs, meetings, resource materials, think tanks, and conferences.

IMPLICATIONS FOR THE FIELD

As chapter 1 points out, the current climate of educational policy in the United States is linked to broader social and political movements, including the trend toward performance-based outcomes and accountability. As an example of where policy affects practitioner learning directly, the evidence-based practice movement places national emphasis on shoring up professional knowledge and skills. Rather than view this emphasis as a deficit-based approach to remediate what is lacking, the evidence-based practice decision-making process empowers practitioners to use the best available evidence to make informed decisions. Communities of practice offer an alternative to the perspective that evidence is generated, organized, disseminated, and translated by a few professionals for the many professionals who need to apply it in their daily work with children and families. Instead, members of practice communities may engage in generating, organizing, disseminating, and translating evidence themselves. Depending on how the community evolves, the outcomes of their activity not only can influence their own practice but also can contribute to the knowledge base that guides the practice of a much larger professional community, as we saw in the consultation example. Let us

consider four challenges of using communities of practice to build the
evidence base in early intervention and education:

- identifying, connecting, and learning from existing communities
  of practice

- implementing effective strategies for harvesting and building the
  evidence and linking those to an appropriate scope of work

- creating effective organizational structures that support group processes
  and

- using technology to extend and enhance communities in cyberspace.

Identifying, Connecting, and Learning From Existing Communities

As was the case with the consultation group, there are productive communities of practice already at work in our field. That is, groups of diverse stakeholders in early intervention and education likely are working
collaboratively to study common issues to further the professional development of their individual members, to innovate practice more broadly at some
level, or both. Chances are that these groups do not identify themselves as
"communities of practice" and may not share information about their activities outside their groups. Because our professional field is in the early stages
of describing the concept and its potential, there is only a limited shared
understanding, vocabulary, and dialogue about communities of practice. Our
first challenge is to promote more discussion of the approach to identify
current activities that seem relevant and promising as well as supports for
those activities.

Implementing Effective Strategies for Identifying and Building Evidence

Members also need strategies that they can use within their community of
practice to identify existing evidence from the three sources discussed in
chapter 1: family or consumer values and wisdom, professional values and
wisdom (craft knowledge), and empirical science. In other words, they must
learn how to learn using the resources of the group. At a minimum, this effort
would begin with the values, knowledge, and research of the members themselves, but it necessarily would include also the values, knowledge, and

research recognized by the field at large. A potential pitfall of communities of practice is that members will depend too much on local knowledge. In fact, the comparison of current understandings and practice against those recommended by professional standards often creates the catalyst for professional growth. The challenge for communities of practice is to know where they are and where they are going in such a complex undertaking. Members not only must focus on the processes they use to discover and communicate their content and the content itself but also must have conversations about what is a manageable scope of activity for their community, given their interests and resources. They must decide whether their goals include sharing knowledge, reconstructing knowledge, generating new knowledge, or some combination, and they may want to consider how potential outcomes related to many bite-size activities over time compare with those of longer term, more complex projects.

Creating Effective Organizational Structures That Support Group Processes

Communities of practice are affected by (a) the interrelationships among the community of practice, (b) the members' philosophies about their practice and their dispositions toward learning and collaborative inquiry, and (c) many wider contextual influences such as the sociocultural environment in their respective workplaces and policies affecting the professional field at large. One challenge in considering the notion of creating communities of practice where they have not been identified naturally is the lack of sufficient information about what types of organizational structures will guarantee the sorts of organic and shared processes described in Wenger's (1998) three dimensions of being a community of practice (Hodkinson & Hodkinson, 2003). Beyond the general expectation that members will share a common interest in examining and improving practice, what else should be considered in organizing a community of practice? For example, what member characteristics (e.g., short-term versus long-term commitments to the community, whether members are professionals or consumers, area of expertise or discipline), resources (e.g., administrative support, time, communication tools), and group strategies (e.g., leadership, problem-solving approaches, renewal) should be promoted, given the purpose of the community?

Using Technology to Extend and Enhance Virtual Communities

Given the state of technology and the fact that, by definition, communities of practice transcend geographical and organizational boundaries, we must ask, Under what circumstances are virtual communities likely to be productive? An abundance of literature is emerging that explores the capacity of computer-based, knowledge-networking tools to foster the establishment of social relationships in which people can construct understanding and knowledge collaboratively as opposed to knowledge management tools that simply focus on routing or transmitting information (see, e.g., Renninger & Shumar, 2002). Nolan and Weiss (2002) offered a daunting list of questions that they called "a thin representation of the complexities" related to how members of virtual communities can find sites, access software, and learn how to learn the "netiquette" required be a member in good standing (p. 315). Their questions include issues related to who initiates the online community and why; the knowledge and skills necessary for access; the communication and regulation of protocol and social norms; the nature of online interaction among members; the ways members enable their own purposes to be served within the community; and the indicators of success, stagnation, or failure of the community. In the field of early intervention and education where face-to-face communities of practice are just emerging, we face perhaps our most exciting, yet most demanding, challenge in knowing how to establish, extend, and enhance communities in cyberspace.

DIRECTIONS FOR RESEARCH

The preceding discussion of implications prompts many directions for future research about communities of practice. The field could profit from continued explorations into theoretical groundings, especially those related to the contributions of activity theory, and is wide open to empirical findings concerning the processes and outcomes of communities of practice. Most basically, in documenting the activities of communities of practice related to our understanding and implementation of evidence-based practices, we should consider a broad range of methodologies to answer questions such as the following:

- What strategies can members of communities of practice use to share and co-construct evidence related not only to family and professional values and knowledge but also to empirical science?

- What factors support and sustain communities of practice in early intervention and education? What incentives promote the allegiance of professionals to communities of practice?

- What types of exchanges (e.g., information exchanges, support or assistance, companionship, etc.) create a sense of belonging to a community of practice?

- What relationship does community-based learning have to individual and group learning?

- What types of interaction and knowledge exchange occur at the periphery of communities of practice? What strategies support knowledge exchange among different communities?

- How can computer technology transform communities of virtual strangers into communities of social relationships bound in a common pursuit of knowledge?

- How effective are communities of practice (compared with traditional models) in generating new ideas, improving practices, and improving child outcomes?

CONCLUSION

One limitation of current efforts to shrink the distance between research and practice may be the episodic format of action research and other projects described as "partnerships" between researchers and teachers. Although in some cases existing relationships may have led to collaborative inquiry, few could argue with the fact that opportunities for ongoing communication and shared experiences between researchers and practitioners are largely missing in our field. The dominant approach to the continued professional development of practitioners involves relatively short-term, small-scale learning opportunities, even as we struggle away from the old metaphor of learning as acquisition toward a newer view of learning as participation. Communities of practice offer the promise of (a) individual learning as a result of social processes and (b) group learning that holds the potential to advance the field as a whole. This chapter described similarities and differences among three communities of practice in early intervention and education and offered speculation about what would maximize the potential of communities of practice to build the base of evidence that informs not only local practice but also recommended practice for the field at large.

REFERENCES

Barab, S. A., & Duffy, T. M. (2000). From practice fields to communities of practice. In D. H. Jonassen & S. M. Land (Eds.), *Theoretical foundations of learning environments* (pp. 25–55). Mahwah, NJ: Erlbaum.

Barnett, W. S., & Frede, E. C. (2001). And so we plough along: The nature and nurture of partnerships for inquiry. *Early Childhood Research Quarterly, 16*, 3–7.

Becker, T. (1991). Knowledge utilization: The third wave. *Knowledge, 12,* 225–240.

Book, C. L. (1996). Professional development schools. In J. Sikula (Ed.), *Handbook on research in teacher education* (2nd ed., pp. 194–210). New York: MacMillan.

Boyer, E. L. (1990). *Scholarship reconsidered: Priorities of the professoriate.* Princeton, NJ: Carnegie Foundation for the Advancement of Teaching, University of Princeton.

Bromme, R., & Tillema, H. (1995). Fusing experience and theory: The structure of professional knowledge. *Learning and Instruction, 5,* 261–267.

Brown, A. L., & Campione, J. C. (1996). Psychological theory and the design of innovative learning environments: On procedures, principles, and systems. In L. Schauble & R. Glaser (Eds.), *Innovations in learning: New environments for education* (pp. 289–325). Mahwah, NJ: Erlbaum.

Brown, J. S., & Duguid, P. (1991). Organizational learning and communities of practice: Toward a unified view of working, learning, and innovation. *Organizational Science, 2,* 40–57.

Buysse, V., Sparkman, K., & Wesley, P.W. (2003). Communities of practice in educational research: Connecting what we know with what we do. *Exceptional Children, 69*(3), 263–277.

Buysse, V., Wesley, P. W., & Able-Boone, H. (2001). Innovations in professional development: Creating communities of practice to support inclusion. In M. J. Guralnick (Ed.), *Early childhood inclusion: Focus on change* (pp. 179–200). Baltimore: Brookes.

Buysse, V., Wesley, P. W., Keyes, L., & Bailey, D. B. (1996). Assessing the comfort zone of child care teachers in serving young children with disabilities. *Journal of Early Intervention, 20*, 189–203.

Calhoun, E. F. (1994). *How to use action research in the self-renewing school.* Alexandria, VA: Association for Supervision and Curriculum Development.

Carnine, D. (1997). Bridging the research-to-practice gap. *Exceptional Children, 63*, 513–521.

Cochran-Smith, M., & Lytle, S. (1993). *Inside outside: Teacher research and knowledge.* New York: Teachers College Press.

Cochran-Smith, M., & Lytle, S. (1999). Relationships of knowledge and practice: Teacher learning in communities. In A. Iran-Nejad & D. Pearson (Eds.), *Review of research in education* (Vol. 24, pp. 249–306). Washington, DC: American Educational Research Association.

Cousins, J. B., & Simon, M. (1996). The nature and impact of policy-induced partnerships between research and practice communities. *Educational Evaluation and Policy Analysis, 18*, 199–218.

Darling-Hammond, L. (Ed.) (1994). *Professional development schools: Schools for developing a profession.* New York: Teachers College Press.

Engestrom, Y., Miettinen, R., & Punamaki, R. (Eds.). (1999). *Perspectives on activity theory.* Cambridge, UK: Cambridge University Press.

Englert, C. S., & Tarrant, K. L. (1995). Creating collaborative cultures for educational change. *Remedial and Special Education, 16*, 325–336.

Eraut, M. (2002, April). *Conceptual analysis and research questions: Do the concepts of "learning community" and "community of practice" provide added value?* Paper presented at the Annual Meeting of the American Educational Research Association, New Orleans, LA.

Fenstermacher, G. D. (1994). The knower and the known: The nature of knowledge in research on teaching. In L. Darling-Hammond (Ed.), *Review of research in education* (Vol. 20, pp. 1–54). Washington, DC: American Educational Research Association.

Fernandez, C. (2002). Learning from Japanese approaches to professional development: The case of lesson study. *Journal of Teacher Education, 53,* 393–405.

Fernandez, C., Cannon, J., & Chokshi, S. (2003). A U.S.-Japan lesson study collaboration reveals critical lenses for examining practice. *Teaching and Teacher Education, 19,* 171–185.

Fuhrman, S. (1994, April). Uniting producers and consumers: Challenges in creating and utilizing educational research and development. In T. Tuijnman (Ed.), *Educational research and reform: An international* perspective (pp. 133–147). Washington, DC: U.S. Department of Education.

Gallagher, D. (1998). The scientific knowledge base of special education: Do we know what we think we know? *Exceptional Children, 64,* 493–502.

Greene, K. (2004). Professional development in inclusive early childhood settings: Can we create communities of practice through lesson study? Doctoral dissertation: University of North Carolina at Chapel Hill.

Han, E. P. (1995). Reflection is essential in teacher education. *Childhood Education, 71,* 228–230.

Hanks, W. F. (1991). Foreword. In J. Lave & E. Wenger, *Situated learning: Legitimate peripheral participation* (pp. 13–24). Cambridge, UK: Cambridge University Press.

Hatton, N., & Smith, D. (1995). Reflection in teacher education: Towards definition and implementation. *Teaching and Teacher Education, 11,* 33–49.

Hausman. C. S., & Goldring, E. G. (2001). Sustaining teacher commitment: The role of professional communities. *Peabody Journal of Education*, 76(2), 30–51.

Hiebert, J., Gallimore, R., & Stigler, J. W. (2002). A knowledge base for the teaching profession: What would it look like and how can we get one? *Educational Researcher, 31*, 3–15.

Hodkinson, P., & Hodkinson, H. (2003). Individuals, communities of practice, and the policy context: School teachers' learning in their workplace. *Studies in Continuing Education, 25*, 3–21.

The Holmes Group. (1990). *Tomorrow's schools*. East Lansing, MI: Author. (ERIC Document Reproduction Service No. ED328533)

Hood, P. (2002). *Perspectives on knowledge utilization in education*. San Francisco: West Ed.

Hummel, H. G. K. (1993, December). Distance education and situated learning: Paradox or partnership? *Educational Technology*, 11–22.

Journal of Curriculum Studies. (2004). 36(2).

LaBoskey, V. K. (1994). *Development of reflective practice: A study of preservice teachers*. New York: Teachers College Press.

Lave, J. (1988). *Cognition in practice: Mind, mathematics, and culture in everyday life*. Cambridge, UK: Cambridge University Press.

Lave, J. (1991). Situating learning in communities of practice. In L. B. Resnick, J. M. Levine, & S. D. Teasley (Eds.), *Perspectives on socially shared cognition* (pp. 63–82). Washington, DC: American Psychological Association.

Lave, J. (1997). The culture of acquisition and the practice of understanding. In D. Kirshner & J. A. Whitson (Eds.), *Situated cognition: Social, semiotic, and psychological perspectives* (pp. 63–82). Mahwah, NJ: Erlbaum.

Lave, J., & Wenger, E. (1991). *Situated learning: Legitimate peripheral participation*. Cambridge, UK: Cambridge University Press.

Lesson Study Research Group. (n.d.). Database of U.S. lesson study groups. Retrieved February 12, 2005, from www.tc.edu/lessonstudy/support_consult.html

Lewis, C. (2002). *Lesson study: A handbook of teacher-led instructional change.* Philadelphia: Research for Better Schools.

Lewis, C., & Tsuchida, I. (1997). Planned education in Japan: The case of elementary science instruction. *Journal of Educational Policy, 12,* 313–331.

Little, M. E. (2000). Preparing for changing educational roles: Creating and learning from within the public schools. *Childhood Education, 76,* 307–311.

Marshall, S. P., & Hatcher, C. (1996, March). Promoting career development through CADRE. *Educational Leadership,* 42–46.

National Academy of Education. (1999). *Recommendations regarding research priorities.* New York: The National Academy of Education, New York University, School of Education.

National Research Council Committee on a Feasibility Study for a Strategic Education Research Program. (1999). *Improving student learning: A strategic plan for education research and its utilization.* Committee on a Feasibility Study for a Strategic Education Research Program. Commission on Behavioral and Social Sciences Education. Washington, DC: National Academy Press.

National Research Council Committee on Scientific Principles for Education Research (2002). *Scientific research in education.* Washington, DC: National Academy Press.

Neilson, S. (2001). Knowledge utilization and public policy processes: A literature review. London: International Development Research Centre.

Nolan, D. J., & Weiss, J. (2002). Learning in cyberspace: An educational view of virtual community. In K. A. Renninger & W. Shumar (Eds.), *Building virtual communities: Learning and change in cyberspace* (pp. 293–320). Cambridge, UK: Cambridge University Press.

Palincsar, A. S., Magnusson, S. L., Marano, N., Ford, D., & Brown, N. (1998). Designing a community of practice: Principles and practices of the GIsML community. *Teaching and Teacher Education, 14,* 5–19.

Palsha, S., & Wesley, P. W. (1998). Improving quality in early childhood environments through on-site consultation. *Topics in Early Childhood Special Education, 18,* 243–253.

Patterson, L, Santa, C., Short, K., & Smith, K. (Eds.) (1993). *Teachers are researchers: Reflection in action.* Newark, DE: International Reading Association.

Pea, R. (1999). New media communications forums for improving education research and practice. In E. Lagemann & L. Schulman (Eds.), *Issues in education research: Problems and possibilities.* San Francisco: Jossey-Bass.

Renninger, K. A., & Shumar, W. (Eds.) (2002). *Building virtual communities: Learning and change in cyberspace.* Cambridge, UK: Cambridge University Press.

Richardson, V. (1994). Conducting research on practice. *Educational Researcher, 23,* 5–10.

Rogoff, B. (1994). Developing understanding of the idea of communities of learners. *Minds, Culture, and Activity, 1,* 209–229.

Ruthven, K. (2002). Towards synergy of scholarly and craft knowledge. In H. G. Weigand, A. Peter-Koop, N. T. Neill, K. Reiss, G. Törner, & B. Wollring (Eds.) *Developments in mathematics education in German-speaking countries: Selected papers from the Annual Conference on Didactics of Mathematic* (pp. 121–129). Potsdam, Germany: Franzbecker Verlag, Hildesheim.

Schoenfeld, A. H. (2004). Multiple learning communities, students, teachers, instructional designers, and researchers. *Journal of Curriculum Studies, 36,* 237–255.

Schön, D. (1987). *Educating the reflective practitioner: Toward a new design for teaching and learning in the professions.* San Francisco: Jossey-Bass.

Senge, P. (1990). *The fifth discipline: The art and practice of the learning organization.* London: Century.

Southwest Educational Development Laboratory (SEDL). (1996). *A review of the literature on information and knowledge dissemination*. Austin, TX: Southwest Educational Development Laboratory (SEDL), National Center for the Dissemination of Disability Research (NCDDR).

Stamps, D. (1997). Communities of practice: Learning is social. Training is irrelevant? *Training, 34*, 34–42.

Starkey, K. (1996). *How organizations learn*. London: International Thomson Business Press.

St. Clair, R. (1998). On the commonplace: Reclaiming community in adult education. *Adult Education Quarterly, 49*, 5–14.

Stepanek, J. (2001). A new view of professional development, *Northwest Teacher, 2*, 2–5.

Valli, L., Cooper, D., & Frankes, L. (1997). Professional development schools and equity: A critical analysis of rhetoric and research. In M. W. Apple (Ed.), *Review of Research in Education, 22*, 251–304.

Wenger, E. C. (1998). *Communities of practice: Learning, meaning, and identity*. Cambridge, UK: Cambridge University Press.

Wenger, E. C., & Snyder, W. M. (2000). Communities of practice: The organizational frontier. *Harvard Business Review, 78*(January–February), 139–145.

Wesley, P. W. (1994). Providing on-site consultation to promote quality in integrated child care programs. *Journal of Early Intervention, 18*, 391–402.

Wesley, P. W., & Buysse, V. (2001). Communities of practice: Expanding professional roles to promote reflection and shared inquiry. *Topics in Early Childhood Special Education, 21*, 114–123.

Wesley, P. W., Buysse, V., & Keyes, L. (2000). Comfort zone revisited: Effects of child characteristics on professional comfort in providing consultation. *Journal of Early Intervention, 23*(2), 106–115.

Wesley, P. W., Buysse, V., & Skinner, D. (2001). Early interventionists' perspectives on professional comfort as consultants. *Journal of Early Intervention, 24*, 112–128.

Wesley, P. W., Dennis, B., & Tyndall, S. (1999). *QuickNotes: Inclusion resources for early childhood professionals* (2nd ed.). Lewisville, NC: Kaplan Press.

Willinsky, J. (2001). The strategic educational research program and the public value of research. *Educational Researcher, 30*, 5–14.

Yoshida, M. (1999). Lesson study: A case study of a Japanese approach to improving instruction through school-based teacher development (Doctoral dissertation, University of Chicago, 1999). Digital Dissertations, AAT 9951855.

Zeichner, K. M. (1994). Personal renewal and social construction through teacher research. In S. Hollingsworth & H. Sockett (Eds.), *Teacher research and educational reform* (pp. 66–85). Chicago: The University of Chicago Press.

CHAPTER 6

ESTABLISHING THE EVIDENCE BASE FOR AN EMERGING EARLY CHILDHOOD PRACTICE: RECOGNITION AND RESPONSE

Mary Ruth Coleman, Virginia Buysse, and Jennifer Neitzel

In this chapter, we share our experience in using an evidence-based practice framework to conceptualize an early intervening system called Recognition and Response. The conceptual framework for the Recognition and Response system is being developed through a collaborative effort with grant support from the Emily Hall Tremaine Foundation (http://www.tremainefoundation.org). This collaboration involves the FPG Child Development Institute at the University of North Carolina at Chapel Hill, the National Center for Learning Disabilities, the National Association for the Education of Young Children, the Communication Consortium Media Center, and five state partners (Arizona, Connecticut, Florida, New Jersey, and Maryland). Collectively, these organizations and partners bring expertise in learning disabilities and early childhood education as well as diverse perspectives from research, policy, and practice in both fields. The president of the Emily Hall Tremaine Foundation charged this group with the tasks of (a) examining the evidence base for establishing an early intervening system that could be applied to early education settings and (b) building the components of the system in a way that addressed critical contexts and issues within the early childhood field.

The work is being accomplished through two primary activities: (a) a comprehensive and systematic review of the literature and (b) a series of meetings and discussions with the collaborating organizations and partners that has evolved into a community of practice. A third activity, evaluating the model, represents an important future goal for this initiative.

Before this experience, each of the authors had used many of the activities that we have described in this chapter to review the literature, build consensus, as well as validate our research methods and findings. None of us, however, had understood fully how these activities fit together within an evidence-based practice framework, nor did we comprehend the implications of applying this framework as a means of weighing research evidence against other sources of evidence, most notably, professional and family wisdom and values. Having immersed ourselves in the evidence-based practice literature, we were convinced that this approach could provide a powerful lens through which to develop and evaluate innovations in the field. It was surprisingly easy to convince the funder and other partners in this endeavor that establishing an evidence base for an emerging practice offered a unique opportunity to build a solid foundation for a new area of practice right from the beginning. Because we made a conscious effort to apply an evidence-based practice approach to this work from the onset (rather than back into evidence-based practice and reframe our work in these terms after the fact), and because our state partners were beginning to implement Recognition and Response practices before all of the evidence was in, it occurred to us that we were building the airplane while we were flying it.

The purpose of this chapter is to offer one example of how an evidence-based framework can be used to conceptualize and evaluate an emerging area of practice. Rather than being an academic exercise, this effort reflects our actual struggle in moving evidence-based concepts from theory into practice. Our challenge was to develop the process for establishing an evidence base while working simultaneously to apply this evidence to create an actual set of practices called Recognition and Response. This chapter will present both the process we used and the findings that evolved from this process. We begin with a review of the issues surrounding response to intervention (RTI) and major trends in the early childhood field that served as an impetus and context for developing the Recognition and Response system. Next, we summarize the collaborative efforts and the process used to integrate the best available research with professional and family wisdom and values. Finally, we share some reflections and evolving lessons from an initiative that is far from completed. Our intention is not to offer these ideas as a blueprint for others who wish to engage in similar work but, rather, to present our experiences as a way of illuminating the issues and challenges involved in adopting an evidence-based practice framework and to promote a discussion about ways to improve the reliance on evidence to support innovation in the early childhood field. Although current policies emphasize the need to determine what works, primarily as this relates to existing practices, the Recognition and Response initiative focused on building the knowledge base through innovations that lead to new and improved practices for children and families.

THE RTI MOVEMENT

In this section, we offer a brief but fairly comprehensive review of issues surrounding RTI. We do so for two reasons: (a) RTI served as the primary impetus for developing a comparable approach for use with younger children and (b) the theoretical, conceptual, and empirical foundations of RTI represent important sources of evidence for an emerging area of practice that focuses on helping parents and teachers recognize learning difficulties as early as possible (before beginning kindergarten) and to respond in effective ways.

The Recognition and Response system originated from the RTI model, which emphasizes prereferral prevention and intervention for school-age children who may be at risk for learning disabilities. RTI now dominates national discussions on the identification of learning disabilities, with entire journal issues devoted to this topic (*Journal of Learning Disabilities*, 2005, Vol. 38, No. 6; *Learning Disabilities and Practice*, 2003, Vol. 18, No. 3; *Learning Disabilities Quarterly*, 2005, Vol. 25, No. 1).

Before RTI, most states defined learning disabilities in a manner that hinged on establishing a discrepancy between children's intellectual abilities (IQ) and their achievement, performance, or both. The problems with the so-called discrepancy model, which requires waiting until the gap between IQ and achievement is wide enough to measure—often not until the second or third grade—are well documented in the literature (Conyers, Reynolds, & Ou, 2003; Fuchs, Mock, Morgan, & Young, 2003; Kavale, Holdnack, & Mostert, 2005; O'Connor, 2000; Speece & Case, 2003).

RTI can be distinguished from the discrepancy model in that it allows for early and intensive interventions based on learning characteristics and needs and it promotes a collaborative approach to delivering supports and services (Fuchs, 2003; Vaughn & Fuchs, 2003). The major premise of RTI is that early intervening services can both prevent academic problems for many students who experience learning difficulties and differentiate which students actually have learning disabilities from those whose underachievement can be attributed to other factors such as ineffective instruction. In addition, because RTI includes an emphasis on the quality of the general education curriculum, the model offers potential benefits to every student and not only to those who experience some type of learning problem.

Although several variations of the model have been proposed, in general, RTI is based on several phases, or tiers, of increasingly intense interventions that guide its implementation in the schools (Blankstein & Cocozzella, 2004; Fuchs, 2003; Marston, Muyskens, Lau, & Canter, 2003; O'Shaughnessy, Lane, Gresham, & Beebe-Frankenberger, 2003). In Tier I, all students are screened to determine whether the curriculum and instruction offered in the general education program are sufficiently supportive to meet the educational needs of most children. If 80% of the children in a particular classroom meet predetermined benchmarks in academics and behavior, then the general education curriculum is presumed to be of sufficient quality. If the 80% criterion is not met, then classroom-level intervention to improve the quality of instruction should be implemented.

In Tier II, enhanced instruction within the general education classroom is used to address the needs of students who do not make adequate progress in Tier 1. Teachers are encouraged to intervene with these students by modifying the curriculum or by using differentiated instructional methods such as small-group instruction or peer-mediated strategies.

In Tier III, teachers implement individualized instruction for students who fail to make adequate progress during Tier II. The RTI approach assumes that a small proportion of students (perhaps 5%) may not respond to any of these interventions. These students may have specific learning disabilities and should be referred for special education services. Figure 6.1 illustrates the hierarchy of tiers for implementation within RTI.

Figure 6.1. Hierarchy of Tiers for RTI

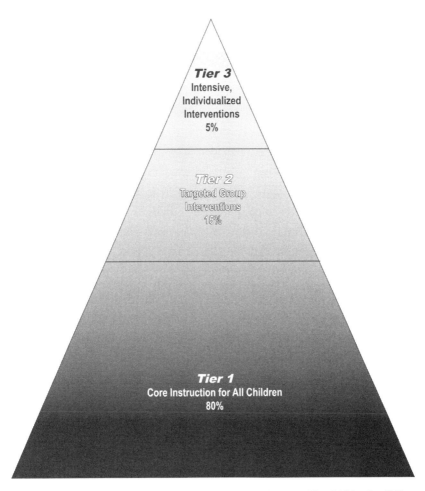

Adapted with permission from *The National Association of State Directors of Special Education*, 2005.

Other essential features of RTI include collaboration between classroom teachers and specialists as well as the problem-solving process, the use of continuous progress monitoring, research-based curriculum and instruction, and systematic assessment of the fidelity with which instruction and interventions are implemented (Fuchs & Fuchs, 2002; Fuchs, Fuchs, & Speece, 2002; Fuchs et al., 2003). Continuous progress monitoring of student performance is used to make data-based decisions across key dimensions of teaching and learning that include the effectiveness of the general education curriculum, the need to provide enhanced instruction for some students, and the timing and intensity of these interventions. By monitoring a student's learning and comparing it with that of peers receiving the same instruction, teachers can determine whether the student's academic level and growth rate is indicative of a learning problem. Most of the research-based instructional practices evaluated within RTI have been used primarily to address reading difficulties, largely because this area represents the primary instructional need for the vast majority of children identified with learning disabilities. Consequently, much less is known about the application of RTI to address children's problems in other academic areas or in behavior.

Prompted in part by the growing movement in the learning disabilities field to replace the discrepancy model with an early intervening system, the reauthorized Individuals With Disabilities Act (IDEA) of 2004 included the RTI approach as one option that schools can use to identify students with learning disabilities. The new language in the legislation is as follows:

> SEC.614. EVALUATION, ELIGIBILITY DETERMINATIONS,
> INDIVIDUALIZED EDUCATION PROGRAMS, AND EDUCATIONAL
> PLACEMENTS
>> (b) EVALUATION PROCEDURES.—
>>> (6) SPECIFIC LEARNING DISABILITIES. —
>>>> (A) IN GENERAL. —Notwithstanding section 607(b), when determining whether a child has a specific learning disability as defined in section 602 (29), a local educational agency shall not be required to take into consideration whether a child has a severe discrepancy between achievement and intellectual ability in oral expression, listening comprehension, written expression, basic reading skill, reading comprehension, mathematical calculation, or mathematical reasoning.

(B) ADDITIONAL AUTHORITY. —In determining whether a child has a specific learning disability, a local educational agency may use a process that determines if the child responds to scientific, research-based intervention as a part of the evaluation procedures described in paragraphs (2) and (3).

On the basis of what is known about RTI for school-age children, the Recognition and Response early intervening system is being developed and validated for use with younger children (3- to 5-year-olds) enrolled in various types of early education settings. In addition to the unique developmental needs of very young children, key contexts in the early childhood field were an important consideration in conceptualizing the Recognition and Response system.

MAJOR TRENDS AND CONTEXTS IN THE EARLY CHILDHOOD FIELD

This section provides an overview of several trends or contexts in the United States that have focused national attention on early education issues and have helped to influence attitudes about the importance of services for very young children and families: (a) the emphasis on high quality early care and education programs, (b) the school readiness movement, (c) the national prekindergarten movement, and (d) the prevention and early intervention service system. Each of these areas reflect key contextual factors that are being considered and weighed against other sources of evidence in our efforts to build an early intervening system for young children. These contexts were the early childhood issues and trends that lingered over all of our deliberations with the collaborating organizations and partners.

The Emphasis on High Quality Early Care and Education

The quality of early care and education has been at the forefront of research in the early childhood field for several decades. Mounting empirical evidence suggests that the quality of early childhood programs is an important determinant of children's social, language, and cognitive outcomes, as well as their school readiness skills (Bryant, Burchinal, Lau, & Sparling, 1994; Bryant, et al., 2003; Burchinal, Roberts, Nabors, & Bryant, 1996; Cost, Quality, & Outcomes Study Team, 1995; Howes, Phillips, & Whitebook, 1992; Lamb, 1997; Peisner-Feinberg, et al., 2001; Phillips, McCartney, & Scarr, 1987; Whitebook, Howes, & Phillips, 1989).

Conceptualized broadly, the definition of quality encompasses all aspects of children's surroundings, care, education, and experiences that are beneficial to their development and well-being. The features of high-quality programs cited most frequently include curriculum content and learning processes that cultivate school-related skills and knowledge, qualified teaching staff and supervisors, low teacher–child ratios and small class sizes, reflective teaching practices, intense and coherent programming, and collaborative relationships with parents (Love, Schochet, & Meckstrom, 1996; National Research Council, 2001; Phillipsen, Burchinal, Howes, & Cryer, 1997).

Program standards and practice guidelines identify the characteristics of programs and specific teaching practices that define high quality early childhood programs. Examples include the NAEYC Early Childhood Program Standards and Accreditation Criteria (NAEYC, 2005), the DEC Recommended Practices (Sandall, Hemmeter, Smith, & McLean, 2005), the Head Start Performance Standards and Head Start Child Outcomes Framework (revised in 1998).

As a part of a high quality program, early childhood teachers are expected to implement a curriculum that aligns with program and early learning standards and to make sound educational decisions for all children (NAEYC, NAECS/SDE, 2003). The proposed Recognition and Response system could enhance program quality by helping teachers identify significant concerns for individual children who may require more focused interventions, by offering them teaching strategies to address these individual needs, and by providing approaches for monitoring and evaluating the effectiveness of these instructional approaches.

The School Readiness Movement

In 1991, national attention was focused on school readiness through the establishment of six national education goals, with the first one being "All children in America will start school ready to learn" (National Education Goals Panel, 1991, codified in the Educate America Act, Pub. L. 103-277). Goal one was eventually defined as including the following dimensions of school readiness that have become widely accepted in the early childhood field: physical and motor development, social and emotional development, approaches toward learning (i.e., creativity, initiative, attitudes, task mastery), language, cognition, and general knowledge (Kagan, Moore, & Bredekamp, 1995; Love, 2001; Meisels, 1999). In 1998, the National Education Goals Panel further defined school readiness by noting the need for *ready schools*—the notion that it was not sufficient for all children to be ready for school but that schools also must be ready to meet the needs of all children.

Several recent publications have affirmed that earlier work, noting, for example, that children's readiness for school is made up of multiple components and shaped by many factors, including children's environments and early experiences (McLanahan, 2005; National Governors Association, 2005; Rhode Island KIDS COUNT, 2005). Other conclusions offered by these sources include the following: (a) experiences during the first 5 years of life provide the foundation for language, reasoning, problem solving, social skills, and behavioral and emotional health; (b) school readiness efforts must recognize that young children vary in their early experiences, skills, knowledge, language, culture, and family background and that gaps in school achievement among children from various groups already exist by the time children enter kindergarten; (c) families help prepare young children for school when they nurture, protect, and provide them with opportunities to learn and explore; and (d) schools improve readiness of young children by making connections with early care and education programs and by creating policies that promote smooth transitions to kindergarten.

The transition to kindergarten increasingly is viewed by early childhood experts as a key component of school readiness, largely because school entry is a critical time in children's development and a primary influence on their school careers (Pianta & Kraft-Sayre, 2003). The National Governor's Association (2005) recommended that local schools develop community-wide transition plans in collaboration with prekindergarten and kindergarten teachers, Head Start personnel, child-care providers, administrators, parents, and community members.

Finally, recent policies that emphasize early literacy and children's academic preparation as key goals during prekindergarten appear to be changing the definition of school readiness. In 1998, for example, specific skills in the areas of language, literacy, and numeracy were legislatively mandated to be part of the Head Start Child Outcomes Framework to enhance children's school readiness skills. The No Child Left Behind Act of 2001 (NCLB; Public Law 107-110) includes provisions for an early literacy initiative—the Early Reading First Program, which targets low-income students in prekindergarten who are at risk for reading failure when then enter kindergarten. In conjunction with standards and accountability movement in education, the Good Start, Grow Smart initiative (http://www.whitehouse.gov/infocus/earlychildhood/) has prompted the creation of new state standards to align child outcomes with the curriculum and to assess children's school achievement in prekindergarten.

These early learning standards, guidelines, and interventions likely will influence school readiness strategies and children's learning goals in the future. It is conceivable, for example, that as early childhood programs address early learning standards related to literacy and other academic content areas, the number of young children who exhibit learning difficulties before kindergarten will increase. As a result, there may be an increased need for an early intervening system to ensure that children have a smooth transition to kindergarten and early school success.

The National Prekindergarten Movement

Another important trend in the early childhood field in the United States is the movement to create public early education programs, with most states now offering some form of prekindergarten education to 4-year-olds (and some 3-year-olds). One study found that appoximately 66% of 4-year-olds and more than 30% of 3-year-olds were enrolled in a preschool education program in 2002 but that these programs had not reached all segments of the population equally, nor were these services distributed equally across various regions of the country (Barnett & Yarosz, 2004).

The Multi-State Study of prekindergarten (Clifford et al., 2005; Pianta et al., 2005) reported that 43 states offered prekindergarten in 2001 but also found considerable variability in the way in which prekindergarten programs were being implemented by states on almost every dimension, for example, age of children served, the focus on children at risk versus universal access, the location of programs, program standards, and costs (see entire issue of *Early Developments*, 2005, Vol. 9, No. 1).

With respect to the quality of public prekindergarten programs, the study found that the observed classroom quality was lower than what has been found in other large-scale studies of early childhood programs. This finding was somewhat surprising, given that prekindergarten program standards were high relative to other early childhood programs. The study also revealed that children enrolled in prekindergarten programs spent 44% of their time not engaged in any activity such as pre-reading, language development, math, art, or social studies. Children spent the largest part of their day in routine maintenance activities such as standing in line or eating.

How did the children enrolled in public prekindergarten programs fare? The Multi-State Pre-Kindergarten Study found that on both standardized measures of language and math and nonstandardized measures (e.g., naming letters and numbers, counting, recognizing colors), children made small but meaningful gains. The authors speculated that children's progress could have been greater if all programs had been of higher quality. They also recommended that the results be used to advocate for improved early education services and perhaps to consider a new model of school entry. Other early childhood experts have called for additional discussion to consider voluntary, universal early learning programs versus targeted services for those at greatest risk of poor achievement and to clarify standards for highly qualified teachers as well as the kinds of development and learning that should take place in these programs (Barnett, Brown, & Shore; 2004; Shore, Bodrova, & Leong, 2004).

The Recognition and Response system was envisioned as being beneficial for various types of early childhood programs (e.g., child-care centers and homes, Head Start, private preschools, and state-funded prekindergarten). An opportunity for initial widespread implementation of this approach exists in early childhood settings that offer the highest professional and program standards. In addition, with its emphasis on research-based instruction and assessment as a foundation for supporting the learning of all children, the Recognition and Response system holds the potential to address recent findings regarding the need to improve early childhood program quality.

Prevention and Early Intervention Services

Policymakers recognized the fundamental importance of prevention and early intervention for the most developmentally vulnerable young children with the passage of the Individuals With Disabilities Education Act in 1986 (reauthorized most recently as the Individuals With Disabilities Education Improvement Act in 2004). This landmark legislation established the Part C Infant–Toddler program, which required states to develop a comprehensive system of early intervention services for children from birth to 3 years with developmental delays or disabilities and for their families. States also were given the additional option of including infants and toddlers who were considered at risk of having developmental delays in the absence of early intervention services. Some of the cornerstones of the Infant–Toddler program that have redefined health and human services for young children and families include its dual focus on health and development, the central role of the child's family as a key partner in all aspects service delivery, the emphasis on transition planning, and the need for interagency coordination (Meisels & Shonkoff, 2000).

IDEA also established the Part B-Section 619 Preschool Program that required states to provide free and appropriate public education and related services for children from 3 to 5 years with developmental delays or disabilities. Both programs require systematic efforts to create eligibility criteria, to find eligible children, to develop individualized approaches to intervention, and to provide appropriate services in natural or inclusive settings. However, definitions of developmental delays and disabilities in both programs cover broad areas of performance (e.g., physical disabilities, language delays, sensory impairments) and do not focus specifically on the identification of conditions that may place children at risk for developing learning disabilities.

In accordance with the reauthorization of IDEA, a local education agency (LEA) is allowed to use Part B funds to develop "early intervening services" for students in kindergarten through Grade 12 (with an emphasis on students in kindergarten through Grade 3) who have not been identified as needing special education or related services but who need additional academic and behavioral support to succeed in a general education environment (see IDEA Section 613 (f) (1)). The Recognition and Response system represents a downward extension of the concepts contained within the new provision of IDEA, the goal of which is to help parents and teachers intervene as early as possible, when children first exhibit signs of learning difficulties. The proposed Recognition and Response system should be coordinated with existing prevention and early intervention services for children with disabilities, which currently do not focus specifically on factors that may place children at risk for learning disabilities during prekindergarten.

The RTI movement and major contexts in the early childhood field were all key considerations in our efforts to create early intervening services for young children and their families. The next section describes the conceptualization of the Recognition and Response system that resulted from our review of the literature and ongoing discussions with our partners in this initiative.

RECOGNITION AND RESPONSE: TOWARD AN EARLY INTERVENING SYSTEM IN EARLY CHILDHOOD

The Recognition and Response system is designed to help parents and teachers respond as early as possible to behavioral or learning difficulties in young children who may be at risk for learning disabilities, beginning at age 3 or 4, before children experience school failure and before they are referred for formal assessment and placement in special education. Young children who exhibit early signs or precursors of learning disabilities that have been documented in the literature (e.g., impulsivity, distractibility, speech and language delays, visual and auditory processing delays, phonological processing deficits; Catts, 1991; Lowenthal, 1998) are unlikely to meet the eligibility criteria for having a learning disability under current state and federal guidelines. As mentioned earlier, they may not meet the eligibility criteria because formal identification of a child's learning disability generally does not occur until there is a measurable discrepancy between the child's aptitude and academic achievement, often not until the second or third grade. The Recognition and Response system is based on the premise that parents and teachers can learn to recognize critical early warning signs that a young child may not be learning in an expected manner and to respond in ways that positively affect a child's early school success.

A number of features of the proposed Recognition and Response system make it a developmentally appropriate approach for use with prekindergarteners (i.e., 3- to 5-years-olds). For example, there is limited reliance in the proposed system on formal diagnosis and labeling. Instead, the Recognition and Response system emphasizes a systematic approach to responding to early learning difficulties that includes assessing the overall quality of early learning experiences for all children, as well as making program modifications, tailoring instructional strategies, and providing appropriate supports for individual children who struggle to learn. These practices reflect sound early educational principles for all young children and are not limited to those who require additional supports. Table 6.1 illustrates how the core principles of RTI (National Association of State Directors of Special Education, 2005) relate to core early childhood beliefs and practices in conjunction with the proposed Recognition and Response system.

It is important that the new practices being established for the early childhood field are anchored in existing practices such as RTI, which is supported by an emerging body of empirical evidence and by growing consensus from the education field. However, in its conceptualization of an early intervening system that is tailored to the unique needs of very young children, the early childhood field can offer important contributions that include an emphasis on collaborating with parents and specialists, planning for transitions, and supporting systemic change.

Table 6.1 Core Principles of RTI and Core Early Childhood Beliefs and Practices in Recognition and Response

Core Principles of RTI*	Core Early Childhood Beliefs and Practices**
We can effectively teach all children.	We can teach children with diverse cultural, linguistic, and learning characteristics.
Intervene early.	Intervene early.
Use a multi-tier model of service delivery.	Use an intervention hierarchy.
Use a problem-solving method to make decisions within a multi-tier model.	Use a systematic, collaborative approach in partnership with parents and specialists to address concerns about individual children.
Use research-based, scientifically validated interventions/instruction to the extent available.	Use early education practices that are based on the best available research evidence combined with the field's collective wisdom and values.
Monitor student progress to inform instruction.	Determine whether children are making progress as expected and use this information to make practice decisions.
Use data to make decisions.	Use information from assessments to make practice decisions.
Use assessment to identify children who are not progressing at expected rates, to determine what children can and cannot do in academic and behavioral domains, and to monitor progress to determine intervention effectiveness.	Gather information about children using multiple methods and sources (including parents) and interpret this information to evaluate teaching practices and child progress.

*Reprinted with permission from National Association of State Directos of Special Education, (2005). Response to interventions: Policy considerations and implementation (p. 20). Alexandria, VA: Author.

**Reprinted with permission from Coleman, Buysse, & Neitzel (2006).

A Conceptual Framework for the Recognition and Response System

Figure 6.2 shows the four essential components of the proposed Recognition and Response system: (a) an intervention hierarchy; (b) screening, assessment, and progress monitoring; (c) research-based curriculum, instruction, and focused interventions; and (d) a collaborative problem-solving process for decision-making. This chapter offers only a brief description of each of these components. Future efforts will focus on further developing and evaluating each component as part of an integrated system, particularly with respect to identifying the specific assessment and instructional strategies within each of the tiers of the intervention hierarchy.

Figure 6.2 Recognition and Response System for Early Intervening

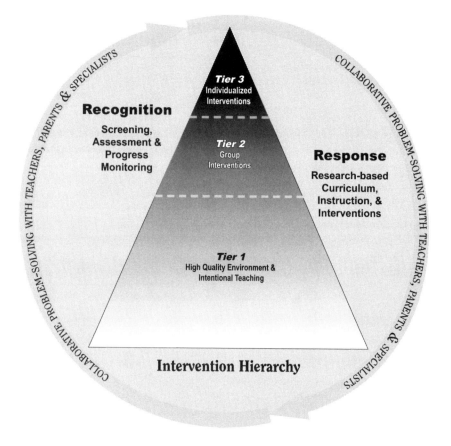

Reprinted with permission from Coleman, Buysse, & Neitzel (2006).

Intervention Hierarchy

An intervention hierarchy reflects increasing levels of intensity of instruction and intervention that correspond directly to children's needs for support.
A teacher's decision to move from one tier to the next is guided by screening
and assessment information as part of a systematic and collaborative problem-solving process that includes parents and specialists. The supports provided to individual children and groups of children are grounded in
research-based curriculum and instructional practices, to the extent that this
is possible.

Tier 1. In Tier 1, a research-based curriculum and effective intentional
teaching strategies are provided for all children. The curriculum and instruction are aligned with early learning standards and benchmarks and reflect
recommended early childhood practices. Universal screening, assessment,
and progress monitoring are conducted in key academic, health, and developmental areas. If most children (approximately 80%) make adequate
progress, it can be assumed that the general early education curriculum is of
sufficient quality. Children who do not make adequate progress in Tier 1 will
require focused intervention at Tier 2.

Tier 2. In Tier 2, teachers provide interventions and curriculum modifications that require minimum adjustments to classroom routines to targeted
groups of children who do not make adequate progress in Tier 1. Group interventions such as introducing vocabulary prior to storybook reading or providing visual cues during circle time can be developed through a
problem-solving process in collaboration with parents and specialists. As in
Tier 1, practice decisions are guided by assessments (e.g., progress monitoring, curriculum-based checklists) and rely on research-based or recommended practices.

Tier 3. In Tier 3, early educators implement more intensive and individualized instruction for children who do not make adequate progress in Tier 2.
Examples of Tier 3 interventions would be the teacher working individually
with a child to reinforce rhyming concepts or helping a child learn to write
her name. As is the case in Tier 2, instructional decisions are developed
through a collaborative problem-solving process and guided by assessments

and research-based or recommended practices. Children who do not make adequate progress in Tier 3 may need to be referred for formal evaluation of learning disabilities.

Screening, Assessment, and Progress Monitoring

An integrated assessment system helps early childhood teachers accomplish the following three goals: (a) make informed instructional decisions; (b) identify strengths, interests, or areas of concern that require focused interventions for individual children; and (c) improve early education programs and interventions (National Association for the Education of Young Children, 2005; National Association for the Education of Young Children & National Association of Early Childhood Specialists in State Departments of Education, 2003; Sandall, Hemmeter, Smith, & McLean, 2005). An integrated assessment plan includes multiple methods (e.g., observations, checklists, rating scales, work sampling, curriculum-based assessments) and sources of information for each child as well as classroom summary profiles. It is important to communicate assessment information with parents in a timely, sensitive manner and to engage parents in making contributions to the assessment process and to the interpretation of the results.

Research-Based Curriculum, Instruction, and Focused Interventions

Providing a research-based curriculum and effective intentional teaching will help to ensure that the majority of children in the class demonstrate growth and development across all domains. The overarching goal of the Recognition and Response is for teachers to use assessment as part of an integrated instructional system to make improvements in the general early education program and to plan more focused interventions for children who require additional supports. Future efforts should focus on identifying standard research-based interventions that would comprise a toolkit from which teachers could extract specific practices (e.g., curriculum modifications, environmental arrangements, peer-mediated strategies, individualized instruction) to respond to individual learning characteristics within each tier of an intervention hierarchy.

Collaborative Problem-Solving Process for Decision-Making

The problem-solving process occurs in all three tiers of the intervention hierarchy and involves (a) defining the problem, (b) analyzing the problem, (c) developing a plan, and (d) evaluating the plan to determine whether it was effective in addressing specific goals (Bergan & Kratochwill, 1990). Key to the problem-solving process is the use of data to inform decisions, thus, creating a dynamic link between "recognition" and "response" that reflects the changing needs of young children. The problem-solving process is collaborative, systematic, and used by teachers, parents, and specialists to make practice decisions and to evaluate their effectiveness for individual children. A particular emphasis should be placed on the specific needs of culturally and linguistically diverse and low income families to ensure their full participation and engagement. This process should also provide transition to kindergarten supports through a careful planning process which includes input from all relevant stakeholders (Dockett & Perry, 2001; Pianta, Kraft-Sayer, Rimm-Kaufman, Gercke, & Higgins, 2001).

Support for Systemic Change

To ensure widespread adoption and implementation of the Recognition and Response system, it will be necessary to create an infrastructure with enough capacity to sustain organizational changes that are made. Included in systemic change are: professional development to ensure that the knowledge and skills needed to implement the changes are mastered; monitoring of early education settings to maintain fidelity of implementation; developing materials that describe and support implementation; evaluating the efficacy of the system to examine the impact of the changes; and creating policies and procedures needed to maintain the system once it is developed.

BUILDING THE EVIDENCE BASE FOR AN EMERGING PRACTICE: THE PROCESS

We have worked to incorporate an evidence-based approach throughout all aspects of this initiative and this effort has been reflected in our decision-making processes and in the scientific rigor of our methods. For example, efforts to reach consensus on key components of the model were informed by our knowledge of the research and theoretical evidence on RTI as well as practice guidelines and program standards that reflected the professional wisdom and values of the early childhood field. Family characteristics and priorities were important considerations in our discussions about the development of observational checklists and tools that would be used in conjunction with the Recognition and Response system. Another example of how the evidence-based practice approach influenced our efforts was the decision to develop a coding system to appraise the quality of the research for all studies included in the research synthesis rather than simply summarize the findings of each study.

In the next section, we describe in more detail the primary activities through which we are establishing the empirical evidence base for the Recognition and Response system.

Conducting a Comprehensive Review of the Literature

To examine the empirical evidence of the RTI model, we conducted a comprehensive review and synthesis of the literature on RTI (see Coleman et al., 2006). Table 6.2 summarizes the key steps in conducting a research synthesis with respect to the Recognition and Response initiative. A literature search produced 14 articles, which addressed issues related to evaluating the efficacy of RTI with children 4–8 years of age. To develop the abstracts for the empirical studies, we followed the recommendations of the National Research Council Committee on Research in Education (2005) for including the following essential elements: background or context, purpose of the study or research questions, setting, research participants, intervention, research design, measures and data analysis, findings or results, and conclusions and recommendations. The abstracts will serve multiple purposes in this initiative. They will be used as part of the process of summarizing and evaluating the empirical and theoretical knowledge base on RTI, and they will be made available on a Web site sponsored by the National Center for Learning Disabilities. These abstracts may be used by other practitioners or parents to obtain information about the key elements of published studies without having to conduct a separate literature search. In this way, the abstracts on RTI

Table 6.2. Steps in Conducting a Literature Review.

1. Identify domains and establish search parameters.
2. Establish criteria for inclusion and exclusion of empirical studies.
3. Prepare abstracts for selected studies and conceptual articles.
4. Prepare summary tables for empirical studies that include recommended key elements: source, authors, title, background or context, purpose or research questions, setting characteristics, characteristics of study participants, research design, independent and dependent variables, measures and data analysis, findings, and conclusions.
5. Use an appraisal system to evaluate the quality of empirical studies.
6. Summarize key ideas and findings; identify strengths and weaknesses of the quality of the research.

can be used to promote knowledge utilization of the research evidence on this topic.

The next steps in reviewing the literature involved creating summary tables to analyze the research methods and findings across studies, and developing an appraisal system to evaluate the quality of the empirical research evidence. The appraisal system addressed recommendations in the literature for assessing quality indicators for various research methods (e.g., experimental and quasi-experimental designs, correlational studies) and established criteria for determining when a particular practice can be considered evidence-based (e.g., there are at least four acceptable quality studies, or two high-quality studies that support the practice; Gersten, Fuchs, Compton, Coyne, Greenwood, & Innocenti, 2005).

The results from the research synthesis indicated that there is an emerging body of empirical evidence to support claims that RTI is an effective method for identifying children at-risk for learning difficulties and for providing specialized interventions either to ameliorate or prevent the occurrence of learning disabilities. Although there was general agreement across studies about the conceptualization of RTI in terms of its key components and tiered implementation, there was less agreement about the nature and focus of specialized interventions, the duration or intensity of the interventions, and the benchmarks used to determine when more intensive interventions were needed for individual children. Despite these limitations, the research synthesis findings suggest that RTI is a promising approach, particularly because of its focus on sound instructional principles such as effectively teaching all children, intervening early, using research-based interventions, monitoring student progress, and using assessments to inform instructional decision-making.

Forming a Community of Practice

Chapter 5 describes what a community of practice is and how these communities work to advance knowledge, improve practice, and support participants in professional growth. In reality, the formation of a community of practice is rarely a neat and tidy process. In the case of the Recognition and Response initiative, the community of practice evolved almost by default. As mentioned earlier, the impetus for this initiative was the funding provided by the Emily Hall Tremaine Foundation to a small group of individuals who represented key organizations in the learning disabilities and early childhood fields and to five state partners. Although the formation of a community of practice was not the initial intent of this initiative, the president of the Emily Hall Tremaine Foundation intuitively understood that bringing together practitioners, policymakers, researchers, and advocates to figure this out was key to its success. The president has remained an active participant, and his insights, questions, and guidance have played a significant role in facilitating a process that will culminate in establishing an evidence base for the Recognition and Response system. Each of the partners in this initiative are making unique contributions through their separate endeavors (e.g., examining the empirical evidence of RTI, developing the tools and measures, and piloting components of the system) and they share the commitment to addressing the issues, dilemmas, and ambiguities that emerge as we work to pull everything together. Our work with the partners has involved extensive discussions and deliberations that have taken place through face-to-face meetings hosted by various collaborating organizations, telephone conference calls, e-mail messages, and Web sites. These discussions, though lively at times, have been conducted with the utmost respect for each of the participants and for the ideas, insights, assumptions, and beliefs that they bring to this experience. These discussions and meetings also have been essential in building the positive relationships among participants that are so important to promoting the open exchange of ideas and to building consensus.

Evaluating the Model

Because our task involved assessing the value of an emerging, as opposed to an established, practice, we determined that the evaluation of the Recognition and Response system would be conducted across several phases. Table 6.3 lists the primary research question associated with each phase of the evaluation. In Phase I, the primary goal is to conduct field tests on the tools and resources developed for each component of the Recognition and Response system (e.g., observational and assessment tools, curricular and instructional practices). Field testing should be implemented in a small number of pilot sites with whom partnerships have been established and with a high level of support and involvement by those conducting the evaluation. The field tests should focus on assessing how the tools and resources are viewed by parents and teachers, whether they are used in the intended manner, and the extent to which they lead to more informed decision making to address children's early learning difficulties. Ideally, the information gained from Phase I activities would be used to refine and improve components of the Recognition and Response system before full implementation.

In Phase II, the goal is to assess the efficacy of the Recognition and Response system in which all of the components have been integrated into a single system. The goal is to determine whether the intervention works under carefully controlled conditions with a high level of support and involvement by the research team. This phase likely will involve conducting an experimental study with implementation fidelity in early education sites that have been carefully matched on key organizational variables (e.g., student and teacher characteristics, size, resources) and randomly assigned to either the intervention or the comparison condition. The research design also should control for any child, family, and program characteristics that could potentially influence study outcomes. Research questions likely to be addressed during Phase II include the following:

- Are the assessments used to recognize early learning difficulties valid and reliable?
- What are the effects of the Recognition and Response system on teachers' classroom practices and the quality of the early education program?
- What are the effects of the Recognition and Response system on parent engagement in their children's early education?

Table 6.3. Primary Research Questions Associated With Each Phase
of the Evaluation

Phase and purpose	Primary research questions
Phase I: Field testing questions	1. Are the tools, resources, and practices being implemented as intended and designed by the research team (implementation fidelity)? 2. Are the tools, resources, and practices feasible, acceptable, relevant, and useful to parents and teachers (social validity)? 3. Do the tools, resources, and practices inform curricular and instructional decisions (evidence-based practice)?
Phase II: Assessing the efficacy of the intervention	1. Does the intervention work under carefully controlled conditions with a high level of support by the research team?
Phase III: Assessing the effectiveness of the intervention (scaling up)	1. Does the intervention work in naturalistic settings when it is implemented by teachers without a high level of support by the research team?

- What are the effects of the Recognition and Response system on child behavior and learning outcomes?
- What are the effects of the Recognition and Response system on system outcomes (e.g., retentions, referrals to special education)?

During Phase III, the primary goal is to understand whether the intervention works in naturalistic settings on a larger scale (i.e., in many different community early childhood programs or public prekindergarten classrooms). Testing the effectiveness of the intervention also involves assessing the extent to which it can be implemented by teachers without a high level of support from the research team. The research questions posed under Phase II are the same as those to be posed under Phase III; only the conditions and level of researcher support change.

A qualitative study also could be conducted to complement information resulting from the experimental studies. For example, structured interviews or focus groups with parents, teachers, specialists, and administrators could be conducted to examine perceptions of the Recognition and Response system in comparison with traditional methods of identifying young children with learning difficulties. Qualitative data would provide essential information with respect to components of the system that were perceived as beneficial for children and families; concrete examples of how the system informed practice decisions; and ideas for improving the system in terms of the usefulness of the tools and measures, the ease in which the system can be implemented, and the relevance of the system for addressing children's early learning difficulties.

SOME REFLECTIONS ON THE PROCESS

This chapter presented our experience in establishing the evidence base for an emerging early childhood practice (the Recognition and Response system) as part of a collaborative initiative. We described the key conceptual, empirical, and policy issues that served as an impetus and context for developing the Recognition and Response system. We also described how the goal of conceptualizing and evaluating an innovative early childhood practice could be informed by an evidence-based approach that relied on the following steps in the process: (a) conducting a comprehensive and rigorous review of the empirical and theoretical literature; (b) creating a dynamic community of practice consisting of key stakeholders who represent practice, policy, and research; and (c) implementing evaluation activities to establish the validity, efficacy, and effectiveness of the intervention.

In reflecting on this experience, one lesson we have learned is that the decision to use an evidence-based approach to support innovation requires a conscious effort to infuse evidence into every aspect of the process. It also requires a reliance on sources of evidence other than research, particularly when the empirical knowledge about an emerging practice is thin or nonexistent. In these cases, collaboration with key stakeholder groups may be even more important, and the process of deciphering professional and family wisdom and values may require additional deliberations, negotiations, and discussions. Although the process may seem unyielding at times, it is vital to specify working assumptions and to resolve debates concerning the strengths and weaknesses of particular approaches or ideas.

The evidence-based process is not a silver bullet, however. Those who intend to apply an evidence-based approach to support innovation in the future will need access to the intellectual and fiscal resources such as those that were available to the partners involved in the Emily Hall Tremaine initiative. Making investments in building the evidence base to support emerging practices right from the start holds the potential to solving one of the most the most daunting challenges in the early childhood field—the need to connect the dots between research, policy, and practice.

REFERENCES

Barnett, W. S., Brown, K., & Shore, R. (2004). The universal vs. targeted debate: Should the United States have preschool for all? *Preschool Policy Matters*, 6. Retrieved April 28, 2005, from the National Institute for Early Education Research Web site http://www.nieer.org

Barnett, W. S., & Yarosz, D. J. (2004, August). Who goes to preschool and why does it matter? *Preschool Policy Matters*, 8. Retrieved April 28, 2005, from http://www.nieer.org

Bergan, J. R., & Kratochwill, T. R. (1990). *Behavioral consultation and therapy*. New York: Plenum.

Blankstein, A. M., & Cocozzella, K. (2004, September/October). Creating a failure-free school. *Principal*, 84(1), 36–41.

Bryant, D. M., Burchinal, M., Lau, L., & Sparling, J. J. (1994). Family and classroom correlates of Head Start children's developmental outcomes. *Early Childhood Research Quarterly*, 9(1), 289–309.

Bryant, D., Maxwell, K., Taylor, K., Poe, M., Peisner-Feinberg, E., & Bernier, K. (2003). *Smart Start and preschool child care quality in NC: Change over time and relation to children's readiness*. Chapel Hill, NC: FPG Child Development Institute.

Burchinal, M. R., Roberts, J. E., Nabors, L. A., & Bryant, D. M. (1996). Quality of center child care and infant cognitive and language development. *Child Development*, 67, 606–620.

Catts, L. P. (1991). Early identification of reading disabilities. *Topics in Language Disorders*, 12(2), 1–16.

Clifford, R. M., Barbarin, O., Chang, F., Early, D. M., Bryant, D., Howes, C., et al. (2005). What is pre-kindergarten? Characteristics of public pre-kindergarten programs. *Applied Developmental Science*, 9 (3), 126–143.

Coleman, M. R., Buysse, V., & Neitzel, J. (2006). *Recognition and Response: An early intervening system for young children at risk for learning disabilities.* Chapel Hill: The University of North Carolina at Chapel Hill, FPG Child Development Institute.

Conyers, L. M., Reynolds, A. J., & Ou, S. (2003). The effect of early childhood intervention and subsequent special education services: Findings from the Chicago child-parent centers. *Educational Evaluation and Policy Analysis*, 25(1), 75–95.

Cost, Quality, and Outcomes Study Team (1995). *Cost, quality, and child outcomes in child care centers: Technical report.* Denver: Economics Department, University of Colorado-Denver.

Dockett, S., & Perry, B. (2001). Starting school: Effective transitions. *Early Childhood Research & Practice*, 3(2), 1–21.

Early Developments. (2005). 9(1).

Fuchs, L. S. (2003). Assessing intervention responsiveness: Conceptual and technical issues. *Learning Disabilities Research & Practice*, 18(3), 172–186.

Fuchs, L. S., & Fuchs, D. (2002). Curriculum-based measurement: Describing competence, enhancing outcomes, evaluating treatment effects, and identifying nonresponders. *Peabody Journal of Education*, 77(2), 64–84.

Fuchs, L. S., Fuchs, D., & Speece, D. L. (2002). Treatment validity as a unifying construct for identifying learning disabilities. *Learning Disability Quarterly*, 25, 33–45.

Fuchs, D., Mock, D., Morgan, P. L., & Young, C. L. (2003). Responsiveness-to-intervention: Definitions, evidences, and implications for the learning disabilities construct. *Learning Disabilities Research & Practice*, 18(3), 157–171.

Gersten, R., Fuchs, L. S., Compton, D., Coyne, M., Greenwood, C., & Innocenti, M. S. (2005). Quality indicators for group experimental and quasi-experimental research in special education. *Exceptional Children, 71*(2), 149–164.

Howes, C., Phillips, D. A., & Whitebook, M. (1992). Thresholds of quality: Implications for the social development of children in center-based child care. *Child Development, 63,* 449–460.

Individuals With Disabilities Education Improvement Act of 2004, Pub. L.

Journal of Learning Disabilities. (2005). 38(6).

Kagan, S. L., Moore, E., & Bredekamp, S. (1995). *Reconsidering children's early development and learning: Toward common views and vocabulary.* Washington, DC: National Education Goals Panel.

Kavale, K. A., Holdnack, J. A., & Mostert, M. P. (2005). Responsiveness to intervention and the identification of specific learning disability: A critique and alternative proposal. *Learning Disabilities Quarterly, 28*(1), 2–16.

Lamb, M. E. (1997). Nonparental child care: Context, quality, correlates, and consequences. In W. Damon, (Series Ed.) & I. E. Siegel, & K. A. Renninger (Vol. Eds.), *Handbook of child psychology: Vol 4. Child psychology in practice* (5th ed., pp. 75–117). New York: Wiley.

Learning Disabilities and Practice. (2003). 18(3).

Learning Disabilities Quarterly. (2005). 25(1).

Love, J. M. (2001, December). *Instrumentation for state readiness assessment: Issues in measuring children's early development and learning.* Paper presented at the Symposium on the State of State Assessments, Atlanta, Georgia.

Love, J. M., Schochet, P. Z., & Meckstrom, A. (1996). *Are they in any real danger? What research does—and doesn't tell us about child care quality and children's well-being.* Princeton, NJ: Mathematica Policy Research. (ERIC Document Reproduction Service No. 415 030)

Lowenthal, B. (1998). Precursors of learning disabilites in the inclusive preschool. *Learning Disabilties: A Multidisciplinary Journal, 9*(2), 25–31.

Marston, D., Muyskens, P., Lau, M., & Canter, A. (2003). Problem-solving model for decision making with high-incidence disabilities: The Minneapolis experience. *Learning Disabilities Research & Practice, 18*(3), 187–200.

McLanahan, S. (Ed.). (2005). School readiness: Closing racial and ethnic gaps. *The Future of Children, 15*(1). Retrieved February 16, 2005, from http://www.futureofchildren.org

Meisels, S. J. (1999). Assessing readiness. In R. C. Pianta & M. J. Cox (Eds.), *The transition to kindergarten* (pp. 39–66). Baltimore: Brookes.

Meisels, S. J., & Shonkoff, J. P. (2000). Early childhood intervention: A continuing evolution. In J. P. Shonkoff & S. J. Meisels (Eds.), *Handbook of early intervention,* (2nd ed., pp. 3–31). Cambridge, UK: Cambridge University Press.

National Association for the Education of Young Children (2005). *Assessment of child progress, A guide to the NAEYC early childhood program standard and related accreditation criteria.* Washington, DC: Author.

National Association for the Education of Young Children and the National Association of Early Childhood Specialists in State Departments of Education. (2003). *Early childhood curriculum, assessment, and program evaluation: Building an effective, accountable system in programs for children birth through age 8.* Position statement with expanded resources. Washington, DC: National Association for the Education of Young Children.

National Association of State Directors of Special Education. (2005). *Response to intervention: Policy considerations and implementations.* Alexandria, VA: Author.

National Education Goals Panel. (1991). *The national education goals report.* Washington, DC: Author.

National Governors Association. (2005). *Building the foundation for bright futures: Final report of the NGA Task Force on School Readiness.* Washington, DC: Author.

National Research Council (2001). *Eager to learn: Educating our preschoolers* (B. T. Bowman, M. S. Donovan, & M. S. Burns, (Eds.). Committee on Early Childhood Pedagogy; Commission on Behavioral and Social Sciences and Education. Washington, DC: National Academy Press.

National Research Council Committee on Research in Education. (2005). *Advancing scientific research in education.* Committee on Research in Education. L. Towne, L. L. Wise, & T. M. Winters, (Eds.). Center for Education, Division of Behavioral and Social Sciences and Education. Washington, DC: The National Academy Press.

O'Connor, R. (2000). Increasing the intensity of intervention in kindergarten and first grade. *Learning Disabilities Research & Practice, 15*(1), 43–54.

O'Shaughnessy, T. E., Lane, K. L., Gresham, F. M., & Beebe-Frankenberger, M. E. (2003). Children placed at risk for learning and behavioral difficulties: Implementing a school-wide system of early identification and intervention. *Remedial and Special Education, 24*(1), 27–35.

Pianta, R., Howes, C., Burchinal, M., Bryant, D., Clifford, R. M., Early, D. M., & Barbarin, D. (2005). Features of pre-kindergarten programs, classrooms, and teachers: Prediction of observed classroom quality and teacher-child interactions. *Applied Developmental Science, 9*(3), 144–159.

Pianta, R. C., & Kraft-Sayre, M. (2003). *Successful kindergarten transition: Your guide to connecting children, families, and schools.* Baltimore: Brookes.

Pianta, R. C., Kraft-Sayre, M., Rimm-Kaufman, S., Gercke, N., & Higgins, T. (2001). Collaboration in building partnerships between families and schools: The National Center for Early Development and Learning's Kindergarten Transition Intervention. *Early Childhood Research Quarterly, 16,* 117–132.

Peisner-Feinberg, E. S., Burchinal, M. R., Clifford, R. M., Culkin, M. L., Howes, C., Kagan, L. S., & Yazejian, N. (2001). The relation of preschool child-care quality to children's cognitive and social developmental trajectories through second grade. *Child Development, 72*(5), 1534–1553.

Phillips, D., McCartney, K., & Scarr, S. (1987). Child care quality and children's social development. *Developmental Psychology, 23*(4), 537–543.

Phillipsen, L. C., Burchinal, M. R., Howes, C., & Cryer, D. (1997). The prediction of process quality from structural features of child care. *Early Childhood Research Quarterly, 12*, 281–303.

Public Law 103-227 (March 31, 1994), 108 STAT. 125.

Public Law 107-110 (Jan. 8, 2002), 115 STAT. 1425.

Public Law 108-446 (Dec. 3, 2004), 118 STAT. 2647, 2704-2706.

Rhode Island KIDS COUNT. (2005). *Getting ready. Executive summary: National school readiness indicators initiative: A 17 state partnership.* Providence, RI: Author.

Sandall, S., Hemmeter, M. L., Smith, B. J., & McLean, M. E. (2005). DEC recommended practices: A comprehensive guide for practical application in early intervention/early childhood special education. Longmont, CO: Sopris West Educational Services.

Shore, R., Bodrova, E., & Leong, D. (2004). Child outcomes standards in pre-k programs: What are standards; What is needed to make them work? *Preschool Policy Matters, 5.* Retrieved April 28, 2005, from http://www.nieer.org

Speece, D. L., & Case, L. P. (2003). Classification in context: An alternative approach to identifying early reading disability. *Journal of Educational Psychology, 93*, 735–749.

Vaughn, S., & Fuchs, L. S. (2003). Redefining learning disabilities as inadequate response to instruction: The promise and potential problems. *Learning Disabilities Research & Practice, 18*(3), 137–146.

Whitebook, M., Howes, C., & Phillips, D. (1989). *Who cares? Child care teachers and the quality of care in America: Final report, National Child Care Staffing Study.* Berkeley, CA: Child Care Employee Project.

MAKING SENSE OF EVIDENCE-BASED
PRACTICE: REFLECTIONS AND
RECOMMENDATIONS

Virginia Buysse and Patricia W. Wesley

Those of us in the early childhood field who embrace the concept of reflective practice understand that it requires us regularly to "step back from the immediate work to consider what it means, how it feels, and what comes next" (Dinnebeil, Buysse, Rush, & Eggbeer, in press). It is particularly important during times of significant innovation and change to create opportunities to express doubt, to examine the potential positive or negative consequences of a particular direction or action, and to pose questions that probe one's values and beliefs in relation to these events (Fenichel, 1992). The evidence-based practice movement represents a dramatic shift in thinking about effective ways of generating, collecting, appraising, and using evidence to make informed practice decisions. In this chapter, the editors of this volume step back from the immediate work to make sense of what we have learned about evidence-based practice and to reflect on what these changes might mean for the early childhood field.

The purpose of this chapter is to highlight the key issues related to evidence-based practice that are raised in each of the previous chapters and then to focus the discussion more specifically on whether and how the early childhood profession could become an evidence-based field. We begin by addressing three broad questions that summarize the primary issues related to evidence-based practice presented in this volume: (a) What is evidence-based practice and how did it emerge; (b) How will evidence-based practice affect the early childhood profession; and (c) What are some promising practices and strategies for implementing evidence-based practice? Next, we offer five recommendations to advance the early childhood field's understanding of these issues and to begin to shift its focus from generating and sharing knowledge to using new knowledge to inform practice decisions. Embedded throughout this chapter are reflections on some of the unresolved issues that the early childhood field must tackle in this regard.

WHAT IS EVIDENCE-BASED PRACTICE AND HOW DID IT EMERGE?

The term *evidence-based* is being used to describe all manner of ideas in the early childhood field and in many other fields, without sufficient attention to what it means and, in many cases, without sufficient empirical support (Hammersley, 2005). In this volume, we proposed the following definition of evidence-based practice for the early childhood field: a decision-making process that integrates the best available research evidence with family and professional wisdom and values. In each chapter, the authors used this definition to examine how an evidence-based framework might influence or reform areas of practice within the early childhood field that are related to research, innovation, knowledge utilization, and policy development. Chapters 1 and 2 traced the origins of evidence-based practice in medicine and explained how the proposed definition for the early childhood profession was based on one used to describe evidence-based medicine—the integration of best research evidence with clinical expertise and patient values (Sackett, Straus, Richardson, Rosenberg, & Haynes, 2000, p. 1).

In her critical appraisal of the evidence-based practice movement, Trinder (2000) wisely noted that the emphasis across disciplines to date has been on the first component of the definition offered by Sackett et al. (2000), that is, gathering and appraising empirical evidence, with randomized controlled trials as the centerpiece of this effort. Still undetermined is whether and how empirical evidence can be integrated with other forms of evidence. The authors of this volume have suggested that evidence-based practice is essentially a process rather than a list of written practice guidelines—that it is a way of empowering individuals to make more informed practice decisions that directly benefit young children and their families. But what guidance can we offer early childhood professionals who desire to implement evidence-based practice in their daily work? No discipline, not even medi-cine in which the evidence-based practice movement originated, has given adequate attention to the complex task of integrating the "hard, high ground of science" with the indeterminate and unpredictable "swamplands of prac-tice" (Schön, 1983, as cited in Trinder, 2000, p. 232). Indeed, this theme is one that reverberates throughout each of the chapters in this volume, and it represents an enormous future challenge for the early childhood field if the goal is to fully embrace the evidence-based practice movement.

The origins of the evidence-based practice movement also can be found in the gap between research and practice—broadened in chapter 4 to include the research–policy divide—which represents another theme of this volume. The problem can be summed up as one in which practitioners do not rou-tinely turn to research knowledge to solve practice dilemmas nor do researchers routinely pose research questions or produce findings that are relevant and useful to consumers. Although the research–practice gap is not a new phenomenon in early childhood, Hiebert, Gallimore, and Stigler (2002) remind us that the evidence-based practice movement has shed new light on an age-old problem.

The standards movement in education is yet another influence that has paved the way for the evidence-based practice movement in the early child-hood field. A focus on establishing what works has created a new demand to demonstrate the direct causal linkages between specific educational or ther-apeutic interventions and progress in children's learning and development (with limited attention given to family experiences and outcomes). In chap-ter 1, we traced the key policies and legislation in the United States that have defined the standards movement in education, the primary goal of which is to create measurable standards that set high expectations for all children, including those enrolled in prekindergarten. (The far-reaching effects of the accountability movement also have been observed in other human service-oriented disciplines; see, e.g., Gilliam & Leiter, 2003.) Although the recent emphasis on standards and accountability can be viewed as an opportunity to make decisions that will improve programs and promote early school success, there are also concerns that the movement could result in developmentally inappropriate assessment and instructional practices for very young children. It is noteworthy that professional wisdom and values (including those of policymakers), more than any other source of evidence, have played a key role in the development of early learning standards. Chapter 4 suggested that future efforts must begin to establish the research evidence base to ensure that expectations for early learning that are generated by the field's collective wisdom are related to children's later learning and adjustment.

HOW WILL EVIDENCE-BASED PRACTICE AFFECT THE EARLY CHILDHOOD PROFESSION?

Snyder examined how evidence-based practice is changing the conduct of research in early childhood (see chapter 2). She identified one of the principal benefits of the evidence-based practice movement, namely, that it has drawn attention to the need for greater scientific rigor, transparency, and relevancy in research. But the movement also has raised persistent concerns about the limitations of relying too heavily on randomized controlled trials to answer the field's most pressing research questions or, even more problematic, the limitations of equating evidence-based practice with randomized controlled trials. In the future, the early childhood field should broaden the scope of research questions and methods that are considered valid within an evidence-based practice framework. A crucial question in this regard is whether evidence produced by randomized controlled studies with population-based samples (and systematic reviews and meta-analyses based on these findings) can be applied in practice to make decisions for individual children and families (Trinder, 2000). At a minimum, broadening the research agenda should involve (a) recognizing the role that values and beliefs play in the conduct of research (Levitt, 2003); (b) assessing the causal mechanisms and processes by which interventions work (or, as Trinder, 2000, so aptly put it, "gain[ing] some understanding of what is occurring within the 'black box' of an intervention" [p. 231]); and (c) demonstrating the effectiveness of interventions in everyday situations (i.e., generalizability).

Although the evidence-based practice movement in early childhood is in an early stage of development, its effect on issues related to knowledge dissemination and knowledge utilization already is apparent. Winton, author of chapter 3, described a number of Web-based initiatives designed to organize and translate research-based knowledge on specific areas of practice, and she identified the most pressing issues and promising strategies to support the use of knowledge by consumers. This trend occurs at a time when the No Child Left Behind Act of 2001 has ushered in a new emphasis on improving teacher quality largely through innovations in professional development that appear promising but, as noted by Cochrane-Smith and Zeichner (2005), have yet to be tested and found effective. A recent publication titled *Losing Ground in Early Childhood Education* (Herzenberg, Price, & Bradley, 2005) found a disturbing decline in the qualifications of the early childhood workforce over the past 25 years, with 30% of teachers and administrators now having only a high school diploma or less education. This study reinforces the need for effective professional development in the early childhood field, but it offers little guidance about whether current evidence-based initiatives that are directed at supporting knowledge utilization will be relevant and effective for practitioners, many of whom have only the minimum professional qualifications. Hiebert et al. (2002) concluded that professional development in education is most effective when it is long term, school based, collaborative, focused on student learning, and linked to curriculum. Whether these characteristics are the most essential components of professional development in early childhood remains unknown. As Winton suggested in chapter 3, the efficacy of promising professional development approaches in early childhood must be evaluated systematically in the future through a line of research that is designed to address particular research goals over time (i.e., assessing an intervention's acceptability, feasibility, fidelity, efficacy, and effectiveness). Future efforts in this regard also would benefit from an examination of theories or conceptual frameworks that could guide the development of innovative models to support knowledge utilization, although the role of theory in establishing the evidence base has yet to be clearly specified within the evidence-based practice movement. Research in fields such as anthropology relies heavily on theory to guide its research questions and the interpretations of its findings, but human service-oriented professions such as education or social work routinely overlook the contributions of theory in establishing the evidence base.

Finally, we examined traditional assumptions and processes by which selected policies in early childhood have been developed, and we then contrasted those frameworks with policymaking that is done from an evidence-based practice perspective (see chapter 4). Policymakers value research more than any other stakeholder group except researchers and are likely to look to science for guidance in making policy decisions. Nevertheless, policymakers also get caught up in the "familiar collision between science and politics" (Feuer, Towne, & Shavelson, 2002, p. 5). Whereas the goal of science is to promote a culture of free inquiry to address a range of questions and issues, political realities almost always demand evidence and accountability from policymakers. One the one hand, despite powerful voices that insist that policies and practices must be evidence based, policymakers face enormous hurdles in making decisions when the empirical evidence is weak or non-existent. On the other hand, by emphasizing areas in which research evidence is absent or thin, we risk overestimating the value of research to dictate specific solutions to complex problems. As Garrett and Islam (1998) noted, the principle value of research with respect to policymaking may be to illuminate issues as well as to define the scope of problems and possible strategies that respond to these problems. Viewed from this perspective, research reviews and syntheses, rather than individual research studies, may be most useful to policymakers. Indeed, Hammersley (2005) concluded that research reviews (those that include an assessment of scientific rigor) represent an essential bridge linking research, policy, and practice whereas individual studies are only steps toward sound empirical evidence, not reliable independent bases for decisions.

WHAT ARE PROMISING PRACTICES AND STRATEGIES FOR IMPLEMENTING EVIDENCE-BASED PRACTICE?

In chapter 5, we described communities of practice as a promising strategy for integrating research and practice through participation and relationships among people with diverse expertise, all focused on a common desire to improve practice within a particular area. We traced the origins of the communities of practice approach in anthropology and education, distinguished that approach from other community-centric approaches to collaborative inquiry and learning, and identified some of its key elements in terms of membership, purpose, and activities.

The communities of practice approach, as it relates to establishing the evidence base for the early childhood field, provides the following principle benefits: (a) it alters the notion that evidence is generated, organized, and translated primarily by those who exist outside of the world of practice; and (b) it advocates for the need to connect individual and collective learning that occurs within communities of practice with the larger professional community to advance knowledge for the field as a whole. Through efforts such as broad-based review groups within the Cochrane Collaborative in medicine, the evidence-based practice movement gives lip service to involving consumers to generate, assemble, and use evidence; however, as Trinder (2000) observed, it is not clear yet how consumer perspectives can inform a scientific process. The challenge for the early childhood field will be to find ways of authentically integrating the world views, experiences, and priorities of families and practitioners with those of scientists and policymakers. Communities of practice hold tremendous potential to meet this challenge. Coleman, Buysse, and Neitzel, authors of chapter 6, offered one real-world example of how they are using a community of practice to conceptualize an emerging area of practice called Recognition and Response in an attempt to involve key stakeholders in building the evidence base for an early intervening system.

Other examples of communities of practice within the early childhood field are presented in chapter 5. The emerging lessons and experiences from these examples may be valuable to others who are interested in creating communities of practice to advance knowledge and understanding in a particular area of practice. In the future, it will be necessary to evaluate through research the specific ways in which communities of practice generate and disseminate useful forms of practice knowledge.

RECOMMENDATIONS FOR THE EARLY CHILDHOOD FIELD

In this section, we build on the five recommendations offered in chapter 1 that are related to adopting an evidence-based practice framework. The recommendations incorporate ideas from each of the chapters and those from disciplines outside of early childhood that have grappled with these issues much longer than our field. We also include our own observations, reflections, and questions about the enormous task of establishing an evidence base to inform practice and about what the implications are for the profession.

Recommendation 1: Reach Consensus on the Meaning of Evidence-Based Practice

Should early childhood be an evidence-based field? On the one hand, one could argue that it is simply too early for the early childhood field to reach consensus on the meaning of evidence-based practice. We are still in our infancy in terms of understanding the implications of adopting an evidence-based practice approach and incorporating it into everything we do on behalf of young children and families. On the other hand, there appears to be not only widespread acceptance but also policy support for the notion that the early childhood field can no longer operate strictly on the basis of ideology and collective wisdom, but must integrate scientific research into its decision making.

Primarily because individuals have begun using the term *evidence-based practice* without paying attention to what it means, the early childhood field must reach consensus on the meaning of this term. Currently, the field is experiencing a great deal of confusion, particularly among practitioners and administrators, about the meaning of evidence-based practice and how that term differs from other terms used in conjunction with written practice guidelines such as the Division for Early Childhood's recommended practices and the National Association for the Education of Young Children's developmentally appropriate practice guidelines (see chapter 2). There is also confusion, particularly among policymakers and researchers, about how to distinguish the terms *evidence-based, research-based,* and *scientifically based;* these terms are sprinkled liberally throughout various publications in the early childhood field and used interchangeably, even though they have quite different meanings (see chapter 2). Drawing on information presented in chapter 2, Table 7.1 provides the key components of these terms to help the reader differentiate the various phrases that are being used in conjunction with evidence-based practice.

Table 7.1. Terms Related to Evidence-Based Practice

Term	Key components
Evidence-based	• A process for making decisions • Integration of best available research with professional and family wisdom and values
Research-based	• Associated with the best available research component of evidence-based practice
Empirically based	• Associated with the best available research component of evidence-based practice
Scientifically based	• Associated with the best available research component of evidence-based practice • Applies the highest standards of scientific rigor
Recommended practices[a]	• Systematically promulgated lists of practices or treatment protocols based on scientific and experiential knowledge • Designed to help make practice decisions
Clinical practice standards (or guidelines)	• Systematically promulgated lists of practices or treatment protocols based on scientific and experiential knowledge • Designed to help make practice decisions under specific circumstances
Developmentally appropriate practices	• Broad-based practice guidelines or philosophical statements that reflect what is known about children's development and learning, their individual characteristics, and their social and cultural contexts.

Note: [a]The term *best practices* is sometimes used to refer to *recommended practices*, but because practices continue to evolve as new evidence is found to support or refute them, the authors of this volume prefer the term *recommended practices*.

The definition of evidence-based practice for the early childhood field that has been proposed by the authors of this volume aligns closely with the definition set forth by Sackett and his colleagues in medicine, but it differs from the one proposed for education because it includes not only the wisdom of both families and professionals but also the core values of those groups. Consequently, we recommend that the field work to reach consensus on a definition of evidence-based practice—perhaps beginning with an examination of the definition proposed here—through a collaborative effort that involves multiple professional organizations within the early childhood field (e.g., Division for Early Childhood of the Council for Exceptional Children, National Association for the Education of Young Children, ZERO TO THREE, Head Start) and a process that includes broad stakeholder involvement and methods of building consensus.

Recommendation 2: Make the Standards of Evidence Explicit

The early childhood field must reach agreement on what constitutes evidence and whether various forms of evidence will be given equal weight (Davies & Nutley, 2002). What happens when the evidence is ambiguous, contradictory, or difficult to interpret (The Urban Institute, 2003)? In areas in which conventional wisdom conflicts with science, how will these conflicts be resolved? For example, how should a child-care provider resolve two conflicting sources of evidence: the mental health consultant's advice concerning the importance of responding immediately to an infant's needs (for which there is ample empirical support) and the parent's deeply held conviction that responding too quickly may lead to spoiling her baby? Even more challenging, how would the child-care provider resolve a question that stems from a conflict, not between science and values, but between her own values or beliefs and those of someone else? From an evidence-based framework, the issue here is not one of knowing effective strategies for resolving conflicts, although that ability is an undeniably important skill, but rather, the issue is one of whether the field can provide adequate guidance to practitioners about how to weigh the evidence from different sources. Does research evidence always trump other sources of knowledge? Or, alternatively, should research play a stronger role in medicine and, conversely, professional and family wisdom play a stronger role in fields such as education and social work

(Hammersley, 2005)? Even if the early childhood field ultimately decides to offer guidelines about how to determine the strength of various types of evidence, the goal should not be to reduce this extremely complex task to a game of rock, scissors, paper. In other words, it would be dangerous to decide a priori that mediocre research evidence outweighs strong conventional wisdom or that a moderately well-formulated theory should take a backseat to the local cultural context.

As we search for answers, it may not be particularly helpful to look to the broader evidence-based movement because the movement to date has been more explicit about the role of research in establishing the evidence base as compared with other sources of knowledge. However, the question of how to weigh various sources of evidence must be part of future efforts designed to identify the standards of evidence. Definitive answers about how we will become an evidence-based field are not available at this time; however, we are beginning to identify some of the most pressing questions in this regard. These questions include the following: (a) Is it possible to link evidence, policy, and practice in a coherent fashion; (b) Is it possible to integrate various sources of evidence in a way that points to a specific action; (c) Can evidence really tell us the best thing to do in a particular situation; and (d) What are the particular implications of using evidence-based practice for each of the stakeholder groups (i.e., researchers, policymakers, and practitioners)?

Drawing from Hammersley's (2005) suggestion that practice is necessarily a matter of judgment, we propose the conceptual framework displayed in Figure 7.1 for applying evidence to make informed practice decisions in early childhood.

Figure 7.1. A proposed model for applying evidence to inform practice decisions.

Another issue that is related to this discussion concerns the need to find acceptable methods for generating new knowledge in the field. Davies and Nutley (2002) noted the need for additional clarity about the relative worth of different research methodologies and suggested that the emphasis be placed on how various methods make complementary versus competing contributions to knowledge. Hammersley (2005) cautioned that an overreliance on randomized controlled studies as the only means of generating research evidence in fields outside of medicine is problematic because treatments cannot be standardized in the same way (e.g., early childhood professionals must adapt their behaviors to the needs of children and families rather than follow a standardized set of procedures), nor can outcomes be measured as reliably. Davies and Nutley also recommended that the generation of knowledge begin with an examination of where the gaps in knowledge exist and what way would be best to address them from a consumer perspective rather than start from a research agenda that has been developed by researchers or policymakers. Because what works in the early childhood field is highly context specific and influenced by many competing variables (as is the case within the broader social science field), it is essential that research questions and methods be derived from the problems of practice that hold the most relevance for practitioners and the children and families whom they serve.

Recommendation 3: Develop Information Systems to Promote Knowledge Dissemination and Utilization

In recent years, there has been a proliferation of Web-based initiatives under the banner of evidence-based practice, all directed at organizing and translating research-based knowledge. Many of these efforts reflect time-limited projects that are funded through grants from governmental or private organizations, the products of which receive no external review or official endorsement from a federal agency or professional organization—an important point that may not be completely transparent to the average consumer who visits a Web site. In addition, these initiatives have adopted different areas of emphasis (e.g., early intervention for children with disabilities, child care, social-emotional development), use different standards of evidence or research appraisal systems, and produce research synthesis products through different methods. Currently, the field has devoted most of its efforts related to establishing the evidence base to developing research reviews and syntheses, gathering information, creating databases, and developing appraisal systems. Far less is known about the process by which this information is diffused throughout the field and is adopted or rejected by its members (Rogers, 1995 cited in Davies & Nutley, 2002). Although the systematic dissemination of what is known in the early childhood field is a worthwhile goal, more attention must be given to the following activities: (a) coordinating knowledge dissemination and knowledge utilization efforts across different sectors of the field and professional organizations, (b) applying uniform standards of evidence and methods for generating reviews and syntheses, (c) identifying areas of practice in which additional research or syntheses of available research are needed, (d) offering guidance and support to practitioners and parents about how to utilize the knowledge from research syntheses, and (e) evaluating all of these efforts related to knowledge utilization to determine their relevance and effectiveness. Finally, the necessity of conducting exhaustive reviews on every topic; the time involved in doing so; and the costs of building a comprehensive, integrated information system also must be addressed in future discussions (Hammersley, 2005).

Recommendation 4: Identify Ways of Involving Consumers as Participants in Establishing the Evidence Base

In fields within medicine and the biological sciences, practitioners generally function within a scientist–practitioner model that promotes an understanding of the potential of their work to advance the field as a whole. By contrast, most practitioners within the early childhood field are only peripheral participants in the scientific and policy communities (Wesley & Buysse, 2001). For the most part, the result of this separation that exists among research, policy, and practice endeavors is that professional activity entails applying methods and strategies that have been discovered and found effective by those outside of the practice world. Reflective practice in which professionals work collaboratively to view their daily experiences through a process of observation, inference, and the testing of hypotheses is one means of helping practitioners integrate research knowledge with situated practice (Fenichel

& Eggbeer, 1991; MacKinnon & Erickson, 1992; Schön, 1987), but it does not allow them to participate directly in making discoveries that are most relevant for advancing knowledge for the field.

Various approaches have emerged to promote collaborative research between those whose primary responsibility is research and others who work directly with children and families, administer programs, or who serve in other pivotal roles—most notably, parents. As noted in chapter 5, these approaches, which include professional development schools and participatory action research, have not completely addressed the need for consumers to engage in mutual analysis of one another's experiences and observations as a way to continually refine practice and co-construct knowledge. Compared with other collaborative research–practice approaches that appear in the literature, communities of practice offer the most promise for engaging practitioners and families in establishing the field's evidence base (Buysse, Sparkman, & Wesley, 2003).

How does the field begin a process that requires us to rethink the way in which we generate, share, and use knowledge? The following ideas offer some possible directions in this regard: (a) incorporate a community of practice perspective into existing local research and practice activities by drawing on mutual interests and shared goals and by linking ideas with the broader professional community; (b) create partnerships between preservice professional development programs in higher education and community-based early childhood programs; and (c) develop a professional culture at every level in which evidence is valued and used as part of a decision-making process. A report by the National Research Council Committee on Scientific Principles for Education Research (2002) titled *Scientific Research in Education* outlined the importance for the U.S. Department of Education to invest in an infrastructure that builds connections between researchers and practitioners. Some of the purposes for building the type of infrastructure mentioned in this report included providing relevant insights from consumers that might otherwise be missed, establishing mutual trust and working relationships with schools and communities, and infusing knowledge of the complexities of educational practice in research designs.

Recommendation 5: Align Professional Development With Evidence-Based Practice

Finally, if the early childhood profession can reach consensus on the need to become an evidence-based field and if it can agree on what evidence-based practice means and how that concept will be implemented in practice, then there will be a need to align professional development with all of these ideas. Already there are indications that the early childhood field is moving in this direction. Efforts are under way within the Division for Early Childhood of the Council for Exceptional Children, for example, to establish the evidence base of its professional development standards. However, much more must be done in this regard. The conclusions of Cochrane-Smith and Zeichner (2005) with respect to the current knowledge base on professional development suggest that embracing an evidence-based approach will be a massive and time-consuming undertaking. It will involve examining whether there is sufficient evidence that professional standards or competencies are embedded throughout academic training programs—not just listed in every course syllabi but actually used to guide the content and format of professional development. Ultimately, it will be incumbent on the field to demonstrate whether academic training leads to improved professional practices in practice settings (which points to the need for valid methods of measuring these results), and whether these practices also lead to better outcomes for children and families. All of these efforts will require that faculty in institutions of higher learning develop effective methods of infusing an evidence-based approach into their coursework and field-based experiences. They will need to develop strategies for helping students acquire the knowledge and skills required to search and appraise the research evidence and to integrate these findings with the field's collective wisdom and values. In addition, faculty will need to find effective ways of helping students learn how to apply various sources of evidence to make practice decisions that are tailored to the needs and priorities of individual children and families. Individuals who organize and deliver professional development as part of in-service or continuing education programs face a similar set of challenges.

In moving toward an evidence-based practice framework, the field must avoid the potential pitfall of becoming overly prescriptive in its approach to professional development, of "manualizing" practices, that is, focusing on doing to an extent that it overshadows the process of understanding (Trinder, 2000). The world of practice is complex and not easily reduced to a set of guidelines or standardized ways of behaving and being. Consequently, professional development programs must continue to acknowledge the uncertainty that exists in practice situations and the importance of professional judgment and flexibility in making decisions that address not only these uncertainties but also the individual characteristics of children and families.

CONCLUSION

In this chapter, we reviewed and reflected on the major issues and challenges that the early childhood field faces in adopting an evidence-based practice approach. Although these issues have not exactly converged to create the "perfect storm" within the early childhood professions, they have produced enough turbulence to rattle some widely held assumptions about how practice knowledge is generated and used, and by whom. The field is at such an early stage in thinking about evidence-based practice that the champions and critics of this approach have not yet emerged, making it difficult to assess the potential long-term effect of the movement. For this reason, we are grateful for the wisdom of scholars from other professions, particularly those in the United Kingdom (Davies & Nutley, 2002; Hammersley, 2002, 2005; Reynolds, 2000; Trinder, 2000), all of whom have far more experience in observing and critiquing the effects of evidence-based practice than we do. A review of this scholarly work suggests that adopting an evidence-based practice approach in our field may include, but not be limited to, the following potential benefits:

- Knowledge, rather than authority, is privileged. The emphasis on gathering and disseminating what is known makes knowledge transparent and accessible to anyone who desires it.

- Practices that are found to be effective are promoted for immediate adoption; practices that are found to be ineffective are identified and excluded.

- The long-standing gaps among research, policy, and practice are addressed.

- Parents and practitioners are empowered to rely on evidence to make informed practice decisions and to participate in generating new knowledge.

A review of the same scholarly work suggests that evidence-based practice can include, but is not limited to, the following potential risks or challenges:

- The world of practice is more complex than the one rendered by evidence-based practice, making it difficult to reduce the implementation of knowledge into the five-step process used in medicine (i.e., posing a question related to practice; tracking down the evidence; appraising the evidence; integrating research with experience, wisdom, and values and applying it to practice; and evaluating the results).

- There is too much research evidence, much of it of low quality, to organize and distill into useful information for practitioners.

- There is unevenness of research evidence, with little or no research on some topics and too much in other areas, but again, much of this information may not be relevant for practitioners.

- Some effective interventions will be ignored because they lack evidence whereas others may be promoted, not because they are more effective, but because there is sufficient evidence available.

Becoming an evidence-based field will require that professionals learn to think critically, analyze alternative perspectives, and pay close attention to the reasoning process as well as the actions that result from that process (Gambrill, 2000). Thinking critically should lead us to pose a series of questions to help make decisions about virtually everything we do: which interventions and services to use, what levels of services to offer, who should provide the services, how progress will be tracked, whether the hoped-for results are reasonable and measurable, how to involve consumers in generating knowledge that is relevant to practice, and so forth. The list is endless. As professionals pay attention to opposing viewpoints to bring clarity to these issues, they must continually check their own assumptions about what evidence-based practice means against the perceptions and assumptions of others (e.g., practitioners, administrators, researchers, policymakers, supervisors, mentors, professors). Adopting evidence-based practice inevitably will involve a willingness to take risks in an effort to honor our commitment to discover the best possible array of services and supports for young children and their families (Gambrill, 2000).

In our view, another important consideration in future discussions will be whether evidence-based practice applies equally to all professions, including those within the early childhood field in which the nature of the work can be described most accurately as the art of practice rather than the science of practice (Schön, 1987). One concern that has been raised is that the emphasis on science within the evidence-based movement could detract from the emotional, caring, and supportive aspects of some professions (Trinder, 2000).

Despite these concerns, there is little doubt that the evidence-based practice movement has responded to some of the most significant problems that we now face—by promoting the systematic dissemination of what is known, by drawing attention to the need for more scientific rigor, and by advocating for increased participation among consumers in establishing the evidence base (Trinder, 2000). In the future, if we decide to go forward, it will be necessary to shift the focus from gathering and appraising the evidence to helping consumers implement this knowledge in practice.

REFERENCES

Buysse, V., Sparkman, K., & Wesley, P. W. (2003). Communities of practice: Connecting what we know with what we do. *Exceptional Children*, 69(3), 263–277.

Cochrane-Smith, M., & Zeichner, K. (2005). Executive summary. In M. Cochrane-Smith, & K. Zeichner (Eds.), *Studying teacher education: The report of the AERA panel on research and teacher education* (pp. 1–36). Mahwah, NJ: Erlbaum.

Davies, H. T. O., & Nutley, S. M. (2002). *Evidence-based policy and practice: Moving from rhetoric to reality.* (Discussion Paper 2). University of St. Andrews: Research Unit for Research Utilisation.

Dinnebeil, L., Buysse, V., Rush, D., & Eggbeer, L. (in press). Teaching skills for effective collaboration. In P. J. Winton, J. McCollum, & C. Catlett (Eds.), *Effective professionals: Evidence and applications in early childhood and early intervention.* Washington, DC: ZERO TO THREE Press.

Fenichel, E. S. (1992). *Learning through supervision and mentorship: A sourcebook.* Arlington, VA: ZERO TO THREE/National Center for Clinical Infant Programs.

Fenichel, E. S., & Eggbeer, L. (1991). Preparing practitioners to work with infants, toddlers, and their families: Four essential elements of training. *Infants and Young Children, 4*(2), 56–62.

Feuer, M. J., Towne, L., & Shavelson, R. J. (2002). Scientific culture and educational research. *Educational Researcher, 31*(8), 4–14.

Gambrill, E. (2000). The role of critical thinking in evidence-based social work. In P. Allen-Meares & C. Garvin (Eds.), *The handbook of social work director practice* (pp. 43–64). Thousand Oaks, CA: Sage.

Garrett, J. L., & Islam, Y. (1998). *Policy research and the policy process: Do the twain ever meet?* (Gatekeeper Series 74). London: International Institute for the Environment and Development, Sustainable Agriculture and Rural Livelihoods Programme.

Gilliam, W., & Leiter, V. (2003). Evaluating early childhood programs: Improving quality and informing policy. *Zero To Three, 23*(6), 6–13.

Hammersley, M. (2002). Evidence-based practice in education and the contribution of educational research. In L. Trinder & S. Reynolds (Eds.), *Evidence-based practice: A critical appraisal* (pp. 163–183). Oxford, UK: Blackwell Science.

Hammersley, M. (2005). Is the evidence-based practice movement doing more good than harm? Reflections on Iain Chalmers' case for research-based policy making and good practice. *Evidence and Policy, 1*(1), 85–100.

Herzenberg, S., Price, M., & Bradley, D. (2005). Losing ground in early childhood education: Declining workforce qualifications in an expanding industry, 1979–2004. Washington, DC: Economic Policy Institute. Retrieved September 28, 2005, from www.epi.org/content.cfm/ece

Hiebert, J., Gallimore, R., & Stigler, J. W. (2002). A knowledge base for the teaching profession: What would it look like and how can we get one? *Educational Researcher, 31*(5), 3–15.

Levitt, R. (2003). GM crops and foods. Evidence, policy and practice in the U.K.: A case study (Working Paper 20). London: ESRC U.K. Centre for Evidence Based Policy and Practice.

MacKinnon, A., & Erickson, G. (1992). The roles of reflective practice and foundational disciplines in teacher education. In T. Russell & H. Munby (Eds.), Teachers and teaching: From classroom to reflection (pp. 192–210). London: Falmer.

National Research Council Committee on Scientific Principles for Education Research. (2002). Scientific research in education (R. J. Shavelson, & L. Towne, Eds.). Committee on Scientific Principles for Education Research. Washington, DC: National Academy Press.

No Child Left Behind Act of 2001, Pub. L. 107-110, 115 Stat. 1425 (2002).

Reynolds, S. (2000). The anatomy of evidence-based practice: Principles and methods. In L. Trinder & S. Reynolds (Eds.), Evidence-based practice: A critical appraisal (pp. 17–34). Oxford, UK: Blackwell Science.

Sackett, D. L., Straus, S. E., Richardson, W. S., Rosenberg, W., & Haynes, R. B. (2000). Evidence-based medicine: How to practice and teach EBM. Edinburgh, UK: Churchill Livingstone.

Schön, D. (1987). Education the reflective practitioner: Toward a new design for teaching and learning in the professions. San Francisco: Jossey-Bass.

Trinder, L. (2000). A critical appraisal of evidence-based practice. In L. Trinder & S. Reynolds (Eds.), Evidence-based practice: A critical appraisal (pp. 212–241). Oxford, UK: Blackwell Science.

Urban Institute, The. (2003). Beyond ideology, politics, and guesswork: The case for evidence-based policy. Retrieved August 21, 2005, from http://www.urban.org/url.cfm?90036

Wesley, P. W., & Buysse, V. (2001). Communities of practice: Expanding professional roles to promote reflection and shared inquiry. Topics in Early Childhood Special Education, 21(2), 114–123.

About the Editors

Virginia Buysse, PhD, is senior scientist at the FPG Child Development Institute and research associate professor in the School of Education at the University of North Carolina at Chapel Hill. She has directed research projects on a variety of topics, including early education programs for children who are English language learners, friendships in young children with and without disabilities, early childhood inclusion, parent leadership development, professional development, and models that support collaboration and change such as consultation and communities of practice. Dr. Buysse serves on the editorial boards of *Exceptional Children, Journal of Early Intervention, Infants and Young Children, Topics in Early Childhood Special Education, and Young Exceptional Children*. She also serves as co-editor of *Early Developments*, a national publication of the FPG Child Development Institute.

Patricia Wesley, MEd, is senior scientist at the FPG Child Development Institute at The University of North Carolina at Chapel Hill where she is also clinical instructor in the School of Education. Following a decade as the director of an inclusive preschool, in 1990 she became the director of Partnerships for Inclusion, a state-wide training and consultation project supporting the inclusion of children with disabilities and their families in all aspects of community life. In this role, she has developed, implemented, evaluated, and published several models of technical assistance to promote high quality inclusion including a framework for on-site consultation in early childhood programs, a community forum model to raise awareness about special needs, and the project's own organizational structure and approach to evaluation.

INDEX